SPEECH
COMMUNICATION

SPEECH
COMMUNICATION

A Basic Approach

FOURTH EDITION

ERNEST G. BORMANN
University of Minnesota

NANCY C. BORMANN

HARPER & ROW, PUBLISHERS, New York
Cambridge, Philadelphia, San Francisco,
London, Mexico City, São Paulo, Singapore, Sydney

1817

Sponsoring Editor: Louise H. Waller
Project Editor: Jo-Ann Goldfarb
Cover Design: Miriam Recio
Text Art: J & R Technical Services, Inc.
Photo Research: Mira Schachne
Production: Jeanie Berke
Compositor: ComCom Division of Haddon Craftsmen, Inc.
Printer and Binder: R. R. Donnelley & Sons Company

SPEECH COMMUNICATION: A Basic Approach, Fourth Edition

Library of Congress Cataloging-in-Publication Data

Bormann, Ernest G.
    Speech communication.

    Includes bibliographies and indexes.
    1. Oral communication.   I. Bormann, Nancy C.
II. Title.
P95.B67 1986   001.54′2   85-21988
ISBN 0-06-040867-7

85 86 87 88 9 8 7 6 5 4 3 2 1

CONTENTS

PART TWO
INTERPERSONAL AND GROUP
COMMUNICATION

PREFACE

Speech Communication, in its fourth edition, is a brief, clear, readable book for the basic performance course in interpersonal, small-group communication, and public speaking. We have kept in mind that for many students the first course will be their only chance to make a systematic study of this vital area of oral communication. We have kept the emphasis of previous editions on public speaking without slighting interpersonal and small-group communication.

This revision is based on the most recent communication research and theory. Included are findings from the research literature relating to nonverbal communication, interpersonal and small-group communication, persuasion, and audience analysis. We have also retained the time-tested basics from the study of rhetoric, rhetorical criticism, and public speaking. We have worked to present this material in as lively, basic, and practical a way as possible.

Our guiding assumption is that speech communication has a core of basic information that applies to various communication forms and situations. By initially learning the fundamentals, readers can then apply them to the demands of daily communication. One good way to learn many of the basics relating to audience analysis, listening, organization, clarifying ideas, supporting arguments, and developing persuasive messages is through exercises in public speaking.

First we introduce the field of speech communication. The instructor can then work with the class to prepare exercises and assignments in two-person communication—such as the job interview—in small-group panels and forums and in public-speaking exercises and assignments. Each chapter is self-contained, and those who prefer a different order of chapters can easily assign them to meet a particular syllabus.

We did not increase the size of the fourth edition. Added material is balanced by cuts of the previous materials. We eliminated the chapters on criticizing communication, on supporting material, and on persuasion but included pertinent discussions from these chapters in new ones on the informative speech, the argumentative speech, and the persuasive speech.

Another major addition is the material on communication perspectives and models that supplements the basic Source-Message-Channels-Receiver (SMCR) model presented in previous editions. We have also added a discussion of recent developments in interpersonal communication, including empirically based approaches as well as the relationship perspective. The chapter on organization has been amplified.

Over the years we have sought the advice and help of teachers who worked with the earlier editions of this book in order to make it an even more useful teaching resource. Many of these instructors teach basic speech communication courses in community colleges, liberal arts schools, and state universities. We have put our emphasis in this revision on those topics where we found the needs of beginning students in these various classes overlapping. We have kept the growing need for meaningful, marketable communication *skills* strongly in mind and have adapted to growing student interest in education useful for career preparation.

The teachers we have consulted advised us that, above all, we should stress solid information the student can use throughout life, restrict its scope to essentials, and keep it businesslike, practical, and as free of jargon as possible. They advised us to write a readable book, with useful information that students can absorb and will find useful. Don't oversimplify, they've told us. Students want to improve their skills, but they do not want to be talked down to with a three-easy-steps approach. We have tried to follow this advice.

Finally, we would like to thank our reviewers who commented on the text as it was being prepared. These include Arlie Daniel, East Central University; Marsha Vanderford Doyle, University of South Florida; Bena Harper, Oklahoma State University; Don B. Morlan, The University of Dayton; Olaf E. Rankis, University of Miami; William Schenk-Hamlin, Kansas State University; and Janice Schuetz, University of New Mexico, Albuquerque.

We would also like to thank Ellen Bormann for her editorial assistance in preparing the book.

Ernest G. Bormann
Nancy C. Bormann

SPEECH
COMMUNICATION

Part One

THE BASICS

chapter 1

Developing a Positive Communication Attitude

Talking and listening are among the most important things we do; yet we begin talking and listening at such a young age that we often take oral communication for granted. Our communication skills and our feelings about communication are so ingrained that we seldom think about them and analyze what they are and how they might be improved.

Sometimes the hardest thing we have to do is to talk to someone or to a group of people. Usually those moments when we cannot talk easily are the very times we want most to talk smoothly, clearly, interestingly, and convincingly. Why do we feel tense and excited when we think about talking in certain situations in general or to certain individuals and groups in particular? Tension comes when much is at stake, when we feel failure will be unpleasant, perhaps even punishing to us, and when success will be pleasant and rewarding. The body alerts itself for verbal battle or for flight.

The fight or flight response is an old one that we have inherited from our prehistoric ancestors, who often faced personal danger. Whether they stood and fought or turned and ran, their bodies needed to be keyed up for maximum physical effort.

Our bodily symptoms when we become alerted to a communication situation where much is at stake tend to vary from person to person; they usually include such things as sweaty palms, increased heartbeat, dryness in the mouth, and shortness of breath. We often report these feelings with such clichés as "I had butterflies in my stomach" or "My heart was in my throat."

A number of investigators have studied the relationship between the emotional feeling people report they have and physical measures of bodily changes such as increased heartbeats. These investigations reveal that some subjects will interpret such arousal as a positive and pleasurable emotion, while others will interpret the same physical changes as anxiety, fear, or dread.

A good way to understand how vital speech communication is to you personally and how you tend to interpret the physical tension associated with it is to set down your own feelings over the last couple of days. Did you get churned up in an argument with a friend, with a date, with your wife or husband? Did you dread having to talk to an intimate friend or relative about something important? Did you feel nervous and excited in class because you wanted to say something but were afraid of what others would think of you? Were you ill at ease at a party where you did not know anybody? Did you turn your face away and avoid having to talk to somebody because you felt that particular conversation might be uncomfortable? More to the point, how did you feel about the prospect of taking a course in speech communication, where you might be asked to participate in interviews, discussions, and exercises in which you would have to talk up? Or were you looking forward to, or dreading, a situation where you might have to get on your feet and speak to an audience?

Among the important mental barriers to the study and practice of speech communication are the ways in which many people swing between blaming all problems on communication difficulties—viewing communication as so important that it is fearsome, or pretending that talk is such an everyday occurrence (nearly all of us have been talking since we were babies) that it is a relatively simple and unimportant matter not worthy of much careful study and practice to sharpen skills.

In this chapter we discuss the development of a positive, realistic communication attitude—the first step to learning how to be a better communicator. We will examine two aspects involved in developing a positive attitude. First, we will discuss the development of a realistic understanding of the importance of communication to your career, to your role as a citizen in society, and to the quality of your personal life. Second, we will consider the need for a realistic understanding of the complexity of communication in all contexts in order to develop a positive communication attitude.

Developing a positive attitude helps you to become a better communicator. (Stewart, The Picture Cube)

THE IMPORTANCE OF COMMUNICATION

The Economic Importance of Communication

Most college students have already experienced the communication difficulties and special needs they find when they move outside the home and school and into the world of work. Suddenly, in your first job interview, you must present yourself as a person and a commodity at the same time; you are a particular person, but you are trying to sell your skills to somebody who needs those skills.

Face to face with a prospective employer, we all become acutely aware of the importance of basic communications skills in getting and holding a job. But while the job interview may be a particularly graphic example of the importance of communication in business, industry, government, education, and the professions, every work situation demands a wide variety of speaking abilities.

People in management positions discover that most of what they do in their jobs is communication. After all, a supervisor seldom moves a subordinate around physically. Management requires the ability to organize, coordinate, delegate duties and responsibilities, and integrate the efforts of a team. All of these managerial tasks require the ability to communicate clearly and persuasively with subordinates.

We need communication skills to help us move through what is popularly called the maze of bureaucratic red tape whether we are trying to register for classes, get a computer error changed at a large corporate bank, or deal with governmental agencies at the city, county, state, and national levels.

Frequently we find ourselves in positions where we must meet the public either as part of a service industry or in a sales capacity. Meeting the public requires skill in opening conversations and giving clear directions or providing information quickly and interestingly. To be a successful salesperson, one needs a high level of speaking fluency and skill in the use of techniques of persuasion.

Communication ability is vital when spending the money we have earned on the job. Wherever we go, we are encouraged to buy something. Billboards, television and radio commercials, newspaper and magazine ads tell us how to spend our money. Persuasive messages are everywhere. We need to know about persuasion not only to be persuasive but also to be able to spot a phony ad, an illogical argument, or a shoddy appeal to our emotions.

The Importance of Communication to Citizenship

Huey Long, a colorful southern politician in the 1930s, gained a large following during the Great Depression with his slogan "Every Man a King." In a very real sense, every citizen is ideally a ruler in a representative democracy. The basic assumption of our government is that with freedom of speech, of press, and of assembly, all points of view will be given an opportunity to be heard, and that the people, once they have heard the competing positions debated, will have the wisdom to choose the best policies and the best representatives.

The leaders in a democracy must be skilled communicators. Democracy has historically encouraged the study and practice of open communication in the making of decisions and plans. Our earliest and still some of our most sophisticated ideas about communication were first developed in the Greek states several thousands of years ago; they had their greatest development in the democracy of Athens and were further refined in Rome during the days when the Roman senate held power. Totalitarian governments have historically discouraged the study of communication skills by most citizens and tried to keep such skills in the hands of a select few working to enforce the power structure.

Citizens must be skilled in debate and discussion of public issues to be participants in the democratic processes. Informal discussion in the home or on the job about various candidates and political programs are important to intelligent voting. Citizens must also become good consumers of political communication and media coverage of the campaigns.

We should be aware that candidates often hire ghostwriters to help them prepare messages for the public. At best the ghostwriter helps the candidate frame his or her ideas in more effective language; at worst the ghostwriter provides both ideas and language that may fool the public into thinking a poor candidate is a good one.

Most politicians running for important public office now use the lastest persuasive campaign techniques developed by advertising agencies and public-relations firms to plan and produce their television advertising and help them with their other promotional communication. How can voters know for whom they are voting under such circumstances? The best answer is we must be fully informed and knowledgeable about political communication.

Communication and Individual Fulfillment

Human beings have a basic urge to communicate and, more than that, to generate words and images, to dramatize for the pure joy of playing with language and with ideas. Even when we are resting, our minds think up symbols, and we fantasize by means of an internal monologue in which we are both the playwright creating the script and the puppeteer pulling the strings and reading lines.

When people find themselves thrown together by accident or for purely social reasons, they feel the urge to talk to one another. Idle chitchat can be playful and great fun. Wordplay and small talk provide pleasant moments for all of us.

Most people gain satisfaction from creative activity—from discovering a new idea or product or way to do something or from writing a poem or a good letter or from finding a new route for getting from one place to another. Talking to people can be creative. We try out ideas in a tentative way on people who have similar interests and abilities. We "brainstorm" or "kick ideas around" or try out wild and far-out notions on close friends.

Finally, some of the best and most satisfying moments come when two people transcend their self-centeredness and reach a high level of understanding. One of the warmest rewards in life is to really know another person. In the search for identity and fulfillment the ability to communicate at the highest level is a basic requirement.

THE COMPLEXITY OF COMMUNICATION

Many of us find the theories of the natural sciences such as physics and chemistry difficult and complex. We also find some of the more advanced mathematical proofs full of complex detail and hard to follow. Technically trained people often regard their specialty as complicated—whether it be double-entry bookkeeping, subatomic physics, or computer programming —but when they move into a supervisory position where their main duties require communication skills, they often develop the mistaken attitude that communication is a relatively simple matter.

On the contrary, communication events are much more complicated than those studied in the natural sciences. For example, take the Newtonian conception of gravity and how it works. Do you consider the study of gravity a complex undertaking? Consider, instead, that a relatively simple formula describes how gravity works in the attraction of two objects to each other; the operations of gravity are usually linear, steady, dependable, and predictable.

Now consider two people walking to class who meet in the hallway of a classroom building and stop to chat. Instead of a simple, steady relationship, consistent through time, their communication will involve a host of relationship factors. They may be friends, enemies, or acquaintances. They may wish to know each other better, or they may wish they could ignore one another, but for some reason based on past communication they cannot. One may have higher status than the other in a group or organization to which they both belong.

Not only is their social relationship a factor in their communication, but there are such universal human difficulties as each of them having different experiences, meanings associated with words, interests, general abilities, and communication skills. Even with the best of intentions and a good set of relationship factors they would face a complicated process of achieving understanding.

Suppose now a third person walks up and joins in the conversation. If we were to add a third object to the formula regarding the influence of gravity on two objects, the formula would become more complicated, but nothing like the complications added to our two-person conversation when a third individual joins in. With three objects one must compute the vectors of forces operating in the gravity system, but the relationship remains linear, steady, and predictable. The addition of a third person to the two-person communication adds such possibilities as the new member liking one of the original pair but not the other, or the newcomer being of lesser status than either of the other two. Imagine now what happens when someone gives a speech to several hundred or a thousand people in a church or auditorium, or when a discussion panel appears on a television program watched by millions of viewers.

If communication is so complex and important why do so many mature people view getting a committee of people together to make an important decision and lay important plans in a meeting lasting several hours as a relatively simple matter? Often such simplistic attitudes stem from the tendency to take flight from the painful realities. Many people have never studied communication in a systematic way. Becoming realistically aware of the nature of communication would be a threat to their self-image. Because they have proved their competence in so many areas they cannot believe that something they think is so simple as communication can be the root of so many of their problems. Many of the unpleasant things that are happening to them could no longer be blamed on forces outside their control such as the immaturity and meanness of others, or the fates, or their bad luck, but they would have to face up to the fact that they are ineffective communicators and what is required is the study of the principles and theories coupled with sufficient practice of the skills.

We have noticed this tendency particularly among business and professional leaders who have come to us for consultation and advice on their communication problems. People who have spent years becoming experts in a technical field and have then become managers involved primarily in communication, sometimes hardly using their years of technical training from day-to-day, often lack knowledge and training in communication and are thus ill qualified to carry out many of their new duties. Such people become enormously frustrated. A typical way for them to save their self-images under these circumstances is to reject the importance of communication and to scapegoat those around them as being incompetent.

The rejection often takes the form of assuming communication is a simple matter. They ask us as communication consultants for easy formulas. "I have someone working for me who always dominates the staff meetings. What can I do to stop him from talking so much?" In this case what the managers want is a brief three-step recipe that they can follow to assure that the talkative group member will keep quiet when they want him to. If we suggest that the talkative member is part of a very complicated communication system in which the manager is a vital part, and that changing that system will require as a start some basic reading on small group communication, managers often say they have more important things to do with their time. Though they realize that their technical competence was built on years of study and practical experience, they feel communication skills, "people problems," everyday person-to-person talk should be simple and "straightforward."

Likewise the student who says, "I don't know why it is, but whenever I take Mary out somewhere we never seem to have anything much to say to one another—what can I do to become a better conversationalist?" would like a brief formula that would assure success because his attitude is that communication is relatively simple. There are as many books claiming shortcuts to "better communication" as there are books on how to improve your golf swing. In both cases, there are no easy answers, no shortcuts. An analysis of the complexities of both is a start. We will outline for you basic theories and research that the study of communication has found sound and practical over the years. We will suggest exercises which you can use, again and again, depending on what you feel your communication needs are. Everyone can learn more about what good communication should be and everyone should be able to learn to communicate better. Yes, communication is complex. It is also like any learned behavior, a skill you can work on once you learn more about the many factors involved.

KEY IDEAS

- Management is largely communication.
- The ability to communicate is vital for all jobs that require a person to meet the public.
- The ability to listen, to understand, and to critically evaluate persuasion is economically important to us as consumers.
- Democracy has always encouraged the study and practice of real communication.
- A citizen in a democracy has to be more responsible, more politically knowledgeable, and more skillful in communicating than citizens do in most other forms of society.

- Communication events are usually much more complicated than those studied in the natural sciences.
- Despite the complexity of communication many poor speakers take flight from their inadequacies by developing the attitude that communication is a simple matter.

SUGGESTED PROJECTS

1. Think of a person you know who, in your judgment, communicates exceptionally well with others. Pick a personal acquaintance, not a public figure. What qualities does this person have that contribute to his or her skill in communication? What sorts of things does this person do that others seldom do? After providing a thorough description of this "unusually good communicator," compare yourself with this person. Be frankly candid. Make a list of the qualities you already possess that help you as a communicator; make another list of the things you should work on to improve your ability. Do you feel you have any habits that you particularly need to work on and change in order to improve your ability to communicate?

2. Estimate how much time in a typical day you spend reading, writing, speaking, and listening. Keep a personal log of these communication experiences for one 24-hour period. Further classify your communication within this period by type—social conversation, business communication, school-related communication, communication related to self-fulfillment, and multimedia communication. Keep the log with you and record your communication each hour; be accurate and complete. Afterward make a percentage scale approximation of your typical daily communication interaction. What percentage of your day do you spend reading, writing, speaking, and listening? Were you aware of any times during the 24-hour period when you consciously avoided a communication situation? If so, be specific as to what and why.

SUGGESTED READINGS

Hiemstra, Glen E., and Ann Q. Staton-Spicer. "Communication Concerns of College Undergraduates in Basic Speech Communication Courses." *Communication Education* 32 (1983): 29–37.

Modaff, John, and Robert Hopper. "Why Speech is 'Basic'." *Communication Education* 3 (1984): 37–42.

Weitzel, Al R., and Paul C. Gaske. "An Appraisal of Communication Career-Related Research." *Communication Education* 33 (1984): 181–194.

chapter *2*

Perspectives on Communication

When people talk together, we can think of what happens as a communication event. In this book we will examine the communication events that are most important in our daily lives, including such things as two-person talks to deepen relationships or work through interpersonal problems, small-group meetings and conferences to transmit information and do common tasks, and more formal occasions when one person delivers a carefully prepared message to an audience.

We have difficulty studying communication events because in all the settings we have mentioned, so much is going on when people talk with one another that we have trouble keeping track of everything. Communication events have the characteristics of a dynamic process. By *process,* we mean a series of give-and-take moves by which some end is reached. By *dynamic,* we mean the process unfolds and changes over time. Processes contain forces that push and pull the parts and set them in motion. Sometimes we are caught up by the way a speaker seems to be center stage; sometimes one member of a discussion is speaking in dramatic terms and we forget that the listener is also influencing the event and that the occasion makes a difference as well. The expectations of the people who are communicating with one another also play a part.

Three elements of a public-speaking situation are the speaker, an audience, and an occasion. (Preuss, Jeroboam)

In this chapter we present three important perspectives on communication. The first perspective is that of *relationship communication*. The relationship perspective stresses the human aspects of communication and how social relationships and social contexts affect understandings, feelings, and misunderstandings. The second perspective is that of *message communication*. The message communication perspective provides a general approach to a process of communication that stresses the high fidelity transmission of information and is applicable to almost all communication occasions. The third perspective is that of *public speaking*. Public speaking, with some modifications sometimes called *presentational speaking* in the modern organizational context, is an important way to systematically study and practice oral communication.

THE RELATIONSHIP COMMUNICATION PERSPECTIVE

Whereas the public-speaking and message communication perspectives both emphasize communication as a means to an end, as a way to do other things, the relationship perspective emphasizes communication as vital to human relationships and often a positive value in and of it-self.

The relationship perspective has a transactional model of communication in which the participants cease to play games with one another and are authentic and honest. They take risks and reveal their authentic selves and in the process they build trusting relationships. The recommended communication attitude is that one should deal with others as authentic human beings and not as things or machines to be manipulated. Good communicators are not wearing the masks or playing the roles that often make people less than human and shield them from contact with others.

The participants often disclose their feelings to one another. Self-disclosure is risky, and as they begin communicating about themselves in authentic ways, they also practice active and empathic listening. The communication climate is warmed by congruent, honest, and open communication.

A strong and good self-image is an important ingredient in ideal relationship communication. One way to build a good self-image includes self-disclosing communication—opening oneself up to others and receiving frank and honest feedback, and then using the feedback as the basis for learning and growth. Feedback in the relationship perspective refers to all the verbal and nonverbal responses that express feelings or reactions to another person's communication and behavior.

The relationship perspective assumes "You cannot *not* communicate." The point of the aphorism is that all responses to a participant in a communication setting can be interpreted (and often are) in terms of relationships, feelings, and attitudes. For the message and public speaking perspective the notion that one cannot *not* communicate is simply wrong; observation of the world around us reveals many situations where high-fidelity transmission of meaning cannot be achieved.

The relationship perspective rejects the purposive, intentional, approaches to communication aimed at achieving audience response or control of the receiver. The perspective focuses on how people can unintentionally arouse meanings and feelings in others. It also stresses the meanings people often infer from the entire context of communication. The relationship perspective broadens the concerns about communication context and as a result stresses the importance of nonverbal communication.

THE MESSAGE COMMUNICATION PERSPECTIVE

The message perspective is based on a model that consists of a communication source encoding a message with some intent and transmitting the message through channels to a receiver who decodes it. Berlo in his book *The Process of Communication* was one of the early developers of the SMCR model of communication. Figure 1 presents the basic model.

The *S* stands for *source.* The source is the person or group who decides to communicate with some other person or persons. If you meet someone in the hall and say "Good morning," you are the source of the communication.

The *M* stands for *message.* In our example the message is the words *good* and *morning,* plus the way you gesture and emphasize the words to indicate, "I really mean it is a pleasant morning" or "I am glad to see you again" or "I am saying these words because I always say these words even if the day is lousy and I feel terrible."

The *C* stands for *channel* or channels through which the message moves. Television messages come through channels. People can receive messages by way of their senses—sight, smell, taste, hearing, and touch. Thus, a message may travel through several channels at the same time, as is the case with television, where a viewer both sees the picture and hears the sound. You are most likely to hear, see, or read a message, since the most popular communication channels are through the ears and the eyes.

The final letter, *R,* means *receiver.* The listener or viewer is the receiver of the message. When you greet someone in the hall you are the *source;* the words and the way you say them are the *message;* the message goes through the *channels* of sound (hearing) and light (sight) to the *receiver.*

Now that you know the SMCR way of looking at communication events, you can examine different situations and decide whether they are complete examples of the process of communication. For example, if John telephones Mary for a date, is that communication? Is there a source? A message? Channels? A receiver? All the parts are there: John is the source, what John says is the message, the channels are the telephone and hearing, and Mary is the receiver. Take another example. The national committee of a political party buys time on a television network and runs a short political announcement on nationwide TV. Again all the parts are there. The national committee is the source; the television waves, television set, sight, and hearing are the channels; and the people at home who see and hear the announcement are the receivers. A candidate for student-body president is talking from the auditorium stage to an assembly, urging the audience to vote for a platform to improve the school. The candidate is the source, the message is what he says and the way he says it, the channels are the light waves (sight) and sound waves (hearing), and the students in the auditorium are the receivers.

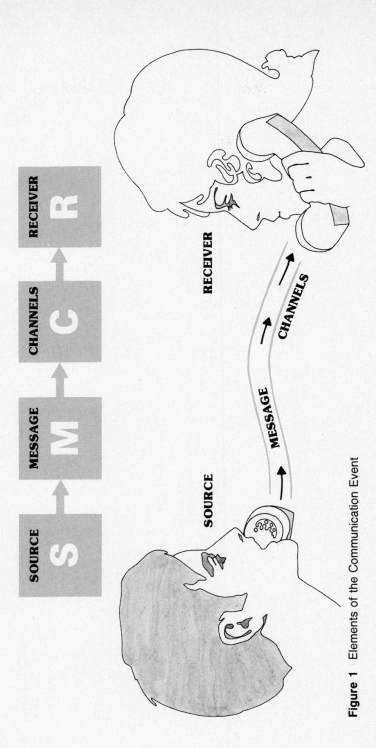

Figure 1 : Elements of the Communication Event

17

The message perspective to the study of communication covers every sort of communication. We have seen the four basic parts in a telephone call, a television message, and a public speech. If we learn how the spark plug works to cause the gas to explode in an engine cylinder, we know a lot about many different car engines. In the same way, if we learn about the source of messages, we know a good deal about many different kinds of communications. We can say the same for what we learn about messages, channels, and receivers

To illustrate the message communication model, we will use the basic situation of a two-person conversation. Our approach is to describe an ideal communication event, which contains all the possible parts operating under good conditions. A good communication model contains all the main parts of a typical conversation in standard form, in their usual places, functioning at peak efficiency.

Assume a situation in which one person wishes to give another person important information. The first person arranges for a conference with the second. The person who calls the conference has something he wishes to discuss, and he tells the listener about it. If the listener understands the message, the first person has succeeded in communicating with the second.

Our model of a communication event perhaps seems relatively cut and dried. Actually, what happens when two people talk with each other is very complicated. Probably the two people in our hypothetical conference spent some minutes passing the time of day before the source began to talk about his business.

Perhaps the person who requested the appointment was a worker who wanted to talk to the boss about a raise, or it may have been the boss who wanted to talk to the worker about improving performance on the job. In either case, the fact that one was boss and the other worker would affect the communication. We could develop a long list of things that affect the two people.

Probably the first message failed to achieve a meeting of minds, and the participants had to try again and again to come to an understanding satisfactory to both.

Because of the unpredictability of human beings, we must describe many possible choices and behaviors to explain adequately the process of human communication. We will begin our explanation with a simplified situation and then move to the more complex. We start with the simplified situation in which the receiver is completely predictable. We are referring to the process by which a person talks to a machine.

Assume that we want to talk to a microcomputer. The first step is to decide what we want the machine to do. We then plan a message to reach our goal, put the message into symbols the microcomputer can understand, and taking care that each sentence is in the correct form, and that no information is left out, we type the message on the keyboard and put it into the computer. The computer accepts the message until it comes to a sentence with a mistake in it. Perhaps we forgot to put in a comma where we should have. The computer's display panel shows that we have made a mistake. We then go back to the message, check the sentence, discover the mistake, put in the comma, and retype the data into the computer. Now the computer understands; it keeps on in this way, either understanding completely or stopping and asking for a correction or for new information. Thus we work together with the machine to achieve understanding.

Remember that we defined process as a series of give-and-take moves by which some end is reached. The linking between the human being and machine is a communication process. Note that when we talk to the computer we start the communication and continue it until the computer fails to understand a part of the message. The back-and-forth part of the process is clear because the machine displays an error statement indicating that it fails to understand. Although we start the process, and the machine is helping us reach the goal, we still have to talk the machine's language and follow the rules of the machine's thinking if we are to succeed.

When the computer indicates it does not understand a message, it feeds back information to the programmer to clear up the misunderstanding. *Feedback* consists of information about the errors in the message that enables the programmer to clear up the machine's lack of understanding.

Feedback plays an important part in the message perspective on the communication process. We can explain feedback in much the same way that we used SMCR to refer to the parts of the communication event. We will use the letters AGP as the key to the process of feedback. The *A* refers to an *actor* (a person or thing) that does something to reach a *goal (G)*. The *P* indicates the *perceptor* built into the actor to provide information on how he or she is doing in order to correct mistaken attempts to reach his or her goal. We will examine some simple events in which feedback is important and then show how it works in communication.

Let us say you see a pencil on the desk and decide to pick it up. You stretch your hand out for the pencil, and as you watch your hand you see that you are going to overreach the pencil, so you tighten certain muscles in your arm and shoulder and slow down the movement. You keep watching your hand and now see that you have slowed down too much, so that your hand will fall short. Again you adjust the push you give your hand until your fingers land on target and you pick up the pencil. One action loops back and causes another.

Does the situation of picking up the pencil contain the necessary parts for a feedback loop? You are the *actor* (person or thing) with the *goal* (picking up the pencil), and you sense (the *perceptor*) through your eyes information about how your arm is moving in comparison with where it ought to be if you are to reach your goal. Using the information you get from watching the path of your hand, you change your reach to hit directly on target. The situation illustrates all the parts, AGP, of feedback as presented in Figure 2.

To return to the person talking with a microcomputer, notice how the person *(A)* has a goal *(G)* of programming the computer to solve a problem or process data. The person sends the computer messages, and the computer sends back information when it fails to understand. Thus the programmer can perceive *(P)* the actual level of understanding in the machine and check it against what is needed to reach the goal.

One important feature of the feedback loop is that only one person or thing has the goal. The pencil does not have a goal; the computer does not set up a different goal and fight the programmer over what they ought to do as a team. (You know, of course, of dramas based on the idea that our machines begin to have goals of their own and start to take over the world, but up to now such stories remain science fiction.) In this simplified situation, feedback is information that enables the source to modify the message so the receiver understands it and the goal can be reached.

When people communicate with one another, the process is similar, but it is highly complicated by the fact that when another person is the potential receiver we cannot predict behavior as completely as we can the response of a machine. The message source begins a communication event with another person much as a programmer begins talking with a computer. The message source has some end she wishes to reach and keeping in mind the receiver's ability to use language and his way of thinking, the source plans a message to reach her goal and speaks to the receiver.

The largest difference between person-to-machine and person-to-person communication is the machine's willingness to be bossed around to achieve the programmer's objective and a person's tendency to resist being the receiver of messages.

In our model of the process of communication (Figure 3), an important element is the fact that the message source has an end in view and sends out messages to achieve that goal. The communication process is a step-by-step, give-and-take interaction between source and receiver by

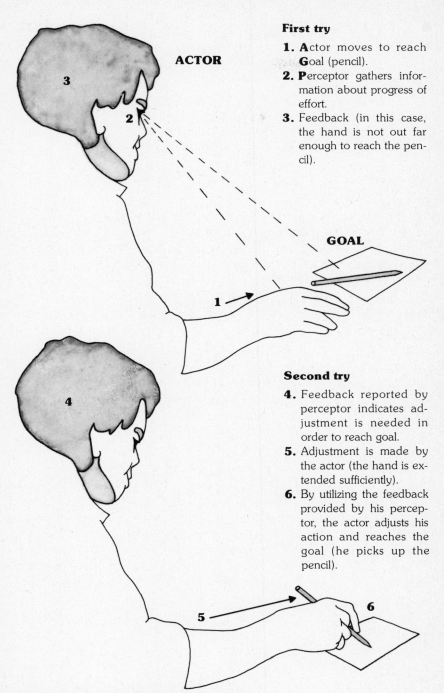

First try

1. **A**ctor moves to reach **G**oal (pencil).
2. **P**erceptor gathers information about progress of effort.
3. Feedback (in this case, the hand is not out far enough to reach the pencil).

ACTOR

GOAL

Second try

4. Feedback reported by perceptor indicates adjustment is needed in order to reach goal.
5. Adjustment is made by the actor (the hand is extended sufficiently).
6. By utilizing the feedback provided by his perceptor, the actor adjusts his action and reaches the goal (he picks up the pencil).

Figure 2   The Concept of Feedback (AGP)

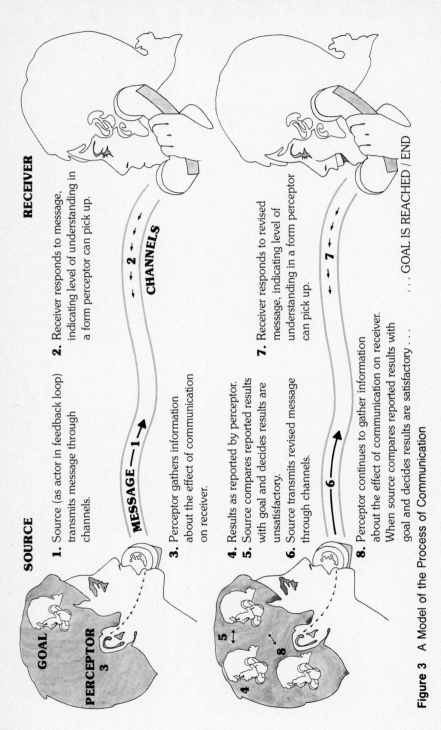

SOURCE

RECEIVER

1. Source (as actor in feedback loop) transmits message through channels.

2. Receiver responds to message, indicating level of understanding in a form perceptor can pick up.

MESSAGE — 1 →

← - 2 - ←
CHANNELS

3. Perceptor gathers information about the effect of communication on receiver.

4. Results as reported by perceptor.
5. Source compares reported results with goal and decides results are unsatisfactory.
6. Source transmits revised message through channels.

7. Receiver responds to revised message, indicating level of understanding in a form perceptor can pick up.

← - 7 - ←

← 6 —

8. Perceptor continues to gather information about the effect of communication on receiver. When source compares reported results with goal and decides results are satisfactory . . . .

. . . GOAL IS REACHED / END

GOAL

PERCEPTOR
3

Figure 3   A Model of the Process of Communication

which the source reaches the desired goal. The idea of feedback includes the notion that the source receives information so he or she can correct attempts to reach the goal. The programmer gets error statements from the computer so he can rephrase his program until the computer understands it. The computer is willing to take the programmer's directives and accepts the programmer's goal without question. When the target for the message is another human being, the receiver often is not willing to be controlled and does not accept the objectives of the source.

What often happens in conversation between people is that after a first attempt by one person to be the source of messages in a communication event, the other person tries to be the source also. When both try to be the source, neither gives the other feedback. The result is a battle over who will control the situation and whose ends will be achieved by the talk.

Even when a person willingly accepts the listener's role and tries to achieve understanding, the response of a human being is much more complex than that of a machine. A person who listens to a message must, like the machine, receive the sentences in the right form, made up of words that can be understood. If you understand computer language, you can always tell when somebody has made a mistake in writing a sentence because the machine accepts only messages put in precisely the right form. A message for a computer is like an arithmetic or geometry problem in that you can tell whether the message can be understood simply by checking its form. But people can understand messages whether or not they are expressed in proper grammar. Of course we cannot put together just any bunch of English words and expect people to understand them. Within limits, our grammar must be correct to be understood. We are not talking about the difference between "it don't make no difference" and "it doesn't make any difference." Our point here is that, in order to be understood, we have to put our ideas into the right form according to some basic rules of American English.

Even when communication does not at first appear to make sense, people will try to find out the meaning of grunts, one-word exclamations, unstructured poetry, and ideas expressed in improper grammar. In that respect, people are much different from computers, and while the difference is helpful because it enables people to talk about complicated ideas and complex feelings, it is a disadvantage because while the computer never proceeds until it understands completely, people often plunge deeper and deeper into misunderstandings.

Like the computer, human beings can feed back error statements and thus indicate when they do not understand the message. In fact, people ought to be much better than a machine at giving feedback, because they can explain in greater detail exactly what they do not understand. In practice, however, people are often much worse than a machine at providing a speaker with feedback. People often hear only a few words of a message and then get the idea that they know what it is all about without listening to the rest. ("I know, I know, I've heard it a hundred times," says the teenager as he starts out with the family car.) People often hear what they expect to hear instead of what a speaker is saying. If a teacher assigns a difficult term paper, the student may not hear the assignment. Finally, and most important, people tend not to ask questions even when they do not understand because they are afraid a question may make them appear stupid, or they feel that if they keep quiet, at least nobody will know how little they understand. We are all guilty of using poor communication habits at one time or another.

A model of the complete communication event is useful to the student of communicative interaction (see Figure 4). Remember that we are trying to picture a dynamic process, and a moving picture would do a better job. Without this moving picture, you must add your imagination. The parts of the process are put into the model, but they are actually parts in motion; as you look at the picture, imagine them in a give-and-take, step-by-step way.

Notice that the model in Figure 4 has two new terms to indicate the last important ideas about communication that we need to complete the picture. Between the source and the message we have placed the word *encode* and between the message and the receiver we have placed the word *decode.* We know that special codes or code words are used by soldiers or spies in wartime to keep secrets. Advertising companies sometimes offer decoder rings or other secret code devices as prizes to get children to buy their products. When spies decode a secret message, they discover what it means. The other term, *encode,* is not as widely used, but it means putting the ideas into a code and is the opposite of *decode.*

Look again at Figure 4. Before sources communicate with receivers, they must make a message out of something that can be sensed by the receivers. People who wish to communicate must make some link to establish contact. (Some people believe that contact can be made without going through the senses, and they try to communicate with the spirit world or with others by means of extrasensory perception, or ESP.) When a person makes a message she encodes her ideas into a form the receiver can take in. Breaking the code to understand the message is the decoding process.

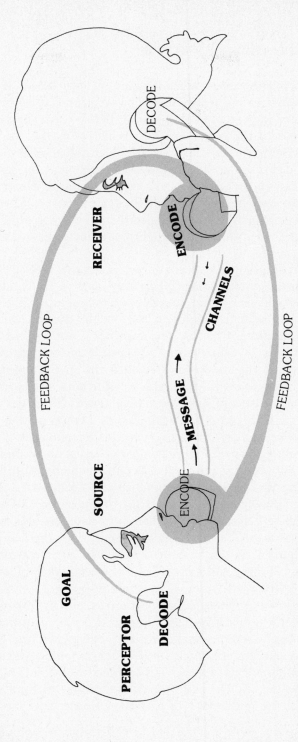

Figure 4 Complete Communication Event

THE PUBLIC-SPEAKING PERSPECTIVE

The basic model of public speaking is a communication situation involving a *speaker,* an *audience,* and an *occasion.* The occasion is something a good speaker must take into account in planning the speech. The audience is an important part of the event, but the speaker must set the action in motion, before the audience can respond. The audience response may modify what the speaker does to adapt to the audience, but the speaker is supposed to remain in control of the communication event.

The speaker may be free to select the *topic* (another basic element of the situation according to this perspective), or the topic may be part of the occasion as when the organizers of the event suggest the topic for the speaker.

The public speaking perspective focuses on the speaker, at center stage, who has studied the audience carefully, and skillfully adapted the topic and supporting ideas to the audience and the occasion. The final part of the model is the *speech,* which results from the dynamic interplay of the parts of the speaking situation. The audience is not passive, but tends to respond positively or negatively to the speech and may provide complications that cause the speaker problems as the speech unfolds. If the audience is hostile to the speaker or the topic or both as the speech gets underway, the suspense and drama are heightened. Moreover, a speech that succeeds against high odds is evaluated as a better speech than one which achieves the speaker's objective with little trouble.

The perspective provides the elements needed to evaluate public speeches. A good public-speaking event is one in which a skillful speaker with a clear purpose analyzes the audience and occasion carefully and wisely, selects a suitable topic, preplans the organization and content of the message, delivers the speech with appropriate gestures and vocal intonations, phrases the ideas in suitable language for the hearers, carefully reads the audience's response, accommodates the ideas to the audience both in the planning and delivery of the speech, and achieves his or her purpose by gaining the suitable audience response.

The perspective provides help for the student by explaining the typical occasions for public speeches and what is usually required to meet those occasions. For example: some occasions call for humor, others for solemnity; some call for argument, others for emotion; some call for information; and others call for moving listeners to action. The perspective also supplies the student with information about such questions as: What is it about the personality of a speaker that makes the audience believe, trust, and accept the individual as authoritative? How does one go about analyzing audiences?

Since the speech itself is the most important part of the public speaking event and is largely under the control of the speaker, much information provided from the public speaking perspective is about aspects of the speech. Information about the speech may include how to select a topic, develop supporting material, organize and adapt the ideas to the audience, phrase the ideas in suitable language, and deliver the speech.

THE USE OF THE PERSPECTIVES

As a student studying the basics of communication in our culture you need to understand the nature and uses of the three perspectives in terms of your communication practice and criticism. The relationship perspective is useful in many interpersonal communication settings. The perspective helps in the study and improvement of family communication, social conversations, the resolution of interpersonal conflict, the development of relationships in more purposive communication such as informal organizational networks, and in processing sessions to improve the social dimension of groups. We use the relationship communication perspective in a number of the remaining chapters of this book, particularly Chapters 4–6.

The message perspective is useful in many purposive, task-oriented communication situations, such as interviews, small-group problem-solving and decision-making meetings, and other organizational communication events. Many communication situations on the mass media are developed from the message perspective and can be evaluated within that framework. We use the message perspective on communication in a number of the remaining chapters of this book, particularly Chapters 7 and 8.

Many occasions are best approached from the public speaking perspective. We use that perspective in a number of the remaining chapters of this book, particularly Chapters 9–18.

KEY IDEAS

- A process is a series of dynamic give-and-take moves by which some end is reached.
- Three important communication perspectives are the relationship, message, and public-speaking approaches.

- The model of the relationship communication perspective consists of several people who drop their stereotyped roles and social masks and cease their game playing to communicate as real, authentic human beings.
- The aphorism "You cannot not communicate" catches the essence of the relationship perspective.
- Feedback in the relationship perspective refers to the response and evaluation of others to an individual's communication.
- The relationship perspective rejects the purposive, intentional approaches to communication aimed at achieving audience response or control of the receiver.
- The relationship perspective broadens the concerns about the communication context and as a result stresses the importance of nonverbal communication.
- The message perspective is based on the SMCR model of communication.
- The SMCR model of the communication process consists of a source encoding a message and transmitting it through channels to be decoded by a receiver.
- During the communication process the receiver feeds back to the source information about what the receiver got out of decoding the message.
- Feedback in the message perspective consists of information about the errors in a message that helps the source clear up misunderstandings.
- One important feature of the feedback loop is that only one person or thing has the goal.
- People have greater potential to provide feedback than machines, but they often fail to do so.
- The basic model of the public speaking perspective involves a speaker, an audience, an occasion, and a speech.
- The public speaking perspective provides the elements needed to evaluate a given speech.
- The public speaking perspective explains the typical occasions for speeches and the usual expectations for those occasions.

SUGGESTED PROJECTS

1. Attend a public speech on campus or in the community. Write a short paper in which you describe the situation in terms of the ideal model of the public-speaking perspective. Evaluate the speech in terms of the criteria for a good public speech. Were there important things happening that the model could not explain?

2. The instructor divides the class into pairs. One of you begins the conversation by playing the role of message source according to the SMCR model. The other person plays the role of message receiver. The student playing the role of message source selects one of the terms from the following list and explains what it means. The student playing the message receiver actively provides feedback until the source has gotten the idea across clearly. You then reverse the roles and whoever becomes the source selects a different concept.

> communication anxiety
> process
> communication model
> encode

After both have been source and receiver, write a short paper in which you discuss how the model of the message communication perspective explains what happened. What was the nature of feedback during your talks? Were there important things happening that the model could not explain?

3. You may keep the same pairs set up in project 2 or pair up with a different member of the class. Either way, make an appointment to have coffee (or?) with the other person sometime outside of class. Allow an hour or more for the talk. Consciously conduct your conversation in the model of the relationship communication perspective. Afterward, separately write a short paper in which you discuss how well the relationship model explains what happened in your conversation. Were there important things happening that the model could not explain?

SUGGESTED READINGS

Bormann, Ernest G. *Communication Theory.* New York: Holt, Rinehart and Winston, 1980.

Carr, Jacqueline. *Communicating and Relating.* 2d ed. Dubuque, Iowa: Brown, 1984.

Jeffrey, Robert C., and Owen Peterson. *Speech: A Basic Text.* 2d ed. New York: Harper & Row, 1983.

chapter *3*

Listening

When we explain the importance of listening, most people say, "You know, you're right! I never thought about it much, but listening is important. From now on I'm going to pay better attention, I'm going to listen better." Like most communication skills, unfortunately, listening is not much improved merely by trying to "listen better."

Speaking and listening are learned skills, learned in much the same manner as reading and writing. The major difference is that we all learn to speak and listen at such an early age, long before starting formal schooling that we tend to feel that everything we need to know about speaking and listening is already learned before we start school; many come to the mistaken conclusion that we do not need to study speaking and listening. We learn to walk and to run long before we enter school, too, but any person with a talent for running dashes can profit from expert coaching and diligent practice, and it is the same with speaking and listening skills.

LISTENING TO PUBLIC SPEECHES

Often members of an audience listening to a public speech do not listen carefully, and as a result they do not comprehend all the ideas in the speech, nor do they critically evaluate those ideas they do comprehend. Some

If you work at listening, you can be rewarded by what you learn from a speaker.
(Carey, Image Works)

members of the audience may be poor listeners because they are taking
flight from the situation, doing anything *but* listen. There are a dozen
places they would rather be and a dozen things they would rather be doing.
Playing the role of listener is a time-consuming, tension-producing job. A
person must often exert effort to keep his attention from wandering.

   If we are at all creative, our attention can find materials more interesting than the speaker's comments. We have a colleague who claims that
for years he has organized his next week's lectures every Sunday morning
during the church sermon. Mental energy that could be used for listening
is often spent in less constructive ways than organizing our week's work,
however; perhaps the speaker has interesting mannerisms of speech or
gesture, and we can count the number of times he says "y'know" or the
number of times he twitches his eyelids, looks at the floor, or tries to put
one hand in a nonexistent pocket in the back of his coat jacket. Perhaps
a young man is attracted to a woman sitting three rows in front of him

in the audience and spends his time thinking how he will get acquainted
with her after the lecture is over.

Deciding to Listen

All too often, our minds drift away from, then back to a speaker; we thus
unthinkingly listen for a while, then fail to do so, then find ourselves back
in the role. It often happens that if we work at listening carefully to the
people we least want to hear, we are amply rewarded by what we learn.
In any case, we would be wise to make a conscious choice about whether
to listen; we should think about whether we will concentrate in a listening
situation and not leave the matter to chance.

Think through your own experiences and list some situations in
which you were unwilling to listen. From time to time the decision not
to listen is probably justified, but the question of when you should be
willing to listen and when not deserves more study than it usually receives.

For the remainder of this chapter we will concentrate our analysis
on those situations in which you have decided that you *will* try to listen.
Even when you willingly take the part of a listener, you will discover that
the role requires some specific skills that need to be understood and
practiced in order to increase listening competence.

Controlling Your Attention

A runner may tire at the midway point in a race but force him- or herself
to continue, despite pain and fatigue. A person listening to a public speech
can do much the same thing by forcing his or her attention to stay on what
is being said. Concentrated effort to focus on the message and understand
it can overcome listening fatigue and the natural tendency of our attention
to wander.

A little practice can help you become aware of those moments when
your attention begins to waver. As you listen, you need to keep part of
your mind on how well you are listening; you can learn to pull yourself
back to the message when you catch yourself losing interest. If the speaker
is developing an idea that seems dull, trite, or uninteresting, or if he or
she is going so slowly that we find ourselves thinking ahead, we may be
tempted to relax and indulge in daydreaming.

One way to keep from drifting away from a dull speaker's slow-
moving train of ideas is to anticipate what point he will make next. By
guessing where he will go, we can arouse our interest in checking to see

if, indeed, we were correct. And if we have guessed correctly, we have then thought about the idea twice and are more likely to remember it than if we had not made the prediction. If we guess incorrectly, we still may wonder why the speaker took the turn he did instead of the one we thought he would take, and in either case, we have tricked ourselves into attending to what he is saying.

Another tactic that can help combat the boredom of listening to a slow speaker is to take 10 to 20 seconds from time to time to review quickly what the speaker has just said. You will find that summarizing from time to time helps you recall the important ideas later.

We have to focus our attention on any message before we can begin to interpret it. You may recall the old story about the farmer who told his neighbor he was going to teach his mule how to drag a log by a chain. After announcing his intention, the first thing the farmer did was pick up a big board and hit the mule over the head with it. "What'd you do that for?" the startled neighbor asked. "I thought you were going to teach him how to drag logs!" "Yup," the farmer said, "but first I have to get his attention."

Focusing on Message Structure

If we now know how to force our attention to the speech, we can learn further techniques of effective listening. We should focus on the structure of the message. People who listen for factual details tend to have trouble recalling the main ideas, and seldom remember many of the facts, either. They thus end up with a vague idea about a mass of undigested material. All of us tend to remember patterns more easily than isolated details. Whole systems of memory improvement depend on connecting the things to be remembered with something we know well. For example, when we meet a number of people at a party and wish to remember their names, if we can connect each person and each name with a house on a street that we know well, we can often recall the names of the persons later. Simply trying to remember a series of names without associations is difficult.

If you practice listening for the main outline or structure of a message, you will find your understanding increasing. You will know that you are a professional listener when you can hear a badly organized message and refit its parts into your own organizational pattern. You may, indeed, be able to recall more of what a rambling speaker said during an impromptu speech than the speaker himself can if you organize the material more effectively than he did.

Controlling Emotional Reactions to Language

Finally, an important key to misunderstanding, even when a person is seeking actively to listen, is related to the connotative aspect of language. Certain words arouse our emotions. Moreover, a speaker's dialect may cause us to respond with anger, suspicion, or fear. The power of words to cause emotional responses is a factor in poor listening. A person in an emotional state is generally upset and acts to some extent as though he were in shock. He loses his ability to think clearly, just as he loses his ability to make small, isolated, subtle physical movements. Even when we want to listen, we may respond emotionally to a word or phrase and lose some of our listening abilities. Just as we lose our ability to make fine adjustments with our fingers when we are nervous and upset, we begin to mishear.

Of course, a certain amount of excitement can improve our ability to listen, just as being keyed up can be used to help us give a better public performance. Excitement, under control, makes us function better. People can experience a considerable level of excitement and high feeling and be keyed up to more efficient use of skills and talents.

In listening as in speaking before an audience, the trick is to be genuinely involved, interested, and efficient. Remember that when you find yourself getting boiling mad, you are also losing your ability to listen well.

After we have learned the techniques of keeping our attention on a message, of structuring the message as we hear it, and controlling our emotional responses to language, we can listen with *understanding*. When we listen to a speech with the aim of understanding, we *comprehend* the message.

Much of the difficulty we experience in working with one another we attribute to communication problems. Marriages are often said to fail because of a breakdown in communication. A colleague of ours argues, in an ironic way, that if it were not for misunderstandings, we would have a world with much more conflict and violence that we do have. He argues that most people filter their incoming communication in such a way that they protect their self-image. Thus they often rearrange what others say so that it fits in with their own comfortable preconceptions, biases, and prejudices. If we always had a clear understanding of what other people were trying to say, he argues, we would come in conflict with them much more often! His point is worth making, if only as an antidote to the popular assumption that communication problems are the basic causes of all conflicts.

Nonetheless, interpreting a speech to mean something other than what the speaker intends can cause difficulty, and most occasions require that we at least comprehend what the other person is saying before the conversation can proceed to either agreement or disagreement.

Listening Critically

Many times we need to do more than just understand what denotative meanings a speaker wishes to convey to us. We must also critically evaluate the speech. We need to examine the speaker's assertions to see if they accurately describe the purported facts. If we can check what is said by observation, we can discover whether the message is true or false. Once we discover a message is false, although we understand what the speaker is saying, we do not accept the statement as an accurate depiction of events.

We should listen carefully and criticize speeches reflecting rumor, propaganda, and persuasion. People encounter rumors frequently and usually listen to them with interest. Rumors are messages in general circulation which cannot be factually confirmed, such as gossip, unofficial messages based upon guesses, or incomplete hints. Many times the rumor relates to official organizational secrets that are of considerable importance to the people in the organization. Rumors in the form of gossip often relate to matters that are socially unacceptable, and thus the concerned parties will keep them secret if possible. Gossip may relate to such things as the boss's wife becoming an alcoholic, the know-it-all neighbor's daughter's illegitimate baby, the professor who passed out drunk at the president's party—the list is endless. Most people enjoy listening to gossip.

If a rumor is the best source of information about something of importance to us, we should try to figure out what the facts are as best we can, remembering how things get distorted as they are passed on by word of mouth.

LISTENING IN INTERPERSONAL COMMUNICATION

How to Listen for Information

One of the important distinctions between the role of message source and that of message receiver in the SMCR model is that the evaluation of good or bad communication is dependent on the ability of the participants to achieve the source's intent jointly. Later, the receiver may legitimately become the source in another, consecutive exchange of information, but for purposes of judging how good or bad a portion of the communication is, we must judge the feedback of the listener in terms of how well it helps the source know that its message has been understood. The critic using the model will judge the fidelity of the transmission in terms of the information the source intended to transmit. Or if the source intended control, the critic will evaluate success in terms of whether or not the message achieved the source's intended control. Therefore, when one person talks with another with the purpose of transmitting information, the problem of whose goal will control the communication must be faced early in the interchange.

When the apparent listener in a communication episode that is getting under way comments in a manner designed to assume the role of a message source, then what the person says and does is not feedback according to the message perspective model of communication. Recall that feedback refers to those verbal and nonverbal cues that the receiver provides about how the message is being decoded. The respondent who tries to assume the role of source encodes a message to achieve a different goal; the comment of the respondent is thus not feedback at all.

Nonverbal communication can help establish that a conversation is to begin, set the ground rules for the talk, and help the participants keep on the track. When you begin to communicate, assuming that you will be allowed to be the message source, you must be very alert to the verbal and nonverbal response of the others involved. In this regard you must "listen" with your eyes as well. You must make sure that your listener or listeners are playing the role of receiver and providing feedback rather than trying to assert a different role.

The Case of the Unwilling Receiver

Often people refer to a situation where nobody wants to be a receiver and everybody wants to be a message source as an instance of poor listening. "We were all talking at once. Nobody was listening. We all had something we wanted to say, and we didn't even hear what anybody else said. We've got to start all over again and *listen* to one another." The problem in such cases probably is not lack of listening skills so much as the unwillingness of the participants to take on the role of receiver at that time. When two people both try to play the role of message source and encode messages aimed at achieving different personal goals, the results do not fit the communication model; instead we have two incomplete communication events that happen to take place at the same time. We have the not unfamiliar spectacle of two people talking past each other, or of two people talking in each other's presence without talking with each other. In terms of the ideal model, two message sources speaking in each other's presence are certainly not communicating. The critic of communication calls such events a failure or a breakdown in communication.

Unwillingness to be the receiver of messages often stems from poor interpersonal relationships, particularly when people are forced by organizational structures to talk over a common task. Above we referred to those informal communication transactions that are signaled and marked by nonverbal communication and tend to be maintained or broken off by mutual agreement. The meetings required by formal structures often cannot be ended in the same way. The doctor and patient may be required to talk about the case history of the patient's illness; the applicant and the personnel director may be required to conduct a job interview; the supervisor and the subordinate may have to discuss the details of a job. Sometimes, two people trying to work on a common task and needing to talk effectively should switch from talking business, according to the SMCR model and adopt the relationship model to discuss their relationship and their communication process. After having created a suitable relationship, they can then switch into the task-oriented interview or conference more comfortably. The person who does not know the one who is the sender of a message may be ill at ease, tense, and unsure and may not be willing to play the role of receiver until the source is better known. The person who is suspicious, hostile, or antagonistic to the message source often refuses to assume the role of receiver, because to do so would be to help the source achieve a goal whereas the last thing the respondent wants is to be helpful. For all these reasons it is vital to remember that listening is not a passive state that just happens; listening is an activity, and a person has to agree to listen, be able to listen, and work at doing it well.

Playing the Receiver Role Effectively

When participating in a conversation for the purpose of exchanging information, you should willingly accept the role and duties of message receiver at appropriate points in your talk. If you anticipate conflict, you should allow the source to develop a complete message first, and then you should provide feedback and work to understand the message until both of you are satisfied that you understand each other. Then if you decide that you are not going to cooperate to achieve the source's intent, you ought to assert yourself clearly in the role of source for another round of communication. Conversely, the other person should willingly assume the role of receiver until your message is understood. Understanding does not assure harmony and cooperation. People may still disagree or grow to dislike one another, but they will do so on a more realistic basis and not because of misunderstandings stemming from lack of communication skills—particularly from either's lack of willingness to play the role of receiver—if they first come to understand one another.

Once you have agreed to play the role of message receiver, the communication skills of good listening come into play. Some of the same psychological powers of focusing attention, searching for structure in the message, predicting and summarizing ideas that were important in listening to a public speech or lecture are equally necessary to the listener in the informal communication event. The receiver tries to attend carefully to what is said, to decipher denotative meanings, and to provide continuous feedback. The speaker, in turn, willingly plays the role of message source, searches constantly for feedback, and keeps encoding new messages to achieve a satisfactory level of understanding. If both source and receiver play their roles willingly and with skill, the whole process becomes a classic expression of the basic model of message communication.

Nonverbal feedback   The communication skills required of an effective receiver of messages include skill in providing nonverbal feedback. Facial expressions are extremely important.

The poker game, which is a situation that puts a premium on bluffing, lying, and systematically misleading other players, also encourages the "poker face," the careful suppression of any facial expression that might give away what cards a player is holding.

The poker face is a liability rather than an asset for the receiver. A skilled receiver makes clear facial expressions and gestures to indicate understanding, acceptance, misunderstanding, or rejection. When participating actively and willingly as receiver, you should smile, frown, look puzzled, allow a look of illumination to spread over your face when you see what the source is trying to say, and so forth. Head nods and shakes are another good technique to provide feedback. One of the authors of this book once took a driving examination for a license and was graded down because he drove across a set of railroad tracks without clearly turning his head first in one direction and then the other, although he stoutly maintained that he had looked carefully in both directions. The tester wanted to see an unmistakable swing of the head, first to the left and then to the right. (Said author then clued in your other author, and when she took the examination later the same afternoon, she looked so long and hard in both directions the tester chuckled and asked, checking the names on his list, "Say, was that your husband earlier . . . ?")

When playing the role of receiver, a person is as active as the individual playing the role of message source. Although the receiver may not say as many words as the source, the receiver will be providing nonverbal feedback continuously; his cues are intentional and done consciously.

Verbal feedback   Verbal feedback, too, is a communication skill necessary for an effective receiver of messages. The receiver can feed back error statements to the source indicating the nature of the problem: "You seem to think I know all about what the group decided last night, but I haven't any idea, really." "I'm confused." "Well, I thought I understood, but now I think it just doesn't make sense. Maybe you'd better . . ." "I don't think I heard that right." Questioning is an important technique for feedback: "What was that last word? Did you say 'would' or 'wouldn't'?" "What do you mean by *entropy*?" "I'm sorry but that whole business about negative entropy confuses me. Would you go over that again, please?" The receiver can also give feedback by repeating, echoing, or rephrasing the message: "OK, now let me repeat what I think you just said." "Just a minute; here's what I got out of that." "Let's see now if I've got that straight." "Do you mean . . .?"

Individuals involved in a conversation that emphasizes information content of messages must take the initiative when necessary and stop the communication flow (just as a computer does, automatically) and indicate to the source, either verbally or nonverbally, (1) that there is a problem (misunderstanding), (2) what kind of problem it is, and (3) where the receiver is in terms of what is understood and what is not.

Creative Listening

Creative listening goes beyond the process of transmitting information from source to receiver. Someone speaks and the listeners not only comprehend and evaluate the comment, but they also sometimes discover meanings in the message that had not occurred to the speaker. They search for nonverbal context and cues and try to understand the feelings implied by the comment as well as the denotative meanings encoded in the words. Much as a creative reader can discover more in a book than the author intended, a creative listener can make a comment that adds new meaning to the original statement. When the listener feeds back ideas into the event, the speaker may be stimulated to see a still deeper meaning in the messages that begin flowing rapidly between or among the participants, generating much increased excitement. Creative listening is an important part of the relationship perspective.

In discussions and conferences, people sometimes find themselves caught up in a chain of fantasies similar to the creative moments individuals experience when they daydream about a creative project or an important problem. Someone makes a suggestion, and the idea is picked up by another participant, then by another, and soon a number of people are deeply involved in the discussion, excitedly adding their reactions and ideas to it. The constraints that normally hold people back are released, and people feel free to experiment with ideas, to play with concepts and wild suggestions and imaginative notions. This sort of idea interplay can also happen between two people who have reached a high level of supportive interpersonal communication.

The total involvement of the listener in communication with others we really care about creates a situation where the flow of meaning is no longer from source to receiver, but where all participants are adding to a common meaning until the result is greater than any one person could have managed by him- or herself. The final growth and insight and learning in such a communication event take place in both the person who originally discussed the topic and the individual who began as a listener. The creative involvement of all participants requires all the communication skills, including the highest levels of listening ability. Interpersonal trust, a positive social climate, skill in expressing ideas, sensitivity to dialect and suggestion, ability at nonverbal communication—all these components are important to the deep and important communication event.

An athlete does not spend all his time running important races at top speed; so, too, we should not hold up the pattern of deep significant communication as the formula for all communication. But when the time is right, and the people are in tune with one another, the deep and significant communication transactions in which we participate are among our most exciting and rewarding experiences.

LISTENING AS A SUPPORTIVE TECHNIQUE

Putting it too simply of course, the clinical psychologist or psychiatrist listens. You pay a great deal of money to have such a professional *lis-*

ten to you. Why? Because the kind of listening they do is a very special kind; they are trained to try to hear what you are *really* saying. There are times when all of us are aware that we are not saying what we really want to say because we are having difficulty getting the words out right, but professional helper-listeners are not listening for the right words. They are listening for the feelings that are being expressed—because the people themselves are sometimes not aware of these feelings, or do not know why they have these feelings or what they mean and why they are bothersome. In any case, professional listening designed to help troubled people and all the research that has resulted from the study of this special kind of therapeutic listening have provided much interesting material for the ordinary person interested in becoming a more effective listener.

Defensiveness and Communication Breakdowns

Much of the material regarding communication breakdowns relates to *defensiveness* and its destructive effect on a person's ability to listen. The first step any good analyst makes is to try to break down the client's defensiveness so that a climate of trust can be built. Because disturbed people are more obviously upset or paranoid than other people, their defensiveness is usually very apparent; they express their defensiveness verbally or nonverbally, either in an outgoing, obvious manner or by retreating into silence.

When people become defensive, their listening ability is lessened. All of us have to maintain sufficient defensiveness to protect our inner images. When we are insecure in a situation, always waiting for evaluation and criticism, we often hear only the "what you did wasn't up to your usual standards," and not the "but then, even second-best from you is better than what most people turn out!" that follows. All of us know people who seem to take nearly everything that is said to them the wrong way—or as we say, "personally." On a bad day even the healthiest of us can feel unduly attacked, and respond defensively when it is not necessary.

Because defensive communication plays a part in everyone's natural communication behavior, but is so often an obvious source of trouble, it has been studied carefully. Jack Gibb discovered certain types of behaviors in messages that appeared to convey attitudes which set up defensive responses to listeners; he also recorded those messages and attitudes that seemed to set up a climate of support and acceptance in listeners. As you might expect, the supportive climates, as he calls them, are mirror images, exact opposites, of the defensive climates.

The defensive climates are generally manipulative in intent and include messages that are (1) evaluative (I'll tell you whether you're good or bad); (2) controlling (Me over you); (3) strategic (I've figured out how to get you to do it my way); (4) neutral (I really don't give a damn); (5) superior (You're a nothing, I'm "it"!); and (6) certain (It's going to go this way, and that's that). Our normal response to anyone communicating these attitudes is to be defensive. The problem, of course, lies in the fact that so often we are unaware of how much of this sort of defense-producing material creeps into our messages. And as listeners, we are often not fully aware why we are not listening well, when, in fact we have become defensive, riled up, angry, and probably hurt.

We all find it much easier to listen to someone whose messages create a supportive climate. Gibb includes among these (1) description (Tell me more about it); (2) problem orientation (What's the problem as you see it?); (3) spontaneity (Hey, let's see what we can do about this!); (4) empathy (You sure feel bad about it, don't you); (5) equality (Two heads are better than one, let's see what we might work out together); and (6) provisionalism (Looks like you feel you could go about it this way, or that way.) These are very brief statements derived from the Gibb article (which we have listed in the Suggested Readings at the end of this chapter), and you may well want to look into his account of defensive communication more thoroughly. Defensive climates are characterized by putdowns of the listener by the source, whereas supportive climates stress equality and a constant reassurance, verbally and nonverbally, that the listener is as valuable a human being as the source and has capabilities and feelings that matter. There is no evaluation of anyone by anyone going on in supportive-climate communication.

In terms of the SMCR communication model, when defensiveness interferes in the channel between the source and the receiver, it is that kind of psychological "noise" that makes good listening and accurate feedback almost impossible. In terms of the relationship communication model, defensive communication builds barriers between people that make trust and openness and authentic interaction difficult, if not impossible. In terms of public speaking, to the extent that any speaker creates defensiveness in his audience, his effectiveness is lessened.

Active Listening

Another form of listening that interests those involved in the relationship perspective of communication is that advanced by psychologist Carl R.

Rogers. Originally conceived as a therapeutic technique for counselors, *active listening* contains principles well worth our consideration as we explore the facets of listening in contemporary communication.

Working with upper-level college students studying small group theory and techniques, we have become increasingly aware of how well the American educational system prepares its students for competition, and how poorly it prepares anyone for the cooperative skills necessary in our increasingly urban society and complex business and industrial organizations. We preach equality and reward excellence; we evaluate one another from babyhood on. Parents criticize so children "can learn." Teachers pit students against one another, "to get a little healthy competition going." Competition exists in most modern societies, in and out of school; but it seems unfortunate to us that the students we encourage to work together, in order to learn firsthand how group dynamics develop and how cooperation must be worked on throughout the class, report that this class is the first in which they *had* to cooperate to make the class work out. Most students have had to live with being ranked since kindergarten. Despite every device educators have come up with (no grades, no "smart" or "slow" groupings, no "failures"), students are constantly told, verbally and nonverbally, where they stand. No wonder our antennae are always out for clues about our personal worth.

We are so used to being evaluated, so used to having our statements accepted or rejected, that when someone actually listens to what we say *without evaluating it in any way,* we want to talk forever. There is an old Spanish proverb, "He who keeps silent consents." When someone listens so nonjudgmentally, we dare to assume he agrees with us, accepts us as we are, is "on our wavelength." This is the core of active listening, and yet there is much more to it. If as a listener you never respond, the person talking cannot be sure how you are responding; your mind could be a thousand miles away, or you could just be bored. The person talking needs some indication that you are empathic to what he says.

If you are listening actively, as Rogers describes the concept, your mind is right with the person who is talking. You are trying to walk that mile in her shoes for the time involved, and you atune yourself to the person to such an extent that you cannot sit in judgment of her because you share her feelings from her point of view. Does it sound a little impossible? Perhaps it would take years of practice to become a totally supportive, nonevaluative active listener, but the basic premises and some of the techniques themselves have proved very interesting and useful to some of our students. They point out the slightly "manipulative" character of the technique. After all, you *do* have a purpose when you practice active listening; you are withholding yourself and your opinions for the express purpose of helping someone else discuss and sort out his or her own feelings and work out his or her own solutions. Even when you are asked, "What do you think? What's your opinion?," Rogers says you must turn the question back to the speaker and give neither negative nor positive evaluation.

Certainly in terms of basic communication skills, to be able to actively listen is extremely valuable, but such listening must be totally honest, verbally and nonverbally. You cannot "con" people by pretending to listen actively; if you try to use active listening as a manipulative tool, as we define *manipulate*—doing things for your own ends, not anybody else's—you will be found out sooner or later.

KEY IDEAS

- Deciding to listen is not enough; guided practice in listening techniques is also necessary.
- Listening is as difficult as reading.
- A listener often must exert effort to keep the attention from wandering.
- We should make a conscious choice about whether or not we will listen to a speaker; we should not leave the matter to chance.
- People who listen for factual details have more trouble remembering what a speaker has said than people who listen for the main ideas.
- If we respond emotionally to a speaker's language, we lose some of our ability to listen.
- We need to understand what the other person is saying before we can intelligently agree or disagree.
- When we listen critically, we need to ask if the denotative meanings are true to the facts.
- Even after you understand a message, you should critically evaluate the propaganda elements within it.
- Feedback only takes place when some participants in the communication willingly try to understand the source's message and systematically provide cues as to how they are decoding it.
- Often what we think of as poor listening is due not so much to a lack of skill as to the unwillingness of the participants to play the role of receiver.
- The unwillingness of the participants to be receivers of messages often stems from poor interpersonal relationships.

- Once you have agreed to play the role of receiver, then the communication skills of good listening come into play.
- Creative listening discovers meanings in a message that go beyond a speaker's intentions.
- When you become defensive, your listening ability is lessened.
- Defensive communications climates often result from manipulative messages that imply evaluation, control, strategy, neutrality, superiority, and certainty on the part of the speaker.
- Supportive communication climates often result from messages that imply description, problem orientation, spontaneity, empathy, equality, and provisionalism.
- Active listening involves an empathic involvement with the other person.

SUGGESTED PROJECTS

1. Make a list of words that tend to make you respond in such a way that you can hardly listen to what comes next.
2. Think back to the experiences in communication you have had in the past week. Write a short paper analyzing your experience as a listener in an important situation.
3. Select a group that is important to you—your family, your fellow workers, or your close friends. Analyze the listening skill of several other people in the group, and then analyze your own listening in that group. Can you suggest ways to improve the others' listening ability, as well as your own?

SUGGESTED READINGS

Gibb, Jack R., "Defensive Communication." *The Journal of Communication* 11 (1961): 141–48.

Nichols, Ralph G., and Leonard Stevens. *Are You Listening?* New York: McGraw-Hill, 1957.

Steil, Lyman K., Larry L. Barker, and Kittie W. Watson. *Effective Listening.* New York: Random House, 1983.

Wolvin, Andrew D., and Carolyn Gwynn Coakley. *Listening,* 2d ed. Dubuque, Iowa: Brown, 1985.

Part Two

INTERPERSONAL AND GROUP COMMUNICATION

chapter *4*

Interpersonal Communication

APPROACHES TO INTERPERSONAL COMMUNICATION

The term *interpersonal communication* has several important meanings in the study of speech communication. One meaning relates primarily to the social scientific study of communication. The study of interpersonal communication includes empirical investigations of such topics as source credibility, language intensity, communicator style, communicative competence, empathy, nonverbal communication, self-disclosure, and communication apprehension. Many of the findings from social scientific research used in writing this book—particularly in regard to the material on listening (Chapter 3), audience analysis (Chapter 9), persuasion (Chapter 16), and nonverbal communication (Chapter 5)—can be thought of as investigations in interpersonal communication.

Another important meaning for interpersonal communication relates primarily to the teaching and practice of the relationship perspective described in Chapter 2. This chapter provides the basics of interpersonal communication in the second sense of the term, namely, how to study, evaluate, and practice relationship communication.

THE NATURE OF THE SELF-CONCEPT

Everyone has a sense of self. Our image of ourselves is important to our mental and emotional health and a basic feature of our interpersonal communication. Your self-concept is essentially the answer you give to the question "Who am I?" Over the years, usually by the process of communication, you begin to define who you are. You define such things as your basic nature, your personality, your roles in life, your hopes and dreams. You may see yourself as a good or poor student, as a survivor or a loser, as a worthwhile person or as "no damned good."

Much of your self-definition came through talking with others in face-to-face situations where nonverbal communication played an important part in telling you how others thought about you and reacted to you. You also got information to help define yourself from feedback, direct or indirect, about what others said of you.

The basic process of naming, or labeling to be discussed in Chapter 12, plays an important role in persuading us about what kind of person we are. The child's mother and a neighbor are having coffee when the child laughs at something the dog does. The mother remarks to the neighbor, "She always was a happy child." The child overhears the comment, hears the pleasure in her mother's voice, and discovers that she is a happy person and that, apparently, it pleases her mother. As she grows up she may hear other members of her family echo this comment that she is a happy person. Gradually she defines herself as a happy person, whereas the family might have named her *moody, sullen, stubborn, competitive, shy, selfish, bashful, unpredictable, or responsible.*

Many times we dramatize who we are in terms of some character in our lives such as a family member or some television or film idol or some teacher or older person we know who becomes the object of our hero worship. "I would like to be like her" becomes "I will be like her" and sometimes "I am like her."

In our fantasies and daydreams we see ourselves acting out scripts that become part of our self-concept either in terms of self-fulfilling prophesies as we work hard to achieve our dreams or as the basis for "I'm no damned good" images when we define our dreams as beyond our reach because of some inner flaws.

Others may also succeed in characterizing us in their communication, so we begin to shape our self-concept along the lines of a person we know personally or have heard a lot about. The father says of the child who has been caught in some mischief, "He's just like his Uncle Harry. We better watch that one or he'll end up in jail." As the child grows up the family members become more and more on the lookout for indications that little Joe is like Uncle Harry, and gradually Joe begins to have an identity and a self-concept modeled partly on his impressions of Uncle Harry. Of course the child may be dramatized as reminding family members of Granddad Flimmerfiddle who was a paragon of talent, social wisdom, and good humor and was a pillar of the community. Our examples may seem far-fetched, but if you think about your own growing-up years you can undoubtedly find various instances where you were labeled as being "like" someone else in your family. How accurate were these labels?

The unfolding process of communication gradually builds up a self-image, and you currently have a self-concept. Although change is possible and sometimes desirable, it is unlikely to happen rapidly. When rapid change does take place, we often say that the person has an "identity crisis." We say that the person doesn't seem to know who he or she is any more. The labels the person gave him- or herself previously no longer seem appropriate. Sometimes, and it appears to occur more frequently during the teenage years and the middle years, people feel they are getting competing messages, conflicting nonverbal cues, about themselves, and they find themselves in a crisis period when their self-identity is less stable and comfortable. During this time they try to redefine themselves in some ways, and even after they become more comfortable within themselves about what kind of people they are, they find it quite a job to communicate their "current" selves to the others in their lives. Since your perception of self is built through the process of communication, it is never totally set, definite. As you interact with others, your self-concept is being confirmed, attacked, changed, and supported through verbal and nonverbal communication.

SELF-CONCEPT AND INTERPERSONAL COMMUNICATION

The concept you now have of yourself plays an important part in your interpersonal communication. We all search messages to determine what they mean in terms of our self-image. Because of this natural protective response, when interpreting a message the listener often reads into the words meanings that have to do with him- or herself as a person. Is the other person saying or implying something about me? Is she saying that she likes me? Is he saying that he dislikes me? That he respects me? Values my work? Thinks my work is mediocre? Thinks that I'm attractive? Wants to know me better? A lot of questions about *me as a person* and my self-concept intrude in my interpretation of the other person's words.

Communicators are often as preoccupied with themselves as listeners are with themselves, and therefore speakers put their own excuses, explanations, interests, biases, and prejudices into the message. A speaker may be wondering about the impression his or her communication is making. Does the listener find me attractive, interesting, and competent? Does the listener see the depth of my feeling? The great humor in my personality? Little wonder that the moments of glimpsing the other person's inner self in the course of our conversations come as seldom as they do. Learning to be meaning-centered is a first step beyond the natural self-centeredness we all bring to communication interaction. Learning further to be listener-centered is an art requiring constant awareness and practice on the part of any person.

THE EIGHT IMAGES IN A TWO-PERSON CONVERSATION

In a given communication event involving two people, the way they perceive each other is as important in their conversation as the way they see themselves. Let us take a situation in which John is talking with Mary. John has an image of himself, which influences his manner and approach to the communication; John also has an image of Mary; John further has a dream image of the way he wishes Mary would see him; and finally, John has an estimate of the way Mary really does view him. Mary, likewise, has a set of images, which mirror those of John. She has a self-image; an image of John; an image of herself that she wishes John to have; and an estimate of the way John does view her. Each person thus has four images of important selves involved in the conversation. If the four images of John and the four of Mary are more or less alike, they can talk in a relaxed and trustful way. You might call this an ideal basis for good two-person communication.

Much communication takes place, however, with one or more of the images in conflict. We will illustrate several possibilities leading to conflict —there are many more, of course—and suggest that you try to see what other images might be out of phase and what other communication difficulties are likely to follow. When John's self-image is much less attractive than the impression he wants Mary to have of him, he may overdo everything because he feels inadequate. He may talk too much, drive his car too fast, and generally come across as overbearing. If John thinks

How you see yourself and how you see another plays an important part in dealing with communication difficulties. (Aron, Jeroboam)

Mary has an attractive image of him as a handsome, brilliant, witty fellow, whereas she really thinks he is plain, dumb, and boring, John will have trouble talking with Mary. Mary's internal response may be, "Brother, does he think *he's* God's gift to women!"

To ask you, particularly if you are in the usual age group of college freshmen and sophomores, to try to figure out what your self-image is and to keep it in mind when communicating with others, is a big order. Learning to know yourself is a lifetime job, but there is no better place than college to start a more sophisticated, systematic examination of yourself and the way you respond. Many college courses have the examination of one's self as the not-so-hidden item on their agenda. Certainly any course in communication must include this probing of one's own basic reactions to life, to situations, and most of all, to people.

SELF-DISCLOSURE

The way to improve the agreement among the various images involved in a conversation is to open oneself up to the other person. We call the revealing of self the process of *self-disclosure*. We know certain things about ourselves, and sometimes we disclose some of these things to another, and sometimes we decide to hide them. Often we hide the unpleasant truths about ourselves to protect the image we want the other person to have of us. We fear the truth will keep us from gaining the liking and respect of the listener. Oddly enough, there are some things about ourselves that we do not know. We may not know, for example, about our little nonverbal mannerisms that disturb other people when we speak. We often do not know what someone else may have told the listener about us.

Therefore, when two people talk with each other, each knows some things about the other. When they share much the same information about themselves and each other, their communication is easier and their talk tends to be free and less protective. Communication becomes protective and less open when one person knows something about the other that is unknown to him, or when one person knows something about himself that is unknown to the other. Take the first instance: Bill knows that Harry has damaged his knee cartilage to the extent that he will never be able to play football again, but Harry does not know his injury is permanent and will partly disable him for life. What Bill knows and Harry does not know makes it difficult for the two of them to have a free and open talk about Harry's future as a professional athlete. Take the second instance: Mary knows something about herself that Ann does not know. Mary knows she is an alcoholic who has controlled her drinking problem through membership in Alcoholics Anonymous. As Mary and Ann discuss plans for a party, the hidden fact of Mary's alcoholism means her communication is always to some extent protective.

When a high level of communication is desirable between two people, the goal of both should be the widening of the area of what they know about one another. Self-disclosure is the technique for such widening or sharing of inner experiences.

SUPPORTIVENESS

How does one go about creating a communication climate in which self-disclosure is possible, even encouraged? Psychologist Carl Rogers, working as a clinical therapist with patients who had mental and emotional problems, used a technique of counseling that he called nondirective. He did not lead or direct the patients in their conversations with him; rather, he encouraged them to pour out things in a free, uncritical, nonjudgmental atmosphere. He learned how to build trust between the patient and himself, so that the patient came to know he could say anything he wished and not be punished for saying it. What Rogers began as a therapy technique, he and others have now modified into a general technique for working with any person to improve communication. Our discussion of active listening in Chapter 3 applies here as well. The heart of the humanistic approach in psychology is to release the human potential within individuals by eliminating the threatening, critical, evaluation communication that brings out a listener's protective filters and produces defensive or counterthreatening messages, and by using, instead, supportive comments to encourage honest discussion.

Because of the manner in which many Americans have come to communicate with one another, we can say that most of us need to develop skills in being consciously supportive of others in those moments of deep and serious talk that are so important to us. We tend to leave things unsaid, to drift through our conversations leaving many loose ends. Through sheer bad habit we often knock the props out from under one another without meaning to do so and sometimes without even knowing that we have done so. A friend of ours who lived in the Middle East for a decade commented, upon returning to live in the United States, that she was more than ever impressed with the coldness and reserve with which we interact socially. "We touch so seldom," she said. "We seem to fear getting personal when people don't want us to, so we stop talking just when people in the Middle East would begin to open up and really help one another. When something really bothers Americans, we tend to clam up." Her comments apply more to the Scandinavian, North European heritage of many people in the Upper Midwest, where the authors now live, than in many other groups of people in our complex, pluralistic society; nevertheless, what she said is true of many subcultures in our country.

The feeling of estrangement that our neighbor found inhibiting upon her return to the United States is sometimes called *alienation*. Today many people feel alienated. All of us are handling more sensory stimuli —in the form of messages, sounds, and emotional assaults—every single day than our ancestors had to handle in a week or more. Much of our interaction grows impersonal because we simply cannot devote our full attention to every new person we meet, every conversation we take part in, and every message we hear on radio or see on television.

Our feeling of alienation is increased by the impersonality of urban life. When several generations of a large family live together or nearby, as they may in a small town and as they did a generation ago in the inner-city ethnic communities, there is a feeling of belonging, of having many people who care how you are, how you behave, what you do, and what happens to you. Today, our mobility from place to place, class to class, group to group has resulted in a loss of the feeling of community. The burden of providing the feeling of closeness and belonging has been placed on the nuclear family. One father and one mother are supposed to give each other and their children all the warmth, support, love, and care each needs. The rising divorce rate is one result. When, for any number of reasons, the family is not able to fill our need for close and important human relationships, we go out into the world somewhat crippled in our ability to interact and communicate with others. We fail to be warm and supportive; others, in turn, fail to be warm and supportive to us. People close emotional doors, begin to turn away, and do not care about one another.

Mutually supportive communication between two people is extremely difficult; certainly the degree of maturity each has attained influences its success. The strain caused by the demand that all the supportive human interaction each of us craves must come from just one other person has led to the development of lifestyles other than the traditional nuclear family. These experimental communes, trial marriages, and multimarriages attest to the difficulties involved when two people interact; many of these experimental lifestyles are attempts to broaden the bases for supportive communication, or in the case of the trial marriage, to acknowledge the possible difficulty of developing a continuing relationship and to give both parties an option to stop it without the legal proceedings of divorce. Despite the development of these new lifestyles, the majority of Americans plan to marry, and the requirements for sustaining a supportive dyadic (two-person) relationship are important for most of us. And to a lesser degree than in marriage, all of us are involved in two-person relationships with family members, good friends, and co-workers.

If we can learn to communicate accurately and meaningfully with those around us, we will find that our skill in human relations is greatly improved. Much of what people feel about us is related to the way we communicate with them. People who make us feel good, we tend to like. People who make us angry or depressed, we tend to avoid. The more genuinely supportive communication we learn to give to others, the more we are liked. If we remember that others want to be talked to as worthwhile persons, we are more likely to be successful communicators. Even if the other persons misunderstand us, if we have made clear, verbally and nonverbally, that we value them, the more likely they are to mention their confusion, to voice their doubts, and generally to disclose their real response to us, often leading to better understanding. Once trust has been established, even unpleasant communication can take place—not without discomfort, of course, but with a feeling of mutual respect.

We believe that good interpersonal communication must be based on trust—which is not necessarily to be confused with liking. Initially we all learn basic communication habits from our own families. If the early examples we use as communication models are good, our chances of being effective communicators are increased. If our parents relate well verbally with each other, they also probably communicated pretty well with us. When the person you should be able to trust most of all, your parent, or if you are married, your wife or husband, lets you down, the experience is a terrible instance of taking an important risk and being punished because of it. If for no other reason than to learn what is considered supportive and what is damaging generally, you can begin to view the interpersonal communication within your immediate family and circle of friends with a better degree of objectivity. Learning what healthy communication is, you can work to build good interpersonal relationships with free and open discussions. In his play *Hamlet,* Shakespeare urged his actors to suit their actions to the words in a play. The advice is good for real-life interpersonal communication as well. If you say one thing and do another, you set up contradictory responses that cause misunderstandings. If you say yes and then do as you say you will, you build trust. If you say "love" and act "hate," you set up discord. In the next chapter we will see the potential for psychological damage in the two-edged message.

THE NATURE OF PERCEPTION

We are all bombarded with a continual stream of stimuli. If we attended to all the messages and signals that hit our sense organs we would be overwhelmed by the buzzing, roaring, snapping, stinking, musky, sweet, sour, flashing, colorshifting confusion. We respond to this overload by selecting out some things to attend to and ignoring the others by pushing them into the background. We can shift our attention so that we bring some of the background into focus, or a sudden movement or loud noise may cause us to do so. We learn to filter out anything that we do not want to see, hear, touch, taste, and feel and ignore it if we can, although some impressions are rudely forced on our attention.

People who suffer from gradual hearing loss often lose the ability to filter out the sounds they want to attend to from the general flow of noise. Because their hearing loss eliminates much of the sound they previously had to push into the background, they no longer need to bother, and they forget how to do it. When they first use electronic hearing aids they often find the rush of many different sounds nerve-racking. Many people cease to wear their hearing aids because all that unfiltered sound is so disturbing. If they try to focus on what another person is saying while a radio is playing, the wind is whistling around the house, and there are traffic noises in the street outside, they cannot filter out the sounds they want to hear and push the rest into the background.

Because we differ in the things we attend to, we differ in our filters and how we perceive the world around us. Look at the vase in Figure 5. Do you perceive it as an attractive or unattractive form for a piece of pottery? When we perceive the world around us, we often make sense out of it by fitting the pieces together into recognizable shapes and forms. We may see a pattern in a series of dots and decide that they fall along a circle, as in Figure 6. We may hear a part of a verse and expect the missing word to complete the proper form of rhyme schemes. For example, if someone says, "Roses are red, violets are blue; I'm all wet and so are . . . ," pausing, we will tend to supply a word which rhymes with *blue*. If the person finishes the thought by saying, instead, ". . . all of us who are running through the sprinkler," the form would seem somehow wrong. We might even have to ask her to repeat the final phrase. In our eagerness to make communication "make sense" (to *us*), we perceive not so much what *is* as what we can understand and utilize. We attempt to organize the often chaotic stimuli into units of information we can use.

Look at the two people in face-to-face conversation in Figure 5. Are they having a friendly talk or are they arguing? Figure 5, like much of our experience of the world, presents several faces, depending on how we look at it and what we expect to see. The angle or slant from which we view something influences what we see. From one angle we see the half-dollar coin as a thin rectangle; from another, as a circle. Equally important is what we expect to see and what we hope to see. When we first mentioned Figure 5, we suggested that you would see a vase. You probably expected to see the vase and that is what you saw.

Figure 5 Form and Perception

Over the years, all of us gradually build up expectations about what we will see and hear under certain circumstances, and we often perceive what we expect or hope to perceive.

In Chapter 3 we discussed how people change the story in the process of retelling it as they pass on rumors. One principle controlling such distortion is that we try to make the story fit our hopes and expectations. People who were certain that Dallas, Texas, was a center of ul-

4 points   8 points   16 points

Figure 6 Pattern Perception

traconservatism in the 1960s often had a first immediate perception of the assassination of President Kennedy as a result of a conspiracy of the radical right.

The way we develop obsessions about certain classes of people or events illustrates how we gradually build filters that help us structure and give meanings to our experiences. An *obsession* is when one idea or thought takes over a person's perception of a number of events or people. While obsessions tend to be extreme, sometimes the extreme case makes the point more clearly than a more average example.

Suppose a man has a near accident with a car driven by a woman. Shaking and angry as he drives on, he tries to make sense out of what happened. An observer, from a different and more neutral vantage point, might say neither driver was at fault, or that the man was more responsible because he made a last-minute turn without signaling. The man, however, might try to explain the occurrence in a way that protects his self-concept as a good driver. He finally decides that the woman was driving recklessly. Still very upset, he notices another car delaying traffic because the driver is timid about changing lanes. "Probably another woman driver," he mutters.

For the next several days the man finds himself watching traffic for further evidence of poor driving by women. (Poor driving by men does not seem to attract his attention.) The harder he searches for poor women drivers, the more he seems to find. Soon he feels confirmed in his judgment that women are lousy drivers and he becomes obsessed with "collecting further evidence."

One evening at a party when he gets off on his obsession, a woman challenges him by noting that she has often ridden in a car driven by his wife and that she finds his wife an excellent driver.

"Yes," he says triumphantly, "but she drives like a man."

Gradually we develop our self-concepts and our perceptual filters—and we *all* have them—by experiencing our world and communicating with others about it. As our filters develop they, in turn, influence the way we communicate. Our perceptions, our self-images, go hand in hand with our interpersonal communication, each influencing and being influenced by the others. As we continue living, filtering our experiences, testing our perceptions through communication with others, we develop patterns of interpretation and denotative and connotative meanings for the words we use. We become islands of meanings trying the best we can to build communicative bridges to and from those around us.

COMMUNICATION ABOUT RELATIONSHIPS

How many times have you heard someone mutter when being called to by another person, "what does he want *now?*" The tone indicates that previous messages from that particular person have been unpleasant and that the intended listener is not willing to enter into a communicating relationship because of too many bad experiences. *Homeostasis* is the tendency to preserve things as they are if we are comfortable and to struggle to get things back into a comfortable state when we are uncomfortable. If you irritate a person, he or she usually tries to get away from the irritation. All communication is potentially irritating, and sometimes punishing. Communication often upsets the status quo, asks us to rethink our pet ideas and prejudices, challenges our self-image, and questions our habits.

Defensiveness

To some extent, all of us adopt a self-protective, wary attitude as we begin to talk with other people. We develop a protective filter through which we hear what is said to us and which strains out meanings that would be too painful for us to admit to our inner selves. The thickness and complexity of the protective filter vary from person to person. Someone who has a good, comfortable feeling about his or her worth as a person has a relatively large screen filter. A person whose self-image has been damaged by the problems of life has a fine-screen filter. Rarely are persons so mature and clear-eyed in their self-awareness that they are able to tell you what all their filters are. Most of us have some degree of self-knowledge, but most of us need to work at becoming more aware of the way we distort our interpretations of messages because of such protective devices. As instructors in colleges and universities who try to tell students about their various inadequacies in communication skills so that they can begin to improve themselves, we have had abundant opportunities to watch the fascinating operation of protective filters and the defensive communication that results. An instructor criticizes a student's speech by first pointing out that certain aspects were good. The student accepts this praise without flinching. Next the instructor criticizes the content and organization of the speech and the articulation of the student. The student immediately says he was nervous, that he was well prepared and had much good information but forgot it because he was nervous.

If the student was well prepared, he should not have forgotten, the instructor persists. The student then says he is working 20 hours a week, had to stay up until three o'clock in the morning to get the speech ready, and was therefore tired and could not do a good job. No matter how the instructor tries to cover the idea that the student has certain inadequacies in his ability to communicate that can be overcome by coaching and practice, the student meets each attempt with an excuse or an explanation that blames the problem on something other than his own inabilities. More than likely, as he leaves the conference, the student thinks to himself, "That instructor just does not like me. Why do I always end up with instructors who pick on me because they do not like me?"

Strange to report, on those occasions when students dared to point out where our teaching was poor and to recommend changes in course procedures, we, too, felt a strong impulse to excuse, explain, and defend what we were doing and how we were doing it.

The Hidden Agenda

Some communication problems come about simply because people avoid talking about what really bothers them. In these instances, people often pretend that when they talk with one another, they are primarily interested in discussing facts, events, and "business." Suppose a teacher and a student have arranged a conference to talk over the student's courses for the coming term. The stated object of the talk is to find out about hours, requirements, and scheduling. To be sure, the topics are important and of concern to both teacher and student. Of equal importance to both, however, are some questions about *self,* and these questions have not been stated. The student may feel isolated and alone in the new environment of the college. He may have liked the teacher's course he took the previous term, and he may have found the teacher an interesting, reassuring person. A personal problem is troubling him greatly. His father has always wanted him to become a lawyer, and he has now decided he does not want to study law. He would like to talk to the teacher about this.

The instructor also has some personal interests she would like to talk about with the student. She has taught the course the student has just completed in a different way, and she would like to have the student's opinion of the course. She has some new projects in mind and would like to ask the student's opinion about them.

Because the stated object of the meeting is to talk about the student's next-term courses, both the student and the instructor feel a certain pressure to stick to the stated business. The conference could very well end with neither of them discussing their other important concerns. We speak of the stated business of a conference, interview, meeting, committee session as the *agenda*. The agenda of the student and teacher we have been discussing concerns what courses the student should take next term. When people talk, they often have hidden items on their agendas. In this example, the student's hidden item was a career problem, and the instructor's hidden item was the student's reaction to the course just finished. Often, bringing what we call the *hidden agenda* into the open through the process of self-disclosure is a good way to improve communication. The responsibility of centering communication interaction on the subject you really want to talk about is *yours*. If you wonder why the other person is acting and talking in unexpected ways, and you sense some hidden agenda item, our advice is simple: *Ask*.

The Importance of Privacy

We have stressed the need for self-disclosure to build trust because too often the importance of the *relationship* between two people trying to talk with one another is overlooked. The need for openness and trust is without question, great. We do not want to leave the impression, however, that maximum self-disclosure, honesty, and openness are desirable at all times and under all circumstances in every communication situation. The thrust toward instant trust is, we feel, being misunderstood and misused by many people. There *are* limits to what we need to tell others about ourselves. Psychiatrists trying to help ill people rebuild a good enough self-image to get by in the world day by day find themselves not only allowing people to keep certain inhibitions, certain established ways of responding to life, but encouraging them to rebuild many of the defenses they found fairly useful before becoming ill. While not all the defenses these people had constructed could be considered good or even desirable, some of these defenses enabled the people to get along. To some extent, all of us have built into our personality structure defenses that enable us to face life. These defenses are there for a reason, and anyone working to break them down had best be prepared to provide replacements or face trouble.

Many people do not care to go about belaboring the world with their innermost thoughts and feelings, and these people should have the right to keep whatever they want to themselves. Few of us who have passed through adolescence do not remember at least one painful truth session with "a good friend," who after telling us all our faults, assured us that "it was for our own good," and left us hanging emotionally, wondering if that was what all our friends thought of us?

Good communication about relationships, we feel, requires restraints and respect as well as, on occasion, self-disclosure. Part of the trust needed in supportive communication comes from knowing that when we are interacting with a person, he will *stop short of hitting below the belt.* He knows the limits of privacy set by me, and he respects them. The woman who tells her husband's secret worry to outsiders is headed for real trouble; so is the husband who repeatedly reminds his wife about her worst habit. This sort of communication hurts and is extremely destructive to the relationship between two people. There are limits in good interpersonal communication, and they are drawn just at that point where we take a swipe at the underpinnings of the personality of the other person.

Differences must be talked out, and verbal battles are useful when they serve the purpose of clearing the air. Verbal battles fought within agreed-upon limits can be useful, even fun, when they help dissipate the natural hostilities generated in any close relationship. Nonetheless, when two people want to maintain good communication, they both have to know where to draw the line. Naturally, as a relationship deepens, each can push the line back a little from time to time, but no matter how close any two people become, each has privacy limits across which no other human should ever intrude.

Airing Grievances

Within a personal relationship with any other person, however, while respecting the limits that he or she places on inner privacy it is still important to express your feelings openly, to be honest about the times when you are hurt or angry. When even the smallest grievance is swallowed, one swallowed word may be added to another, until after a while the load becomes too heavy. Then, when you simply cannot carry those unsaid words around any longer, you will find them tumbling out for almost no reason whatsoever, accusation upon accusation, explosive emotional charges that will strain any relationship. Keeping things to oneself causes inner tension, and when things are left unsaid between two people, at least one of those people is aware of it, if not both. Moreover, the person who is the object of a grudge often fears unspoken words far more than he or she should, imagining them to be far worse than they actually are.

When one of the authors was teaching interpersonal communication for the first time, one of our teenagers picked up the textbook she was using. She seized the notion of "gunnysacking" (carrying all your grudges around with you until you unload them on someone inappropriately) and delighted in accusing her mother of doing just that "all the time!" "But that's the point," her mother said, "Since I do it all the time, that's not gunnysacking." "Yeah," our daughter replied, momentarily resigned, "I guess what you always do to me is more like sandbagging—a few grains at a time."

Relationship communication must be based on openness, trust, a sharing of authentic selves, enough empathy so that you withhold judgments when another person is expressing his feelings, even if they upset you, and an ability to allow other people to grow and mature even if you feel them slipping ahead of you. We wear the lightest reins most easily. If you have sufficient maturity to let those with whom you communicate in close relationships grow, then you will grow with them. Respecting the self you also want respected, you work all the time to keep the channels of communication open between you and those you care about most.

If the best thing life has to offer is a truly delightful relationship with another human being—and we believe it is—relationship communication skills are very worthwhile indeed.

KEY IDEAS

- Our image of ourselves is important to our mental and emotional health and a basic feature of our interpersonal communication.
- A person's self-concept is the answer he or she gives to the question "Who am I?"
- Self-definition often comes through talking with others in face-to-face situations.
- The basic processes of naming and labeling play an important part in telling us who we are.
- Our personal fantasies in which we play leading roles and the stories that others tell about us contribute to our self-concept.
- Participants in a conversation are often worried about their images of themselves and of one another.

- The way two people see each other is as important to their conversation as the way they see themselves.
- One way to improve the agreement among the various self-images involved in a conversation is the process of self-disclosure.
- Self-disclosure is encouraged by supportive communication.
- Good interpersonal communication is based on trust.
- We respond to the overload of stimuli by selectively perceiving part of them.
- Because we differ in the things we attend to, we differ in our filters and how they perceive the world around us.
- Over the years we build up expectations about what we will see, and we often perceive what we expect or hope to perceive.
- We tend to adopt a wary attitude when we begin to talk with other people because we want to protect our self-image.
- Some communication problems come about simply because people avoid talking about what really bothers them.
- Often bringing the hidden agenda of a conference into the open through self-disclosure is a good way to improve communication.
- Many people are unskilled at providing or interpreting feedback in interpersonal communication about relationships.
- Maximum self-disclosure, honesty, and openness are not desirable at all times and under all circumstances.
- Each of us has limits of privacy, which no other human being should try to cross.

SUGGESTED PROJECTS

1. Write twenty brief statements in answer to the question "Who am I?" Analyze your answers and prepare a short message, to be given either orally or as a paper, in which you discuss what your answers mean in terms of your communication.
2. Your instructor will divide the class into pairs and give you a brief period of time for a get-acquainted conversation with another member of the class. Write a short paper in which you describe the image of yourself that you tried to project and the image of yourself that you think the other person, in fact, has of you after the conversation.
3. Recall an important conversation you had with a close friend or family member in which there was a disagreement resulting in part from different perceptions of what happened. Analyze the way differing perceptions influenced the communication.

SUGGESTED READINGS

Adler, Ronald, and Neil Towne. *Looking Out and Looking In.* 4th ed. New York:
    Holt, Rinehart and Winston, 1984.
Johnson, David W. *Reaching Out: Interpersonal Effectiveness and Self-Actual-
    ization.* Englewood Cliffs, N.J.: Prentice-Hall, 1972.
Jourard, Sidney M. *The Transparent Self.* 2d ed. New York: Van Nostrand, 1971.
Rogers, Carl R. *On Becoming a Person.* Boston: Houghton Mifflin, 1961.

chapter 5

Nonverbal Interpersonal Communication

NONVERBAL COMMUNICATION DEFINED

We will define nonverbal communication as (1) what people do (in addition to the words they use) on purpose, intentionally, in order to get something across to others, and (2) what people do out of habit or because of spur-of-the-moment feelings—even if it is without their being aware of it—if other people generally read the same meaning into it. Our perspective in this chapter is that of relationship communication as described in Chapter 2.

While we have limited our definition a good deal so we can emphasize some basics, you should remember that an emphasis on *context* is a good one for the student of contemporary communication. We must remember that others may read more (or less) meaning into our dress, smell, physical appearance, hair style, fidgeting, facial expressions, home surroundings, and office arrangements than we do. The influence of context or scene is important and cuts across all communication situations.

CATEGORIES OF NONVERBAL BEHAVIOR

The technical name for the contemporary study of the nonverbal features of spoken communication related to voice production and the articulation of sounds is *paralinguistics. Para,* a prefix borrowed from the Greek language, in this instance means "beyond." *Linguistics* refers to language. The term *paralinguistics* thus means "beyond language" and refers to that part of talking that goes beyond words.

The technical term for the study of nonverbal behavior that involves the motion of the body is *kinesics.* We define *body motion* to include gestures and facial expressions that support, mimic, or pantomime in parallel with verbal communication and either reinforce or reverse the content of what the person is saying—the overall posture, facial expression, eye movements, and so forth that support, modify, or reverse the content of verbal messages.

The technical term for the category of nonverbal behavior that includes the position of the participants in a communication event in relation to one another and to any other objects around them is *proxemics.* We define *proxemics* to include what is known in theatrical terms as the stage blocking of a play and what theater people call "stage business." A play director will often tell the actors exactly how to stand, move, and gesture in order to communicate the meaning of a scene. Spontaneous and unrehearsed situations are, of course, much more prevalent and are of more interest to us as we look at nonverbal communication.

LEARNING NONVERBAL COMMUNICATION

One question that keeps coming up in the study of nonverbal communication is: To what extent is nonverbal behavior something you are born with because you are a human being, and to what extent is it something you have learned to do? Some studies have tried to see if certain physical actions are always interpreted as "meaning" the same emotion, even when the subjects for the study come from different cultures.

Three factors are involved in the nonverbal communication of each of us:

1. We learn a general way to communicate nonverbally from our particular culture. We learn this general nonverbal language as children, just as we learn to speak in the verbal code of our family. The cultural body language includes such things as how closely people stand when they talk to one another, whether people touch one another when talking, whether people look one another in the eye when they are angry or embarrassed, whether a vigorous nodding of the head accompanies agreement or disagreement.

2. Every individual, within his or her culture, develops a nonverbal language and vocal inflections to help communicate. We may use nonverbal gestures while talking to emphasize our verbal messages, or we may use nonverbal gestures alone to convey our meaning. To some extent nonverbal communication is cultural, but to some extent it is individual and varies from person to person. Some people are skilled and can use nonverbal communication to emphasize, even to contradict, what they are saying.

3. Every person develops characteristic ways of talking and moving, of standing or sitting while listening, and of using the hands while excited. This is highly individual, and often nonverbal communication of this sort is more an interference than a help in conveying meanings to another person. If an individual's gestures call attention to themselves, not to the message intent, these gestures should be modified to allow more meaningful gestures to enhance communication.

Examples of the contextual cultural basis of much nonverbal communication are numerous and striking. Some years ago, middle-class white teachers in urban ghetto schools had difficulty communicating with young black children because they did not understand some of the black nonverbal communication unique to that place and time. The teachers were from a culture in which eye contact while conversing indicated interest, sincerity, careful listening, and genuine concern. The teachers thought of a person who looked down, even away much of the time, as being uninterested or insincere, perhaps even untruthful. The children were from a culture in which eye contact indicated anger. No wonder the children were disturbed by teachers who always seemed to be angry with them!

The Japanese tend to smile in a certain way when apologetic, embarrassed, and disturbed. When a manager in a Japanese factory calls a mistake to an employee's attention, the employee smiles. Before American managers working in firms in Japan learned of this cultural way of communicating, they often were upset by the smile. One manager broke off, reprimanding the employee with a curse, and forbade the employee to smile like that when discussing an important problem.

When you talk with someone from a different culture, whether that culture is within the United States or outside it, you need to be aware that the culture-based silent language of body position, relationships, and motion can hinder successful communication. We have many different cultures within the United States that affect the nonverbal part of communi-

Different cultural backgrounds can make communicating difficult unless nonverbal cues are understood in the cultural context. (Berndt, The Picture Cube)

cation. Some authorities maintain that poverty produces its own culture. We are becoming increasingly aware of, and are emphasizing, cultural differences in the minority groups in our national culture. Regional differences affect communication. The dialects of the Deep South are not just matters of forming sounds; they also relate to the vocal inflections and the body motions that accompany them. The same is true of the Yankee dialects of the New Englander or the speech of the Far Western Mountain Region.

PARALINGUISTIC FACTORS

Proper articulation is a matter of being intelligible—of being able to make all the sounds of a dialect so that someone else can understand them. *Pronunciation* is a matter of being able to use well-made sounds in words, with the emphasis in the generally accepted order for a particular dialect. One might articulate the sounds properly and still mispronounce a word.

The Importance of Articulating Consonants

Consonants are produced by stopping, blocking, or diverting a sound wave. Most consonants are short and cannot be drawn out the way vowels can. Because of the shortness and noisiness of most of them, consonants do not carry the musical or voice quality features that the vowels do. Their main function is to distinguish among the various parts of an oral code such as the English language. The differences among words such as *bit, hit, sit,* and *bit, bill, big* are in the consonants that surround a common vowel.

The consonants often contain less sound energy than the vowels. One of the weakest sounds in English, for example, is the consonant /t/. Because the consonants generally have less energy in them, the listener cannot easily hear them. As a result, the receiver cannot always decode the words; if the consonants are not heard the message is lost. Often we can overhear a conversation without understanding it because all we can distinguish are the vowels, and we hear something like "oh, ee, awww, ooo." On the other hand, we can use the same vowel in every word of a sentence, and if the consonants are clear, we can understand the words even though the conversation sounds strange and stilted. For example, say the following sentence using the same vowel every time. "Mu futhur dummunds thut u gu to culludg."

The lesson to be learned from the nature of consonants is clear. If you want to be understood, in the most basic sense of the receiver's getting the words you are saying, you must articulate consonants clearly. The reason the mumbler is often not understood is that the receiver simply cannot hear the consonants well enough to decipher what words the source is saying.

For example, if you are talking over the telephone and find that because of a bad connection the person on the other end of the line cannot make out the words you are saying, the best procedure is not to yell the vowels more loudly but to articulate the consonants with great care and clarity. The vowels are probably being heard, but the consonants are what counts. Talking more loudly to slightly deaf people often makes them angry, but articulating your consonants more slowly and more clearly helps them to understand.

To communicate effectively, a person must both articulate clearly and pronounce the words correctly. Of the two skills, clear articulation is the more basic. If a person articulates clearly, others will probably be able to decipher the words even though they may wince at the way a dialect's conventions for saying those words are being broken by mispronunciations, but if a person does not articulate well, the receiver may not be able to decode the word the source intends.

Pitch

Pitch is the perception of changes in a sound wave as tones on a musical scale. The pitch of a speaking voice should be neither too high nor too low for general, comfortable use, and every speaker should learn to use variations in pitch to best advantage.

The way a speaker varies the pitch of his or her voice is an important nonverbal technique to emphasize the meaning in a message or to indicate that the meaning one would normally associate with certain words is to be discounted or interpreted as irony or sarcasm. One can communicate a great deal by the skillful use of changes in pitch in such vowels as "oh" or "eee." You can experiment with the usefulness of pitch variations as a nonverbal technique of communication by saying "oh" so that it expresses different emotions and meanings: "How delightful," "I don't believe you," "That's nothing new," or "How disgusting."

Loudness

The ear perceives changes in air pressure in the sound wave as changes in loudness. Loudness levels of voice have one basic and vital function in speech communication. The message must contain enough sound energy to travel through the channel to the intended receiver so that it can be picked up and decoded.

Above the minimum required for decoding, loudness changes provide another technique of nonverbal communication. Loudness variations add emphasis by making certain ideas within a message stand out. A speaker can make important elements in a message stand out by saying them either more loudly or more softly than the surrounding verbal padding. We sometimes forget that speaking for a time at one level of loudness and then suddenly dropping the voice and saying the important words softly can emphasize them as much as suddenly raising the voice to a shout.

Rate

The speed with which one utters syllables and words is the *rate* of speech. Rate is the third major dimension of voice related to nonverbal communication. A rapid rate is usually associated with excitement, danger, the need for sudden action. A slow rate often communicates calm, tiredness, sickness, resignation. Speaking rates tend to vary depending on what section of the country a speaker was brought up in, and much of what we call speech accents are actually variances in rate.

In many respects, variations of rate, like variations in pitch and loudness, function to add emphasis.

Pauses

Pauses can be thought of as part of the rate of utterance, but they play such an important role in the nonverbal encoding of messages that they deserve separate treatment.

Perhaps the most important feature of the pause is its function as oral punctuation. Comedian-pianist Victor Borge had a comedy routine in which he substituted strange and bizarre sounds, such as whistles, squawks, and clicks, for the various punctuation marks. The result was a hilarious example of the fact that the spoken as well as the written message needs to be properly punctuated to carry meaning successfully.

Generally, short pauses are useful as dividing points, to separate short thought units or modify ideas, much as commas are used in writing. Long pauses serve to separate complete thought units, much as periods, question marks, and exclamation points do in writing.

THE FUNCTIONS OF VOICE AND GESTURE

To Enhance the Words

A speaker may enhance or flesh out the words of a message with the nonverbal. The nonverbal can increase the expressiveness of the speaker and can add in making information clear. The message source can repeat meanings (add redundancy) by saying the same things nonverbally as verbally, so that gestures, vocal melody, and words reinforce one another. When the receiver sees gestures that support the ideas he is hearing, another communication channel is being used, which adds more information, thus increasing the chance of getting the idea across from source to receiver.

Body motion may also serve to add to the vocal sounds, to frame or package an utterance for a speaker. The speaker may use head nods, arm gestures, or hand and finger motions to show where a comment begins and ends, to underline or emphasize certain parts of the comment, to indicate complete thought units, to separate modifying words, clauses, or phrases, and to point out which of the expressed ideas are more, and which less, important in relation to one another.

Some gestures serve as a tipoff that a person wishes to speak. Maybe that person will lean forward, make mouthing movements, and tense the body as though to move even farther forward, and others will notice that this individual wants the floor. Once a person starts to speak, he or she may use nonverbal cues such as facial expressions to display emotions and attitudes similar to those encoded in words. The speaker may say, "I don't understand," and accompany the words with a puzzled facial expression. Other gestures may resemble or demonstrate what the speaker is saying. The person returning from a fishing trip says, "You should have seen the one that got away. I swear it was over a foot long," and indicates a size by holding her hands apart. A speaker may say, "I bought that picture in Paris," and point to the picture. A speaker may emphasize the intensity of his verbally expressed emotion or resolve. The coach shouts, "We're going to get going next half or I'll know the reason why!" and kicks a locker or pounds his fist on a table.

To Detract From or Reverse the Words

A speaker may detract from or reverse the verbal message with the nonverbal. The speaker who says one thing verbally and another nonverbally introduces *ambiguity* and makes the message less clear. The speaker implies, "I mean this, but on the other hand, maybe not." On the other hand, a persuasive speaker can use the nonverbal to reverse the verbal for purposes of irony and sarcasm. A skillful speaker can say a great deal with a few words by using irony and satire.

As Feedback

Nonverbal communication can serve a powerful function as *feedback*. Indeed, nonverbal gestures, facial expressions, eye movements, and postures are all among the most useful ways in which someone playing the role of receiver can indicate confusion, understanding, agreement, apathy or lack of interest, involvement, acceptance, or rejection as related to the *content* of the verbal message. Nonverbal communication can function to indicate the subtleties of relationships and can display emotions. Since so much of our social conversation is directed to how people relate to one another, nonverbal expression during the beginning and evolution of inter-personal relationships is extremely important.

Double-Edged Messages

Double-edged messages are communications that say one thing verbally and another thing nonverbally. The double-edged message may have ei-ther a positive or negative function, depending upon the context. The positive functions include the fact that the double-edged message may at one and the same time make one sort of comment on the content of the words and another on the relationship between the speaker and listener. If a woman believes that a man who has just traded in his old car for a newer model has wasted $1000, she may say to him, "You dummy"; but if she smiles and touches him sympathetically as she says it, she expresses her dissatisfaction with this action but indicates that she still cherishes their relationship. By sending the positive relationship message through the more potent means of body motion, she indicates that the relationship is more important to her than her dislike for the thing that he has done. Should she reverse the selection of channels and say, "Aren't you the smart one?" but punctuate the sentence with nonverbal cues which sug-gest, "You dummy! Where are you going to get another thousand bucks?" she achieves sarcasm and indicates that the negative comment (nonverbal) is more important than the positive one (verbal). She may well get an unequivocal message from him, in which the nonverbal supports the verbal to the effect, "What do you mean by that? It's my money, isn't it? If I want a new car, that's my business, isn't it?"

Sarcasm and irony often make points with a sharper cut than long explanations can manage. "How was your date last night?" asks a friend. The woman answers, "He was a nice boy," punctuated with body motion which says that he was nice in the way that a pampered and protected 12-year-old male can be nice, which makes a point with considerable force for the listener who interprets it correctly. The danger, of course, is that the nonverbal part of the message may fail, if not delivered skillfully, to reverse the verbal, and the listener may end up confused. "She says he was a nice boy, but I don't know for sure what she means." One reason why the study of public speaking includes specific training in voice and gesture is to enable its practitioners to deliver double-edged messages effectively.

By using the double-edged message, a speaker can make a statement with irony or sarcasm and leave an escape route in case the results begin to be punishing. The speaker finds it more difficult to "weasel out" of a clear, unequivocal statement. The woman discussing the purchase of the car in the example above can, if she chooses, answer the challenge "It's my business, isn't it?" with, "I said you are a smart one, didn't I?" If she changes the nonverbal way she says the latter sentence so that it is now supportive of the words, she has hinted at her displeasure but escaped from the storm.

The double-edged message can, however, have a negative effect. If people who are in a close personal relationship use many double-edged messages, they may well carry on their power struggles largely on the nonverbal level. They may hint at problems and conflicts but not resolve them. The fact that much of our theory about nonverbal communication has come from psychiatry is an indication of the toll that inconsistent messages can take on the cohesiveness of groups and the emotional and mental health of individuals.

The Double Bind

If a person keeps getting double-edged messages from a friend or relative, the relationship between them is likely to deteriorate; or if the relationship is difficult to break off, the first person is likely to be in a double bind, if the messages are in the form of contradictory instructions: If the person follows the one instruction, the other cannot be followed. One instruction is usually in words and the order is countermanded by the nonverbal. The woman who asks a man "Aren't you going to kiss me?" verbally, but indicates nonverbally, that she'd just as soon he didn't, puts the man in a double bind.

Think how a child often learns from his family to do things that are directly counter to the parents' pious pronouncements. "Don't," a father says, "make the mistake I did and drop out of high school. Get a good education. You can't get anywhere these days without it." At the same time the father says this, however, much of what he does suggests to the son that he thinks reading books is a waste of time, that he views colleges with suspicion, and that he sees college professors as strange, impractical people. The father communicates in a thousand nonverbal ways that he does not believe his own advice, and then this same father is unable to understand why his son quits school just as he himself did. There is much truth in the old saying that "teachers teach as they were taught, not as they were taught to teach." You must be sophisticated indeed in all aspects of communication to be totally aware of what you are communicating, nonverbally as well as verbally, when you send out messages.

PROXEMIC FACTORS

One important factor in the way people communicate with one another relates to where people are in relation to one another. If an employer calls an employee into her office to discuss something in a two-person situation, the arrangement of the furniture and the seating of the two people influence the communicative setting. If the boss sits behind his or her desk and the worker sits in front of the desk, the fact that one is the boss and the other the employee is always part of the situation. With the proxemic nonverbal dimension so strongly a part of the interview, a discussion of personal matters would be difficult. Clearly, the boss who sets up a conference on this basis wishes to keep some distance from the employer as a person and to stress the status difference between them. If the boss comes from behind the desk, pulls up another chair, and sits beside the employee so they can talk at a distance of one or two feet), the situation has been drastically altered by the changed geography of the communicative setting.

The geography of the small group meeting is a fascinating study. In some settings, a place at one end of a rectangular table is viewed as a position of power. Watching the way people sit at a meeting tells a wise observer a good deal about who likes whom and who is competing with whom for position or influence. During the course of the discussion such bodily movements as leaning back in a chair, leaning forward and placing the elbows on the table, turning slightly and pulling away from the speaker, or turning toward the speaker respectively indicate interest, boredom, acceptance, or rejection.

In a large group, the position of the listeners in relation to one another and to the speaker is a matter of considerable importance. If the speaker is located on a stage, standing behind a podium some distance from the audience, the speaker's relationship to the audience not only indicates formality but also stresses the separateness between speaker and audience. Should the speaker jump down from the stage and walk up and down the aisles as he speaks, such bodily movement would communicate a desire to break the public distance and move in the direction of more personal space to convey his message.

The distances among the members of the listening audience also affect the suggestibility of the audience. If a few individuals are scattered throughout a relatively large room, with many chairs empty, the effect is much different than if the audience is packed tightly together with some people sitting on the floor around the edges of the room or standing along the walls. When the audience reacts sharply to a speaker by a sudden tightening of bodily tension on the part of a majority of the listeners, or by a sudden intake of breath, a sigh, a laugh, or a groan, the speaker and the listeners get the message and respond with emotion as well as with interest.

The Functions of Proxemics

To Indicate Boundaries and to Defend Territory   Nonverbal communication can function in terms of *territoriality* and personal space. Recently, evidence has been assembled to indicate that human beings stake out various territories in which they live, work, and play, just as animals do. A student may sit in the same chair every time he attends a given class and be disturbed if someone else takes his territory. People exhibit some of the same behaviors in defense of their territory as other species do. In addition, people act as though they had a bubble of personal space surrounding them that they like to keep free of others. The size of the bubble seems to grow larger or smaller depending on the context and nature of their meetings.

People talking with one another often define territorial limits in a given situation nonverbally. Members of a small discussion group in a classroom will frame or outline the boundaries of their group's territory by the way they arrange the chairs in a circle, by the way they look at one another and away from other people in the room, by the way they hold their arms and legs to protect their turf. When the group finishes its "meeting," the participants often move in ways that say, in effect, "OK, we have finished now, and we give up our hold on this territory." They pull back their chairs, lean back, look around; some may get up, while others stay seated.

To Frame a Communication Event   Body position and motion can serve to indicate that an informal and spontaneous transaction is to begin, can define the details of the order of speaking and listening and the tempo of the give-and-take, and can mark the end of communication. For example, John sees Mary walking down the hall toward him. He slows up, changes direction so he will walk closer to her apparent path, lifts his eyebrows, widens his eyes, raises his head, holds up his right hand, and says, "Hello, how are you?" The way John emphasizes the words and his body motion invite the forming of a transaction. Mary can answer, "Hi." The way Mary acts as she says the word may reject the invitation, and John may swing back on his former path and go on his way. On the other hand, Mary may respond with a big smile, walking directly toward him until she is within three or four feet and then stopping. John may then continue with, "Classes keeping you awake today?" As Mary answers, he notices an acquaintance, Harry, coming down the hall. Harry smiles and says "Hello," but John nods to him briefly over his shoulder, while turning a bit to close off the turf of the twosome he has formed with Mary. Even though Mary has turned with her head up, looking expectantly at Harry, whom she has not met, Harry gets the nonverbal message from John and walks past them. In the same way, after they have chatted and John has indicated nonverbally a desire to extend and make the transaction more intimate and Mary has replied nonverbally that she is not interested in doing so at this time, she may indicate nonverbally that the transaction is coming to a close. John may accept her cues and nonverbally agree, and they will go their separate ways.

To Indicate Interpersonal Relationships Nonverbal communication may also function in relationships that are beginning or evolving among the participants in a communication event. One of the most important ways in which nonverbal messages comment on relationships is in terms of saying "I like you" or "I dislike you." Most people are always on the alert for cues relating to how they are being accepted or rejected by others. Often a verbal response to another person is restricted by custom, norms, or style. The participants in a business meeting are restricted by the norms of our society from saying such things as "You arouse me sexually." Innocuous verbal comments can, however, be accompanied by nonverbal messages that suggest the evolving relationship. Frequently, too, expressing dislike or loathing in verbal messages is "not the thing to do" in many social situations, but nonverbal cues may get the message across nonetheless.

Another important relationship that nonverbal messages often communicate is that of power. If there is a "pecking order" in the relationships of two or more people and they are meeting together, the nonverbal messages often communicate their pattern of dominance and submissiveness. Nonverbal cues often reveal if one participant is of higher status, has fate control over others, or is in a "one-up" relationship.

When status is clear and accepted, the participants who communicate with one another tend to have routine nonverbal patterns that indicate that the power relationships are known and accepted by all involved and that the communication can continue based on those relationships. The members do not have to consciously expend effort in building or rebuilding status relationships. Clear and accepted power relationships tend to free the time of the participants to concentrate on information processing and would thus represent a good situation. In other words, with comfortable and acceptable personal relationships established, participants can keep their minds on the content of the messages and use both the verbal and nonverbal channels to support the same information, with a better chance of achieving understanding. When the relationships are disturbed and begin to get in the way of the work, then our recommendation would be to tend to those relationships and get them back into harmony, so the participants can once again concentrate on the task at hand.

In intimate communication, on the other hand, we tend to emphasize evolving relationships as people grow—for example, from acquaintance, to liking, to love. For the participants, the relationship itself often becomes a focus of concern, and both verbal and nonverbal messages deal with relationship matters.

When relationships are evolving, people emit nonverbal messages that are not routine or habitual: they exhibit courtship cues and cues of rejection or acceptance; they exhibit dominance behavior, conflict confrontation, submission, and so forth as they go about evolving relationships.

KEY IDEAS

- Nonverbal communication consists of the body language and vocal melodies that accompany a speaker's words.
- The technical name for the contemporary study of the nonverbal features of voice production is *paralinguistics*.
- The technical term for the study of body motion related to speech is *kinesics*.
- The technical term for the physical relationships among communicators is *proxemics*.
- We learn a general body language from our particular culture and also develop a highly individualistic way of communicating nonverbally.

- Proper *articulation* is a matter of being understood.
- Proper *pronunciation* is a matter of using the generally accepted sounds in the proper order with the proper emphasis.
- The vowels carry the quality of the voice.
- The main function of the consonants is to carry the code that furnishes the meaning of an utterance. Therefore, if you want to be understood, you must articulate the consonants clearly.
- If you want to have a pleasant and expressive voice, you must articulate the vowels clearly and vary their pitch, loudness, and duration.
- When a person consistently omits and substitutes sounds while speaking, the result is a difficult-to-understand mumble.
- The most important feature of the pause is its function as oral punctuation.
- Nonverbal communication is an important means of providing feedback.
- Kinesics and proxemics may function to enhance words, to indicate boundaries, and to frame a communication event.
- Nonverbal communication often indicates relationships such as liking or disliking, and power and status differences.

SUGGESTED PROJECTS

1. Each student records his or her voice both talking informally and reading. The reading should be from simple prose exposition, *not* dramatic reading. With the help of the instructor and the other students, each class member analyzes his or her nonverbal communication in terms of vocal monotony, flexibility, quality, pitch, rate, loudness, and clarity of articulation. Each student writes a brief paper describing his or her own vocal strengths and inadequacies, and in consultation with the instructor and, if necessary, plans a program of exercises that can be used to improve his or her nonverbal vocal communication.

2. Divide the class into coeducational pairs, if possible. Each pair has two minutes to communicate a mutually agreed-upon emotional relationship between two people, using only a variation in the intonations of the words *John* and *Mary.* No other words may be used. The male member of the pair will say, "Mary," and then the female member will say "John," and they alternate these words for two minutes. Gestures and facial expressions should be kept at a minimum. The situation portrayed could be as impersonal as two strangers meeting on a bus and striking up a conversation, as personal as an intimate family incident, a lover's quarrel, or merely two friends gossiping. The class tries to figure out the relationship between the two people from the verbal intonations alone.

3. Five members of the class are given a current, preferably controversial topic to discuss. They go to the front of the classroom and conduct a brief unrehearsed discussion. Half of the remaining members watch and make notes about the proxemics of the discussion group, their nonverbal gestures, postures, and facial expressions. The other half of the class watches the nonverbal proxemics and gestures of the entire classroom, including the instructor. After the discussion, a general class meeting analyzes the nonverbal dimension of the discussion group and the entire classroom setting.

SUGGESTED READINGS

Birdwhistell, Ray L. *Kinesics and Context: Essays on Body Motion Communication.* Philadelphia: University of Pennsylvania Press, 1970.

Knapp, Mark L. *Essentials of Nonverbal Communication, Brief Edition.* 2d ed. New York: Holt, Rinehart and Winston, 1980.

Leathers, Dale. *Nonverbal Communication Systems.* Boston: Allyn & Bacon, 1976.

Mehrabian, Albert. *Silent Messages: Implicit Communication of Emotions and Attitudes.* 2d ed. Belmont, Calif.: Wadsworth, 1981.

chapter *6*

Communicating
with Another Person

We may talk with another person for many different purposes, including to fulfill social conventions, to escape boredom, to warn of impending disaster, and to get acquainted. We can also talk just for the fun of it. In this chapter we limit our consideration to the more common and important situations in which two people meet with an agreed-upon purpose. We write this chapter from the perspective of message communication in which the participants try to reach a meeting of the minds in order to do a job. The task-oriented two-person conference includes such communication episodes as interviewing, planning, briefing, and coordinating meetings.

COMING TO AN UNDERSTANDING

As you listen to a message unfold, you do not simply absorb the other's meanings. You interpret the message by calling up meanings from your experiences—experiences that have shaped and been shaped in turn by your perceptions—fitting them into the forms suggested by the structure of the message. We come, therefore, to the important question "What are *meanings?*" Philosophers, psychologists, linguists, and communication scholars have puzzled about the meaning of meanings and discovered that the definition is much more difficult than might at first be supposed. For the student of communication who wishes to improve his or her daily conversations with other people the basic question has to be answered, since communication according to the message perspective is the efficient transmission of information and that turns out to be some exchange of meaning.

In two-person conferences, the source encodes a message in words and nonverbal codes. As the speaker talks he or she can watch for the response of the other person. The receiver provides the speaker with continuous feedback as the message unfolds. Since the channels in a face-to-face conversation include both sight and hearing, the speaker can get a reading on the listener's response throughout, at the same time he or she is speaking, from the nonverbal feedback cues of the listener. We cannot stress too strongly that two-person communication provides ideal conditions for close-range continuous feedback. In many communication situations, such as when you are writing a letter, memorandum, or report, or are watching television or listening to the radio, such efficient feedback is missing. The opportunity for high-fidelity communication is greatest in the two-person situation.

When two people talk to each other, the meanings aroused by their interaction are within them. When you talk with another person, what you derive from the talk is something within your consciousness and what the other person derives from the talk is something individual and personal for him or her. We are islands of consciousness and cannot break out of the boundaries of self to experience directly another person's interior life. For example, when you see a color and call it "red," you have learned from experience that when other people talk with you about flowers of that hue, they call them red. You thus come to call flowers of a similar color red. When a man gives his date flowers and says, "These red roses mean something special," she accepts his characterization of the roses as red; whereas had he labeled roses everyone has learned to name *yellow* with the word *red,* she would have corrected him. You know what the word *red* means, in the sense that you agree with others in the presence of a particular flower that it has the property "red." Such agreement is the basis for much common-meaning when we communicate with one another.

However, even after you agree with another person that a rose is red, you have no way of knowing if the red you see is anything at all like the red the other person sees. Logically we have no evidence that when Mr. A talks with Mr. B they may not have radically different worlds of color, sound, taste, and feeling. Mr. A's world may be full of bright and garish colors, while Mr. B's is full of muted tones. Mr. A's world may be a noisy, raucous one, full of violent and clashing sounds, while Mr. B's world is muffled and quiet. Mr. A and Mr. B may agree that the rose is red or that the musician is playing a Beethoven sonata, but in an important sense, neither one can know what the color red means to the other or what the music sounds like or means to the other. The point is made by an old unanswerable question, "How do you tell a color-blind person what 'red' means?"

ENCODING MEANING

Within his island of meanings, the source discovers a desire to tell another person about something. He encodes a verbal message and supports the *meaning* with nonverbal intonations and body language. Quite often the speaker finds that, for what he wants to say, his tools are clumsy. He struggles to find the right names and right properties and relations. He casts about to form the words into the right kinds of sentences. Still he cannot put everything he wishes into his message. His island of meanings is too complicated; the ideas are so complex. He tries to pattern a message that reflects the complexity and the subtle richness of his ideas. The task is difficult. The world within the message source is changing, shifting, dynamic; the language he encodes is frozen once it leaves his lips. The sentences are set, static. He resembles the painter who tries to put a great idea and deep feeling into a series of static forms on a flat canvas. How can he catch the motion, the shifting relationships? The answer is, of course, that he cannot do so completely. The source approximates his ideas and meanings in the form of the verbal and nonverbal message codes.

Some sources encode messages better than others. The encoding of messages is an art that can be learned. Language is limited, but most natural languages are flexible and have great communicative power when handled by a well-trained and talented speaker. The source's language facility, the size of his vocabulary, the rules of his dialect, his creative ability to combine words into novel patterns and to associate ideas and make new meanings by coining figures of speech all affect the kind of verbal message he encodes. Also, some people use nonverbal communication better than others. The source who has a flexible voice and an expressive face and who uses appropriate gestures enhances the effectiveness of his communication.

All of us, when talking with another, encode our messages from within our islands of meanings. We have perceptions, obsessions, biases, interests, prejudices, needs, and wants, all of which affect the way we encode messages. If we are trained as policemen or medical doctors or legal secretaries or automobile mechanics, our training and the kind of work we do begin to enlarge certain areas of our vocabulary and that part of our internal world likewise grows in size and complexity, while the areas we seldom think about or discuss gradually dwindle in our perception. Our ability to talk technically and with understanding and complexity about the things we do most often increases, as our ability to talk about those things we seldom do or think about decreases.

All of us have to accept our ignorance as we communicate with someone else. I know little or nothing of you until you tell me. You are ignorant about me, also. Ignorance is simply what we do not yet know. You are bound to know a great deal about something I know nothing about. If I pretend I am not ignorant about something, I mislead you. We can expect communication problems. We have to learn to broadcast our ignorance on occasion and not try to conceal it. Only when we admit ignorance can someone else begin to tell us about what we do not know. Admitting ignorance is a vital key to providing feedback to improve communication.

DECODING MEANING

The source's problems of finding the right message to communicate his meanings are mirrored to some extent in the receiver. The receiver of any message also has a personal island of meanings. The receiver has a certain language facility, a certain dialect, certain biases, interests, and prejudices. The listener tends to read into the messages those meanings associated with her personal biases and interests.

The receiver finds some parts of the message easy to associate with a denotative meaning. Generally, if a name is specific, such as, "My dog, Rover, sitting over there by the chair," the listener associates a part of her perceptual world quickly and easily, and both the speaker and the listener know what is being discussed. The receiver feels confident that she understands the message, and she may nod her head to indicate understanding. Problems arise because some words are abstract and difficult to associate with a denotative meaning or with connotative meanings. Messages that are not firmly anchored to clear denotative meanings may trigger a large pool of meanings and their emotional associations in the listener.

Just as the speaker finds his verbal and nonverbal codes clumsy for the task of encoding messages, so the receiver finds the interpretation of messages difficult, but it is through this interpretation that human understanding can come about. Perhaps the listener interprets a nonverbal gesture as a clue to some deep and important idea within the consciousness of the speaker. The excitement of discovery regarding a fellow human being begins. The listener strains to find a verbal key to the idea. She asks for more messages. She strives to interpret these and seeks additional comments. She thinks she sees the shape of the idea; she gets a glimmer of the feeling within the source. Somehow she manages some contact through the self-protective walls of biases, dialect, background, interests, and motives. The interchange has proceeded until the two people feel they have achieved genuine understanding. Both are excited, moved, touched by the experience. They have glimpsed the interior island of another person's meanings.

Such moments of high-fidelity transmission of meaning come too seldom for most of us, and little wonder, considering the difficulty of the task and the fact that we often take the skills required for granted. When they come, they provide some of the most rewarding of all human social experiences.

FEEDBACK

Much talking that passes for communication is merely people talking *at* other people, because the speaker and the listener demand neither feedback nor clarification. One of the surprising discoveries of people who study communication is that so many people are so poor at providing and interpreting feedback to aid understanding.

Several important factors operate in two-person communication to keep people from providing the essential feedback. One is the mistaken notion that talking with another person is a simple matter. After all, we reason, we have probably spent more of our total communication time in such two-person talks than in any other form of communication. We ought to be good at it by now, we tell ourselves. Besides the fact that we take such interaction for granted, the situation itself is often informal and relaxed and makes talking seem much less difficult than giving a good formal speech to an auditorium full of people. When we do misunderstand something in an informal conversation, we often blame our failure to find out more on some inherent trait of the other person or some factor beyond our control: "I guess George didn't hear me," "We were interrupted about then, and I guess it wasn't clear," or "I don't know what it is about Lorraine, but she just never can get anything straight."

Another factor that operates to prevent feedback is our assumption that our first attempt to tell another person something has succeeded. We often interpret silence as understanding and acceptance. We even interpret mumbling or other unclear answers as acceptance. Actually, our first attempt to communicate is *likely to fail.* The more completely we have failed, the more likely it is that the listener will greet the communication with silence. Silence itself often should be interpreted as feedback indicating not that the other person understands or agrees with you, but rather that he is confused. If you give a directive to someone else, particularly if you are in a position of authority, you should be as suspicious of a simple yes answer as you are of silence. When a policeman has been called to an apartment because of a domestic argument and he "lays down the law" to the couple and then demands of them, "Now, is that clear," what can their answer be but "Yes." As one young policeman said in class, "And then I had to go back five nights later and spell it out again." He was disgusted, until he realized that he had left little opening for the couple to express their real failure to understand his advice and their refusal to appreciate the need for working out their problems in some way that would not disturb their neighbors at four o'clock in the morning.

An additional factor in poor feedback is concern for protecting the self. We have discussed protective and defensive communication at length in Chapter 4. One of the important effects of the need to defend self is unwillingness to reveal lack of information, knowhow, understanding, or skill by providing feedback. We have to learn to be comfortable admitting what we do not know in any situation.

A final factor in poor feedback is lack of skill. Watch a television play or go to the theater and watch the actors who are not speaking at any given moment. The good performers are acting every minute, reacting to what the speaker is saying, responding nonverbally, *communicating* to the audience what they understand and how they feel about what another character is saying or doing. A good communicator does much the same thing when listening to another person; he or she responds in such a way that the speaker can see and hear and understand his or her response.

COMMUNICATING WITH ANOTHER PERSON
TO DO A JOB

Much face-to-face business and professional communication takes place between two people. Arranging for a small group of busy people to take part in a meeting is difficult and time-consuming. Arranging contacts between two people is often an efficient way to do business. Supervisors in organizations of all kinds do much of their managing in formal and informal two-person conversations.

Busy people often dash from one conference to another. A doctor may see a steady stream of patients during his office hours. A teacher may have counseling sessions with a number of students during the course of a day. A manager may move from a conference with her boss to a telephone conversation with a salesperson from another company to a discussion of a work-related problem with a subordinate to a briefing conference with her administrative assistant. Often, people under pressure feel that the communication events are coming so fast that all they can do is improvise on the spot. They may try to keep up by relying on their instincts and mentioning topics as they pop into mind. Often the off-the-top-of-the-head communication causes misunderstandings and mistakes.

One reason we often feel that little planning and skill are required to talk to another person about a job-related matter is that such meetings resemble the social interactions of passing the time of day. You can chat with a fellow worker about the movie you both saw the evening before while having morning coffee; why not talk about a job-related matter of considerable importance in the same informal, aimless, and casual way? The answer is that even the most casual conversation is a complicated communication situation, as we saw in Chapter 4. To create misunderstanding in a discussion of a movie may not be important, but to fail to communicate on important business or professional matters is often serious.

We could illustrate the basic principles of communicating with another person to do a job with several different types of interviews. We could use the situation where a person is interviewing another for information, such as when a newspaper reporter is preparing a story. We could concentrate on a person interviewing another to sell a product or service. We could use a situation where a supervisor is explaining to a subordinate what needs to be done to accomplish an organizational task.

We will use the job interview to illustrate how to communicate in two-person, task-oriented conferences, because it includes elements from all the above situations. If you are interviewing for a job, you will want to find out important information relating to the nature of the work, the salary, and the fringe benefits. You will also need to persuade the interviewer that you can provide important services for the organization. Often the interviewer will determine the time and place of the meeting, and you will have to adapt to the way the interviewer has planned the session. Many of the principles of communication that relate to the job interview can be adapted easily to other interviews.

THE JOB INTERVIEW

The Function of the Job Interview

The job interview is not an isolated communication event. The interview takes place in a context of a hiring organization. While the interviewer and interviewee may be meeting for the first time, the fact that the meeting may result in a future association of the prospective employee with the organization over a period of time influences the importance and conduct of the conference. The interview must thus be examined in terms of the long-range effects it may have. The person applying for the job may feel anxious because of the future implications of success or failure. The person conducting the interview may feel some tension and take much more care because the interviewer wants to hire a person who will not only do the work required but who will also be able to get along with the others with whom the interviewee would be working. A successful job interview is one in which the "right person is hired for the right job." If the right person is hired, then the interview is often the beginning of some sort of relationship between the person hired and the person who hired him.

The interviewer will usually have some information about the applicant's background before the interview begins. She may know about the applicant's educational background, his age, and his previous work experience and may even have some evaluation of his personality strengths and weaknesses if the applicant has furnished her with recommendations from previous employees or associates prior to the interview. Nonetheless, the interviewer usually will want to check out any information she has prior to the interview with the applicant himself; many a face-to-face interview has made the difference between someone getting hired or being rejected ("He looked good on paper, but . . ."). Particularly if the interviewer knows that the applicant has the professional skills required (has successfully completed the necessary courses or apprenticeship and so forth), the paralinguistic and other nonverbal skills of the interviewee become more important. The interviewer is trying to assess such things as: Will this person be dependable and show some loyalty to the job, or is he self-centered, immature, only looking out for himself, and likely to take off at the slightest provocation? Does this person really want *this* particular job, and if so, why? Is an association between this applicant and the firm likely to be mutually beneficial and satisfying? Call these the hidden agenda of every job interview. Sometimes a direct question regarding these matters will surface, but more often it is a subtle matter of messages sent and received nonverbally.

The job interview may be a first meeting for the two participants, but it may have long-range effects. (© Kroll, 1981, Taurus)

Planning the Job Interview

Both participants in a job interview can benefit from making some plans before the meeting. Many large companies have people who do nothing but conduct job interviews all day. Personnel departments of large corporations develop highly specialized methods of trying to find and keep good employees. Smaller businesses, however, may have someone who is actually very inexperienced and awkward doing the job interviewing; on such occasions the interview can be unsatisfactory, even a painful chore for both parties. As in all other human interactions, the skills of interviewers vary greatly. The student should understand that a "bad interview" can be as much the fault of the interviewer as the applicant, and it never hurts to request a second interview if things did not go well the first time.

Both participants should determine their *objectives* prior to the interview. What, for each, would be the most desirable outcome? The least desirable? The minimum acceptable outcome? Would pushing for the most desirable outcome force a decision that might bring about the least desirable? (If, as applicant, you want the job, and you push the prospective employer for an immediate decision, might that result in a negative decision? Would leaving the outcome for sometime in the future be more in your favor?)

Here are some ideas that both might keep in mind beforehand:

Considerations for the Interviewer

How can I begin the meeting to develop rapport and create a climate in which the applicant will be at ease and be most natural?

Do we have common ground that can serve as a starting place?

What do I know about this person's motives, and interests, knowledge, expertise, habits, and attitudes already?

What major information do I need to get from him during the interview itself?

What is the best order in which to take up the main topics?

How is the applicant likely to respond to the main objective that I have for the meeting?

What resistance can I anticipate?

Considerations for the Applicant

What can I do to help create a comfortable social climate to aid in getting the information I need?

Do we have common ground that can serve as a topic for opening conversation?

What should my approach be? Should I be serious, solemn, wary, friendly, lighthearted, jolly?

What major points about my background, education, desires, hopes, abilities in working with people, do I hope to make?

What major information about the job, working conditions, pay, fringe benefits, and so forth, do I need to know?

If the interviewer gives me a chance to play the role of message source, what is the best order for me to take up the main topics I want to discuss?

How is the employer likely to respond to the main objective I have for the meeting? What resistance can I anticipate?

Conducting the Job Interview

The person conducting the job interview can select one of two general strategies, the directive or the nondirective approach. The *directive* strategy is one in which the interviewer assumes the role of message source and takes control of the channels of communication in order to achieve her goal. The interviewer decides what topics to introduce and in what order, and attempts to keep the interview going pretty much according to her plan. She wants certain information from the applicant and plans the interview to cover the matters she considers important.

The *nondirective* strategy finds the interviewer making only minimal moves to assume the role of message source. Instead, the interviewer is alert for clues from the interviewee as to what role he, as applicant, would like to assume. The nondirective strategy calls for an emphasis on listening and encouraging, being permissive and supportive, and actively seeking the role of receiver whenever appropriate. The nondirective approach is appropriate whenever the employer wishes to learn a lot about the applicant's hopes and fears, personality, attitudes, and general level of articulateness.

For most job interviewing situations, some balance between nondirective and directive interviewing techniques is usually advisable. Even if the interview seems to be largely directive, however, an interviewer aware of good communication will allow the applicant to be the source of communication in appropriate subparts of the interview; even if time limits force an interviewer to stick largely to a prescribed list of questions that her organization always requires, she should build in several opportunities for the applicant to volunteer information or ask questions about matters he wants to know.

Skill in asking open-ended questions that cannot be answered by a brief "yes" or "no" comes with practice. The job interview is almost always face-to-face communication, and nonverbal aspects are very important. Feedback is crucial, verbally and nonverbally, and must be consciously built into the interview. Be aware of your nonverbal communication as well as your verbal remarks; shaking the head, nodding, frowning, smiling, looking puzzled, making questioning sounds, sounds of agreement, enthusiasm—all communicate a great deal about both participants. The amount of comfortable eye contact must be decided throughout the interview. Instantaneous appraisals are being made by both parties, and many people feel the nonverbal messages are more important to the outcome than the verbal exchanges, much as when you decide to vote for one candidate rather than another. "I can't put my finger on it; I just didn't get a good feeling about her. It wasn't her ideas so much as the way she expressed them, I think."

When any two people interact, each is projecting his or her self-image, certainly, but it is the applicant in a job interview who is, literally, selling him- or herself as someone of value to the interviewer and to the organization the interviewer represents. With our cultural bias against bragging, against selling oneself, the competitive aura of a job interview sometimes inhibits an applicant. Much of the popularity of assertiveness training courses in recent years has come about because of people who walked away from some situation feeling, "Darn, *I* could have done that better than she did. Why didn't I speak up and give my ideas?" or "I have to tell people what I can do, tell them my talents; I just get so frustrated all the time because I never speak up in time and someone else always gets the job, or the credit." As assertiveness training developed, it was found that you *can* learn to stand up for yourself with practice, and the job interview is certainly one such place. If you do not communicate your ability and potential as a job applicant, you really cannot blame the interviewer for not having a magic crystal ball that enables him or her to read through your blank, inarticulate projection of yourself.

A good interviewer has something to sell, too, of course; the interviewer is selling the organization and the position. The applicant is selling skills and personality.

KEY IDEAS

- Much business and professional communication takes place face to face in two-person meetings.
- When two people talk to each other, the meanings aroused by their interaction are within each of them.
- We are islands of consciousness and cannot break out of the boundaries of self to experience directly another person's meanings.
- Our interior world is changing, shifting, dynamic; the language we use to encode our meanings is static and therefore never fully adequate.
- The encoding of messages is an art that can be learned.
- The source's problems of finding the right message are mirrored to some extent by the receiver's problems of supplying the right meanings for the message.
- Many people are unskilled at providing or interpreting feedback in task-oriented groups.
- Our first attempt to communicate with another person is likely to fail.
- Silence should usually be interpreted as indicating for the speaker that the other person is confused.
- Both participants in a job interview can benefit from making plans before the meeting.
- Both participants should determine their objectives prior to the interview.
- The person conducting the interview can select a directive strategy in which he or she assumes control of the meeting.
- The person conducting the interview can select a nondirective strategy, which puts an emphasis on listening, being supportive, and seeking the role of receiver whenever appropriate.
- The nonverbal aspects of a job interview are important in terms of the impression that the interviewee makes.
- The applicant's communication will project a self-image, which is important in getting the job.

SUGGESTED PROJECTS

1. This is a job interview exercise. The instructor may have interviewers from companies conduct the simulated interviews. If no outside interviewers are available, the class can be divided into pairs, with one student playing the role of job applicant and the other the role of interviewer. Each pair conducts a job interview in front of the class or

on audiotape or videotape. You are to review your performance and write a short paper of self-evaluation.
2. The class is divided into pairs. One person in each pair selects an important idea or process to explain to the other. The idea should be something that the first person knows from a course he has taken or from a personal experience he has had but the second person has not. The first person acts as a message source and tries to explain the idea or process to the other. The second person concentrates on providing feedback, both verbal and nonverbal, to the first. The second person can only ask these three questions: "What do you mean?" "How do you know?" and "So what?" at the appropriate times.

SUGGESTED READINGS

Goss, Blaine. *Processing Communication.* Belmont, Calif.: Wadsworth, 1982.
Stewart, Charles J., and William B. Cash. *Interviewing: Principles and Practices.* 3d ed. Dubuque, Iowa: Brown, 1982.

chapter 7

Communicating in Work Groups

Our emphasis in this chapter and the next will be upon the task-oriented small group. As a student, you probably attend many group meetings in our society. A student may be a member of an athletic team or club, a neighborhood or street gang, a fraternity or sorority, a political club, a special interest group, a departmental association, or a student cooperative. A student may attend meetings or committees for student government, dormitory groups, student unions, religious foundations, and increasingly, of special groups to prepare projects for class.

In addition to performing duties for an immediate work group on the job, a person who works for a store, a factory, a service industry, or a government agency such as a police force or fire department attends committee meetings, union meetings, and work group sessions. Off the job, a typical citizen takes part in religious groups, political organizations, or groups for other community and voluntary purposes.

Every project to get things done requires working with small groups. If we wish to change our neighborhoods and organize for community power or political power at another level, we must work productively with others in groups.

Despite the importance of working with small groups, most of us take our role in a discussion for granted. Few people have a chance to study group discussion or drill in the techniques of group work in order to become professional communicators in the small-group setting. However, one of the best ways to ensure that the group meetings you attend in the future will be useful and that you will feel satisfied about your contribution to them is to study small-group communication and evaluate critically the dynamics of the meetings you attend.

FUNCTIONS OF WORK GROUPS

A discussion group in our culture is a special form of the work group. Work groups use several different sorts of meetings. If the members come to the meeting with the wrong idea about what the meeting is for and what it will be like, they may be frustrated. For example, if the meeting is just a ceremony to rubberstamp decisions already made and a member comes expecting to change the decision, he or she feels cheated.

Every organization has some meetings that are rituals. A ritual is a set ceremony that has come to be expected at certain times to celebrate an organization or group. In a meeting that is a ritual, people may say one thing and mean another. Some religious rituals contain prayers that the worshipers repeat over and over again, and the meaning of the prayers as expressed in the words is not as important to the worshipers or to the ritual as the act of saying the words over and over again. The ritual meetings of an organization may aid its cohesiveness (its ability to stick together) and ensure that people in authority are recognized. For example, the department heads of a business organization may make an oral presentation of their yearly budgets at a meeting of all the vice-presidents. The meeting is really meant only to rubberstamp decisions already made. Yet the meeting is important to the others in the business. The newcomer who says that the meeting accomplishes nothing and is therefore a waste of time is judging it on the wrong grounds.

Another kind of meeting is the briefing session, used to give members information they need to carry through on plans already made. The objective of the group is clear: the members know what they want to do and need only find out who is to do what, when, and where.

A group discussion may also have the purpose of instructing participants in some concepts or skills they can use in the future. Teachers may use small discussion groups to teach a course in English literature, for example, by dividing up the class and having each group discuss a novel.

A small discussion group may meet to advise the person or persons empowered to make decisions. The person in charge consults or asks the advice of the people in the meeting. A department head at a college or university might ask a committee of students and faculty about changes in course requirements. If the meeting is consultative, the department head does not promise to abide by their advice but does ask for and consider it. The danger in an advice-giving discussion is that if the people who attend do not understand its purposes, they may expect their advice to be accepted, and may feel cheated when it is not: "We spent all that time making that decision, and then they ignored it."

Finally, an extremely important kind of meeting is one called actually to make the decision. Members of decision-making groups often are more fully committed to their decisions and usually work harder to implement them than do the participants in other kinds of groups. One of the most important functions of small groups in many organizations is to provide a way for people to participate in management decisions and to exercise some of the power relating to the use of the organization's resources. The growing use of quality circles and involvement teams in American business firms testifies to the importance of groups that give advice and make decisions.

CHARACTERISTICS OF A GOOD WORK GROUP

The work group is a social event. When several people share ideas or produce a product, a social dimension emerges. The first question in the mind of every person in a new work group is "How do I relate to these other people as a human being?" Every member wants this question answered, and he wants it answered early. Even after he has been in the group for months, or years, he wants the answer repeated from time to time.

If individual members feel that the others like, admire, and respect them, enjoy their company, and consider their ideas important, they can relax and turn their full attention to doing the job. Such an atmosphere of trust and understanding should be the goal of every participant, and *particularly* of every manager, chairperson, moderator, or leader of a work group.

We are discussing only those groups that have a job to do. Inevitably, the members expect, and usually want, to concentrate on the job. If the group is a discussion meeting or conference, they want to start talking about the agenda. If the group is working in an office, the members want to start reading the mail, filing papers, drafting letters, holding conferences. If it is a production group, the workers need to get the machines rolling. The family, too, is a working group; its job is to maintain the living

A work group is also a social event. (Mercado, Jeroboam)

arrangements of its members and manage their day-to-day existence. Many studies have been made of the family as a group. The group's work is hampered by poor plans, misunderstandings, faulty reasoning, inadequate concepts, bad information, and most important, the way directions and orders are given and received. *A whole book could be devoted to the subject of giving and receiving orders.* Orders must be given, but when you give another person an order, the social and task dimensions of your interaction may come into conflict. If the group member thinks the direction indicates that the leader feels superior or is using the group for his own purposes, the order may be misunderstood or disobeyed even though it is a good order.

Morale and Productivity

A good work group has high morale. The members are happy with the group; they enjoy working with the others on the job and are pleased with their place in the group. They receive a sense of belonging and a feeling of personal satisfaction from their roles.

A good group gets things done. It reaches its goals with a minimum of wasted motion. It turns out a large quantity of a high-quality product, wins games, solves problems, or makes good decisions.

Some people think productivity is all that counts, but the individual should gain a sense of satisfaction and worth from his participation in the group. We do not believe that the individual exists solely for the group. The group has certain duties and responsibilities to the individual.

Cohesiveness

Cohesiveness is the key to successful work groups. *Cohesiveness* refers to the ability of the group to stick together. Another term for the same quality is *group loyalty.* A highly cohesive group is one in which the members work for the good of the group. They form a tightly knit unit, and they help one another. They exhibit team spirit. They reflect the motto of Alexander Dumas's Three Musketeers: "All for one and one for all."

Cohesiveness encourages increased and improved communication, morale, and productivity. Cohesive groups do more work, because members take the *initiative* and help one another. They distribute the workload among themselves and take up the slack in times of stress. People in groups with little cohesiveness tend to stand around and wait for assignments. They do what they are told to do and no more. They do not care about the work of others. While members of cohesive groups volunteer to help one another, people in groups with little cohesiveness look out primarily for themselves.

The more cohesive the group is, the more efficient the communication within the group. Cohesiveness encourages disagreement and questions. Both are necessary to communication. Highly cohesive groups disagree among themselves. Individual members of such a group cannot stand by and watch the others do a shoddy job or make a wrong decision. Their group is at stake. They must speak up and do what they can to assure its success. Such disagreements improve the quality and quantity of the work by assuring a high level of communication. Cohesiveness encourages questions, because in the cohesive group all the members know their places and are secure. Their position is not threatened if they admit they do not know something. Indeed, the welfare of the group requires that each member have adequate information. The group rewards questions that help it achieve its goals. Likewise, the important member does not feel insulted when people demand more information. He or she is more interested in the welfare of the group than in his or her own personal feelings. Since the success or failure of a group depends largely on the efficiency of its communication, the cohesive group encourages its members to work cooperatively to achieve understanding.

To build cohesiveness in your group, you need to know some of the dynamics of group process. Every member of the work group is constantly experiencing pushes into and pulls away from the group. The cohesiveness of the group changes from day to day. A unit that is highly cohesive this year—an effective, hard-hitting group—may next year suffer a series of reverses or a change of personnel that causes it to lose cohesiveness and be less effective. If the group comes into competition with similar groups, cohesiveness is usually increased. Athletic teams develop high levels of team spirit and will to win because they compete with other teams in a win or lose situation. Coaches know the importance of cohesiveness and how to build it.

On the other hand, a *competing* group may try to lure individual members away from their group and thus decrease their feelings of commitment. If you wish to examine the cohesiveness of your group, you must look to the other groups that are competing for the loyalty of the members. The attractiveness of the group for a given member is partly dependent on the character of the other groups he or she could join. If another group becomes more attractive, a person may leave his or her original group.

If you want to know how attractive your group is to a member, total the rewards it furnishes that member and subtract the costs; the remainder is an index of group attractiveness. At any given moment, an individual feels the pull of his or her group because it satisfies one or more personal basic needs.

If you understand how a group can satisfy the needs of its members, you are well on the way to understanding how to make a group more cohesive. A group can provide its members with material rewards such as money, with social rewards such as the sense of belonging, with prestige rewards that come from being part of a respected group, with an opportunity to do good work and to achieve, with the chance to fight for a good cause, and with a sense of individual significance and worth. Think of a group you are working with and ask yourself of each member: What is this person getting out of the group? Run down the list. Does the group give the person material rewards, or does it cost him or her money to belong? Does the group give the person social rewards? If you wish to improve the group, the next step is to see if changes can increase the rewards the group furnishes for the individuals who are not committed to the group.

BUILDING A POSITIVE SOCIAL CLIMATE

One way to increase the attractiveness of a group is to build a social climate that is rewarding and fun for all members. When the members of a new work group meet for the first time, they begin to interact socially. They nod or talk to one another. They smile, frown, and laugh. All those things help build a climate that is pleasant, congenial, and relaxed, or one that is stiff and tense. A positive social climate makes the group attractive, builds cohesiveness, and encourages people to speak up and say what they really mean.

Investigations of the social dimension of groups indicate three kinds of verbal and nonverbal communication that build good social feelings among group members and three that build a stiff and negative social setting. The positive communications are shows of solidarity, of tension release, and of agreement. The negative messages are shows of antagonism, of tension, and of disagreement.

Any action or statement you make that indicates to the others that the new group is important to you is a show of solidarity. Raising another's status, offering to help do something for the group, volunteering, or indicating that you are willing to make a personal sacrifice for the group shows solidarity.

The opposite of showing solidarity is showing antagonism to the group or to another person. While shows of solidarity build a pleasant spirit and rapport, shows of antagonism make the others uncomfortable.

People in new groups always feel a certain amount of tension. Embarrassment, shyness, and uneasiness when meeting with strangers are shows of social tension. When a discussion group first meets, everyone experiences *primary* tensions. They feel ill at ease. They do not know what to say or how to begin. The first meeting is tense and cold and must be warmed up. When groups experience primary tension, the people speak softly, they sigh, and they are polite. They seem bored and uninterested. No person is really bored when he has an opportunity to speak up and make a name for himself. Every individual, however, gambles a great deal by plunging into the meeting, by taking an active part and trying to make a good showing. A person who has had success in similar situations in the past may be more willing than others to take this chance. The others may be impressed by her ability and decide they like her as a person; on the other hand, they may be irritated by her, decide she is stupid and uninformed, and reject her. This gamble makes a person feel nervous and tense, and she may take flight from the situation by pretending she is not interested. Do not be misled. The person who seems bored and uninterested is really tense and most interested, particularly in the social setting of the group. If the meeting never releases primary tension, the whole style of future meetings may be set in this uncomfortable mold. It is vital that the primary tension be released early! Tension is released through indications of pleasure, such as smiles, chuckles, and laughs. Members of a new group should spend some time joking and socializing before getting down to business. Judiciously used, socializing is time wisely spent. Once the primary tension is released, however, the group should go to work.

Once people relax and get down to work, new and different social tensions are generated by disagreements over ideas and by personality conflicts. *Secondary* tensions are louder than primary ones. People speak rapidly, interrupt one another, act impatient to get the floor and have their say; they may get up and pace the room or pound the table. When secondary tensions reach a certain level, the group finds it difficult to concentrate on its job. When that point is reached, the tensions should be released by humor, direct comment, conciliation, or confrontation and working through to a satisfactory conclusion. Secondary tensions are more difficult to bleed off than primary ones. There are no easy solutions, but the tensions should not be ignored. They should be brought out into the open and talked over.

Agreement is one of the basic social rewards. When the group members agree with a person, they say, "We value you." When others agree with us, we lose our primary tension, we loosen up, we get excited, and we take a more active part in the meeting. The more people agree, the more they communicate with one another.

Disagreements serve as negative-climate builders. When people disagree, they grow cautious and tense. *Disagreements are socially punishing but absolutely essential to good group work.* They are double-edged. They are necessary to sound thinking. Yet disagreements always contain an element of personal attack. The person who finds his ideas subjected to rigorous testing and disagreement feels as though he is being shot down.

One of the reasons that the number of disagreements increases with a rise in cohesiveness is that groups must develop enough cohesiveness to afford disagreements and still not break up. The rate of disagreements is often highest in the family—the most cohesive unit in our society. How often someone complains, "You're so much nicer with strangers than with the members of your own family!"

Some people try to cushion the hurt in a disagreement by saying such things as "That's a good idea, *but . . .*" or "That's right, I agree with you, *but . . .*" Eventually the others discover that these prefatory agreements or compliments are just ways of setting them up for the knife. They begin to cringe as the ". . . *but* I think we ought to look at the other side of it" hits them. The fact is, disagreements must be understood to mean "Stop, this will not do." When they are thus understood, no amount of kind words of introduction serves to sugarcoat them.

An important way to resolve conflicts is to build group cohesiveness. It helps to do things to knit the group back together after a period of heavy disagreement. Often disagreements increase as a group moves toward a decision. Good groups use positive-climate builders after the decision is reached. They joke and laugh. They show solidarity. They say, "It was a good meeting," "It accomplished something," "Let's all get behind this decision." They compliment the people who advocated the rejected plan. They tell them they are needed, that the group cannot succeed without their help.

Another technique sometimes used by successful work groups is to allow one person to become the "disagreer." He tests most of the ideas, and the group expects him to do so. Whenever they feel the need for disagreements, they turn to him. They reward him by giving him a nickname or by joshing him about how disagreeable he is. Since he plays the role of critical thinker, other members are less hurt by his criticisms, because "After all, he disagrees with everybody."

GROUP ROLES

The first important discovery from research into newly formed (zero-history) groups is that after several hours the members begin to specialize; that is, not every member does an equal amount of the same thing. If we analyze the content of the typical group's communication, we find that some members talk more than others and that members tend to say different kinds of things. Some give more information, some talk more about personal characteristics and social relationships, some make more suggestions about doing the work of the group.

When it becomes clear to a person that she is specializing and when the group discovers that she is doing so, she takes a *place* in the group. She has her particular *role.* Individuals change "personality" as they go from group to group. The college woman who has such a sparkling personality in class and enjoys flirting with the men may be quiet, devout, and reserved with her church circle. She may be ill-tempered and bossy with her family. Think of yourself. In one group you may be a take-charge person who gets things rolling. In another you may be likable, joshing, and fun-loving, but not a leader at all. In a third group, you may be quiet, steady, and a responsible worker.

Principles of Role Emergence

A member's role is worked out jointly by the person and the group. This is the basic principle. We should not blame the group's problems on innate unchangeable personality traits inherent in a troublesome person. Groups can be more neurotic than individuals, and they love to blame their troubles on one member—make him the scapegoat for their failure. If we understand the nature of roles, we will no longer make that mistake. Instead of wishing we could get rid of Bill so we could have a productive group, we ask what the group may be doing to Bill to make him act as he does.

Once everyone has found a place, a second important thing happens. The group judges the relative worth of each role. It gives the roles it judges more valuable a higher status that the others. After a group has been working together for several hours, a trained observer can arrange a status ladder by watching the way the members talk and act. They talk directly and more often to the people they consider important. High-status people talk more to the entire group. The high-status people receive more consideration from the others. The others listen to what a high-status individual says; they often stop what they are doing to come to her; they stop talking to hear her, and they agree more, and more emphatically, with her. The group tends to ignore and cut off comments by low-status members.

Since rewards of much esteem and prestige are given to high-status members, several people usually compete for the top positions. In this competition they come into conflict; there are disagreements. The group's energy is directed to the question of who will win, and attention is drawn away from the work. In extreme cases the struggles become heated, and the group gets bogged down. Every new group must go through a "shakedown cruise," during which the members test roles and find out who is task leader, who is best liked, and so forth. During the shakedown cruise, secondary tensions mount, and people who are contending for leadership come into conflict.

Each contender for a high-status role is led to specialize through both his own efforts and the group's encouragement. The group agrees with him when he does what it wants him to and disagrees when he does not; it thus discourages him from a role it considers unnecessary or unacceptable. A given person does not have a monopoly on the role assigned him in this way, but he fulfills most of that role's functions in the group.

Group stability and communication increase side by side. When a group achieves a stable role structure and a high level of cohesiveness, an increase in feedback usually follows. A person who is strongly attracted to the group and wishes it well wants to maximize communication. She knows the group will do a better job if each member is thoroughly briefed. Therefore, if she does not know something, she is likely to ask. In addition, if she has a stable place in the group, admitting her ignorance does not hurt her reputation. Sometimes bad habits that developed during role struggles carry over, and groups continue to function without adequate feedback. The group should make periodic evaluations of the level of feedback and make conscious plans to encourage it as needed.

Just as the need to appear more knowledgeable disappears with stable structure, so does the need to show off. A person can relax and be honest in a group with a high level of cohesiveness, and the change in attitude allows greater concentration on listening to messages. When roles stabilize, the members no longer feel the need to view each message in personal terms. They no longer think, "Does this message mean so-and-so is leadership material? that he likes me? that he doesn't like me?" Members can become more message-centered, which is the first step to improved listening.

The members of an organization vary in their communication skills. Some may have trouble holding long chains of argument in mind. Achieving effective communication takes considerable time and tension-producing effort. Communication is hard work. Groups should establish the rule that enough time will be allocated and spent (not wasted) to ensure that the proper level of understanding is reached during the meeting.

The presence in a meeting of a person with high formal status in a community or organization immediately inhibits the free flow of communication and feedback. People wait for the high-status person to take the lead; they wait for cues from that person about the proper tone of response. They tend to tell the high-status person only what they think he or she would like to hear. If a feeling of cohesiveness is generated within the work group, the dampening effect of the high-status person can be overcome to some extent. If the others discover the person is sincerely interested in the good of the group, tolerates disagreements, and recognizes the necessity of sound communication, a productive meeting should follow.

The Leadership Role

Of all the roles that emerge in a work group, none has fascinated the philosophers, writers, social scientists, and the average person more than the high-status, influential role of leadership.

In our country we are of two minds about leadership. If a member of a new group suggests that another person would be a good leader, that person's response typically is, "Oh, no! Not me. Someone else could do a better job." Despite such protests, nearly every member of every group would like to lead. We would like right now to dispel that old saying that some people are born leaders and others born followers. This just is not so. All people would like to be leaders and usually are, if not in one group, then in some other group. Some people have more skills in the leadership area than most and become leaders in more groups. But never underestimate the desire of others to take over the leadership role. Publicly, people sometimes do not admit this, but privately they usually do.

Why this ambivalence? On the one hand, our democratic traditions suggest that all people are created equal and that nobody is better than anybody else. We maintain a belief in a classless society and stereotype leaders as people who dominate others and act as though they were better than others. On the other hand, few cultures are so involved in calling for leadership as is that of the United States. From all corners comes the call for better leadership in politics, in government, in business and industry, in religion, and in education. We continually strive to become leaders and managers, to climb to the top of the pyramid and gain all the perquisites (perks) of leadership. We organize and attend leadership and management training courses and programs and read books and articles on how to become leaders. Given such ambivalence no wonder that many people in the United States are fascinated by the role of leader.

The most satisfactory explanation of leadership is that it is a result of an individual's aptitudes (inherited characteristics plus training), the purposes of the group, the group task, the pressures put on the group from the outside, and *the way people in the group communicate with one another as they go about their work.*

Such a contextual explanation provides a more complete view of leadership than other approaches. It includes the idea that some people may be "stars" in the sense that they are by training and inclination more likely to become leaders but it recognizes that individual characteristics alone do not account for the emergence of leaders.

The contextual approach rejects the argument that there is one best style or way of leading such as democratic rather than authoritarian or employee oriented rather than production oriented.

The contextual explanation is also more complete than another popular way of looking at leadership called the contingency approach. The contingency approach suggests that leadership depends on a limited number of factors that make up the favorability of the situation for the leader. In one popular formulation the favorability factors include whether or not the leader has good personal relations with others in the group, whether or not the leader has formal leadership authority, and whether or not the task is an easy one. The contextual approach includes all of these contingency factors but most importantly also includes the internal communicative processes that govern the group's history and behavior.

The contextual approach implies that potential leaders can achieve communicative skills and improve their leadership talents. The approach explains why someone who emerges as a leader in one group may fail to emerge as the leader of a second apparently similar group. The approach focuses research and educational efforts not only on externals but also on group communication processes.

The members of a group spend time and energy on selecting leadership because it is so important to the success of the group. We are touchy about the people who boss us around. We do not like to take orders. If we have to, we prefer a leader who gives wise orders in a way we can tolerate. The leader makes crucial suggestions and decisions about the way the work will be divided and the way the material resources of the group will be distributed. In the end, the group rejects potential leaders until they are left with the person who seems best able to lead *for the good of all.*

Sometimes the struggle for leadership is never resolved. Groups in which this happens become invalids. The members spend their time backbiting and getting back at internal enemies. If, after working together for some time, a group is left with two or three potential leaders, each having substantial handicaps, the leadership question may not be resolved.

KEY IDEAS

- When people must work together, a social dimension results from their communication.
- When someone structures a group's work, the social and task dimensions come into conflict, because giving and taking orders causes social tensions.
- Good work groups have good morale and get things done.
- A highly cohesive group is one in which the members work for the good of the group.

- The more cohesive the group is, the better the communication, because cohesiveness encourages disagreements and questions.
- At any given moment a person feels attracted to a group if it satisfies one or more of his or her basic needs.
- People in new groups always feel some social tension, because they are unsure how the others will react to them as people.
- Persons who seem bored and uninterested at a first meeting of a group are probably tense and most interested, particularly in how the others would view them if they spoke up.
- Agreement is one of the basic social rewards in our society. Disagreements are socially punishing but absolutely necessary to good group work.
- One important fact of group dynamics is that members tend to specialize in doing certain tasks over a period of time.
- When all members have a common expectation about how a person will behave, that individual has a *role* in the group.
- A member's role is worked out jointly by the person and the group.
- Members award a higher status to those roles they judge more valuable to the group.
- Feedback is related to role stability and cohesiveness because a person can ask questions with less fear of losing status in a cohesive and stable group.
- The presence in a meeting of a person with formal status within a community or an organization poses a barrier to successful communication.
- The leadership role is the one that is most fascinating to both the general public and the experts.
- In our culture we both deplore leadership as an undesirable feature of a classless democracy and applaud the successful person who rises to a position of power.
- The members of a group spend much time and energy on the leadership question because it is so important to the successful achievement of group goals.

SUGGESTED PROJECTS

1. Think through your own philosophy of group leadership. Outline on paper its main points and think through how you have been guided in your small-group communication by this philosophy in the past.
2. Students are placed in leaderless groups of five or six. Each group is

furnished with a tape recorder and spends one or two class meetings, which the group records, preparing a panel discussion program on some important public issue to present to the class. The group selects a moderator for the program and, after discussing the topic in front of the class for 30 minutes, throws the discussion open for audience participation. Each member of the group listens to one of the tapes taken during the planning meetings and writes a short paper evaluating the role emergence that takes place during the planning sessions and the actual presentation.

3. Select a small group that you work with on a regular basis. This group could be part of an office or business organization, a committee of students working on a long-term project, a church or social action group—any task-oriented small group. Keep a journal of your experiences in the group. Describe the group's cohesiveness, role structure, and leadership. Where do you fit into the group's role structure?

SUGGESTED READINGS

Bormann, Ernest G. *Discussion and Group Methods,* 2d ed. New York: Harper & Row, 1975.

Bormann, Ernest G., and Nancy C. Bormann. *Effective Small Group Communication.* 3d ed. Minneapolis, Minn.: Burgess, 1980.

Brilhart, John K. *Effective Group Discussion.* 4th ed. Dubuque, Iowa: Brown, 1982.

Philips, Gerald M. *Communication and the Small Group.* 2d ed. Indianapolis, Ind.: Bobbs-Merrill, 1973.

chapter 8

Communicating in Group Discussions

GROUP DISCUSSION

Group discussion refers to one or more meetings of a small number of people who communicate face to face in order to fulfill a common purpose and achieve a common goal.

The small group is an identifiable entity. Authorities differ on details relating to the size of a small group, but the general features are agreed upon. The communication networks and personal relationships that develop while people hold a discussion change when the size of a group is increased, and these changes can be used to describe the "small" group. When a third person is added to a two-person interview, the nature of the working relationships and the flow of communication change; thus a small group is composed of at least three people. The upper size limit of the small group is more difficult to specify. However, when the group becomes so large that it begins to change its patterns of communication, it should no longer be considered a small group. In groups of five or fewer, all members speak to one another. Even those who speak little talk to all the others. In groups of seven or more, the quiet members often cease to talk to any but the top people in the group. As groups become even larger, the talk centralizes more and more around a few people; group interaction falls off. In groups of thirteen or more, from five to seven people hold the discussion while the others watch and listen.

The best size for a group discussion is probably five. Members of groups with fewer than five people complain that their groups are too small and suffer from a lack of diversity of opinion and skill. Groups composed of even numbers of people tend to be less stable and rewarding than groups of odd numbers. A group of five or seven works better than a group of four, six, or eight. On learning this, many people have said when analyzing unproductive groups they have been in, "Well, that was our first mistake! There were ten of us."

CHARACTERISTICS OF THE ONE-TIME MEETING

Students of small-group communications must understand not only that a discussion meeting may serve different functions but also that groups differ in other significant ways. In a group that meets only once, the dynamics of the communication are quite different from those that operate in a group that meets several times. Groups also differ depending on how closely they relate to an organization. A group of students from a speech communication class is different from a standing committee of an academic department composed of students, teaching assistants, and faculty members.

The one-time discussion group is such an important communication event that it deserves some special attention. The people in a one-time discussion group have not worked together before and are not likely to do so again for the purposes under discussion. Some may have worked with others in similar groups and some may know one another socially, but the particular grouping of these five or six people for this particular purpose has not happened before.

CONTRASTS BETWEEN ONE-TIME
AND AD HOC GROUPS

The one-time discussion meeting is different from an ad hoc committee. *Ad hoc* is a Latin term meaning "for this special purpose." An ad hoc committee thus is formed for a special purpose important enough to cause the group to meet for several sessions over a period of weeks or months before it makes its final report. An ad hoc committee is also different from the standing permanent committees of an organization which continue for as long as the organization exists. For example, if a political action group has a standing committee for public education, that committee will function as long as the group continues. However, if a group of people organize a committee to meet and work for several months for the specific purpose of getting a city ordinance passed, that committee is ad hoc.

The one-time meeting is held by people who expect to achieve their purposes in a single meeting. Since its composition is unique, the discussion group has no history, and the people who come to the meeting cannot be guided by past experience with one another in such a discussion. The group holding a one-time meeting has no team spirit, no usual way of doing things, no idea about how the communication and social interaction will proceed.

The first meeting of an ad hoc committee is like the one-time meeting in that its members have not previously met together for this particular purpose. But although the ad hoc committee has no history, it does have a future. The members will be meeting together for a considerable period of time, and the influence of the future expectations produces some important differences between the first session of an ad hoc committee, and a one-time meeting.

As we saw in Chapter 7 the group without a history but with a future is under pressure to test potential leaders and other possibly important members to develop a common way of doing things, to take nothing at face value, and to check reputations, formal status, and assigned structures before accepting them.

One of the most important things about the one-time meeting is the willingness of the participants to accept leadership. Whether the person calling the meeting is a self-appointed moderator or has been assigned to lead the meeting by some organizational unit, the members are likely to accept and appreciate guidance from that individual. The group needs quick help in getting started. Members realize they have little time to waste and tend to accept with little argument the leader's description of goals and his or her methods of getting on with the meeting.

Participants in one-time meetings tend to use any information they have to help form an impression of their fellow committee members. If students in a speech-communication class meet to plan something and discover that one member is majoring in elementary education, another is the president of the freshman class, a third was a beauty contest winner, and so on, they use such information to help them structure their meeting.

Once the discussion is under way, those members who do not hold positions of stature, or who are not known by reputation, tend to be quickly stereotyped. The stereotyping that takes place in the one-time meeting comes from first impressions. Each person makes a quick judgment about every other member and, thus, a person who does not speak for 15 or 20 minutes may be stereotyped as quiet, shy, apathetic, or

The moderator of a one-time meeting is expected to attend to the administrative details of setting up the meeting. (Gatewood, Image Works)

uninterested and be dismissed as unimportant. Another, who speaks loudly, expresses strong opinions, and makes flat judgments, may be stereotyped as bossy or pushy.

The people in a one-time meeting take shortcuts to structure their group into a pecking order, so they can get on with the business at hand. They are willing to risk getting a wrong impression because they are pressed for time and often because they think the purpose of the one-time meeting is less important than that of a discussion group that meets repeatedly.

Members of one-time meetings tend to accept a stereotyped picture of how a meeting should be run. A newly formed group that plans to meet for many sessions works out its own unique ways of getting the job done, but the one-time meeting does not allow enough time to do this. The accepted picture of how a small-group meeting should be conducted—the norms that most North Americans come to accept by the time they reach college—includes the idea that there should be a moderator, leader, or chairperson (depending upon how authoritarian the leadership style is to be) and a secretary or recorder.

The moderator, leader, or presiding officer of a one-time meeting is expected to attend to the administrative details of setting up the meeting place, planning the agenda, sending out preliminary information, and scheduling the meeting.

PLANNING THE ONE-TIME MEETING

If you are assigned the duty of moderating, leading, or chairing a one-time meeting, you ought to do the following things in the planning stage:

1. Determine the purpose of the meeting. Every one-time meeting should have a clear and specific purpose. Make sure the other members know the purpose of the meeting either before it starts or early in the session. You should also make the type of meeting clear to the members: Is the meeting for briefing, instructing, consulting, or decision making?
2. Plan the meeting to achieve the purpose. You should ask such questions as: Where is the best place to hold the meeting? What format will best achieve the purpose? Who should take part in the meeting? Should people with special knowledge be invited? Should some high-status people be invited?
3. Plan the little details. A successful one-time meeting requires time and effort in the planning stages. Do not neglect the small details. If you do, you may save a bit of your own time, but wasting the time of your colleagues in a useless meeting is not wise. Little things such as providing pads and pencils, refreshments, properly arranged and enough seating, all contribute to the success of the meeting. When minor details of administration are handled smoothly, people feel the meeting is important and is going to do significant work.
4. Specify the outcomes of the meeting. Making the outcomes clear is not the same as deciding on the purposes. If plans are to be made, how will they be developed? In detail? In general outline? Decide what decisions can be made in such a meeting, and in what form they should be made.
5. Utilize the results of the meeting. What can be done to follow up and apply the results? Do not let important leads drop at the end of the meeting.

LEADING THE ONE-TIME MEETING

During the course of the meeting the assigned (or elected) chairperson is expected to lead the discussion. The chairperson's duties are commonly understood to include the following:

A. Chairperson's duties in regard to the task
1. Start the meeting
2. Act as pilot to keep the group on course, remind members of the discussion outline, cut short those who wander too far from the outline
3. Help the group arrive at decisions (take votes when necessary)
4. Provide transitions from topic to topic
5. Summarize what the group has accomplished
6. Control the channels of communication to ensure that everybody has a chance to talk and that all sides get a fair hearing; encourage the quiet members to take part and discourage the too-talkative ones
B. Chairperson's duties in regard to human relations
1. Introduce members to one another
2. Help break the ice at the start and relax people so they can get down to business
3. Release tensions and bad feelings that come from disagreements and conflicts of personality or opinion

Assuming the willingness of participants to follow his or her direction, the leader still needs certain basic skills to conduct an efficient meeting. The three basic techniques for this purpose are the question, the summary, and the directive. Summaries are always useful to indicate progress and to orient the group. The democratic style requires more questions than directives; the authoritarian style, more directives than questions.

The first task is to get the group down to business. A certain amount of time should be devoted to getting acquainted, but then the group must go to work. Questions are useful, especially open-ended questions asked in such a way that they cannot be answered with a simple yes or no. An open-ended question can get things started. Early in the meeting, the leader should set the mood for short, to-the-point comments. If the first comment runs too long, the leader may have to interrupt with a question directed to someone else.

The leader needs to watch carefully and make running choices about the drift of the discussion. Is it part of the necessary kicking around of an idea? He or she should not take the easy way out and make the choice strictly according to the agenda. When the leader decides the discussion is wasting time, he or she should bring the meeting back to the agenda. Questions are useful for this: "Can we tie this in with the point about rules in the student union?" "Just a minute, how does this relate to grading procedures?" Summaries can give an overview of the past few minutes of the meeting and bring the group back to the agenda. Finally, a leader may simply assert that the discussion is off the track and direct that the group get back: "We seem to be getting off the subject. Let's get back to Bill's point."

The moderator should not push the group too fast; on the other hand, devoting 20 minutes to material that deserves only 5 produces restlessness and frustration. The leader should watch for signs that a topic has been exhausted. If members begin to repeat themselves, fidget, or pause for lack of something to say, the leader should move to the next item. The summary is the best way to do so. A summary rounds off the discussion of one point and leads naturally to a new one. It also gives the group a feeling of accomplishment.

From time to time, the group needs to make decisions. The leader can help by stepping in at those times and asking, "Are we in substantial agreement on this point?" If the question is important, he or she may call for a vote.

Often some tension-producing behavior creates an awkward moment for the leader and the participants. What we offer here are some hints about how to handle the awkward situation immediately when it crops up in a meeting. One common difficulty for the moderator is the member who talks too much. The leader may break into a long comment by an overtalkative person with a yes-no question and then quickly direct another question to someone else.

> LEADER: Just a minute, Joe; would you be willing to drop that course from the requirements for a major?
>
> JOE: Now, I didn't say . . .
>
> LEADER: I just want to be clear on this. Would you be in favor of that?
>
> JOE: Well, no, but . . .
>
> LEADER: Bill, I wonder how you feel about this?

Sometimes the leader can stop the talkative member by asking for specific information. Interrupting him for a summary is another technique. The leader can then conclude the summary by directing a question to someone else. People usually sit back for a summary. Sometimes the leader simply has to say, "I'm going to ask you to stop there for a minute and hold your next comment. Everyone has not had a chance to be heard on this point."

The member who is too quiet also poses problems. The leader should use questions to draw out the quiet members, asking the nonparticipating person a direct open-ended question, addressing him by name, so that only that person can answer. Do not ask a question that can be answered with a yes or no, and, of course, do not ask a question that the person might be unable to answer for lack of information. Once the quiet member answers, encourage some elaboration on the answer.

PARTICIPATING IN THE ONE-TIME MEETING

The norms of a one-time meeting do not assign specific roles to any group member except the leader. All leadership functions are assigned to the moderator, and other members are expected to follow the moderator's lead and accept his or her directions. When the chairperson recognizes a person, the others are supposed to respect that decision and not interrupt. When the chairperson cuts off discussion on a topic, the others are supposed to accept that decision.

The duties of the participant include the following:

A. Participant's duties in regard to the task
   1. Enter into the discussion with enthusiasm
   2. Have an open-minded, objective attitude
   3. Keep contributions short and to the point
   4. Talk enough but not too much
   5. Speak clearly and listen carefully
B. Participant's duties in regard to social and human relations
   1. Respect the other person
   2. Be well mannered
   3. Try to understand the other person's position
   4. Do not manipulate or exploit the other person

Of course, the model of how a good one-time meeting should proceed differs considerably from the realities of even a short session. Participants do not all willingly follow the assigned moderator even when they know they should. They are, however, much more likely to do so in a one-time meeting than in the first session of a group that will meet a number of times. People in the more permanent group move strongly in the first meeting to test the assigned leader's abilities.

Even in a short meeting, role differences become apparent. A few people speak more than the others, despite the best efforts of the moderator. Some people are silent. Others are humorous and friendly. The generalized picture of a meeting composed of a leader and a group of indistinguishable followers soon changes under the pressure of discussion with a common purpose.

The group discussion, even a short one-time meeting, is an extremely complicated event. The addition of a third person (or several more) to the two-person communication situation adds a good deal more than one-third in additional complexity. The general discussion above of how to prepare for, moderate, and participate in the discussion should be viewed in terms of our knowledge of group dynamics.

If, indeed, a small group meeting is so complicated, why do most people think it is easy to assemble a few people, and, in the course of an hour or two, discuss a series of important topics, make a couple of vital decisions, and adjourn in time for the next class?

The main reason for our too-simple approach to groups is that we have a rather clear idea of what we think a meeting ought to be like, and this clouds our perception of what a group, in fact, *can* be like. Many people think a business or committee meeting should be an efficient, no-nonsense affair. The meeting should be well planned. The discussion should follow the agenda. Everybody should say about the same amount, and everything they say should be to the point and helpful. The members ought to be involved, eager to participate, good listeners and speakers.

The ideal discussion is largely a fiction seldom encountered in real life. Lest you think that our treatment of the one-time discussion reflects only the common stereotype of an ideal discussion, we hasten below to set the record straight. What we have described above are the expectations people commonly have about what moderators and participants should do in preparation for and during a discussion. Below, we describe what, in fact, tends to happen in a discussion.

A REALISTIC PICTURE OF SMALL-GROUP COMMUNICATION

What is a realistic picture of how a good group communicates? Good group communication takes time. Given the complicated communication network that must be developed in a work meeting, we should not expect a group to cover more topics in a two-hour meeting than one person could study and decide about in an hour if that person were working alone. Yet we often expect a group to cover as much work in a few hours as one person would be hard put to accomplish in a day. When we ask a group to do more than it can, it either gets bogged down on the first part of the agenda and leaves some business undone or races through the meeting without dealing adequately with anything. As a result, the people who attend come away feeling the meeting was a failure.

The Limited Attention Span of a Group

Also unrealistic is the notion that a group can organize its discussion so it keeps to the main ideas and moves in a logical, step-by-step way through a series of topics. Individuals have attention spans measured in minutes, and sometimes in seconds. When we listen, read, or think about something in a logical, step-by-step way, we often find our attention wandering. You may read a paragraph and understand it quite well, then halfway down the next page you realize that while your eyes are moving, your thoughts are on getting a drink of water or on the date you are going out with later. Even when people puzzle about an important problem or decision, they often find their attention shifting to other subjects.

Groups, like individuals, have short attention spans. Most groups cannot talk about a topic for much more than a minute before someone changes the subject. Sometimes the group wants to change the subject, because it has finished talking about one topic, and should move on to another, but quite often the person who changes the topic does so while others still want to consider the original subject. Sometimes the new topic is not relevant to the matter under discussion. A short attention span for a group meeting is natural and inevitable, and we must work within the limitations it imposes.

Most of what we have said about a group's short attention span comes from research on what members say during meetings. Investigators have studied a group's communication and noted when the group changed topics. Of course, in any given period of time during the meeting, people may or may not be listening to what is being said. Thus the job of holding everybody's attention is probably even more difficult than the evidence, gathered by looking at the content of the messages, indicates.

Clearly, people in small groups have difficulty keeping their attention on an idea so they all can understand it and give their opinions about it. Yet if the meeting has work to do, they feel pressure to get on with the job. Participants in a discussion with a purpose do not like the aimless skipping from idea to idea that is common in social conversations. If the group has an outline or an agenda for the meeting, the members will keep looking at the plan, using it to measure how well they are doing. When the discussion leaves the agenda, they often comment that the group is getting off the topic or that much still should be done.

Balancing Freedom and Structure

People vary as to how much fooling around they can stand in a meeting. Some are uncomfortable unless the point of the meeting is clear and the outline of topics is specific. They want the group to stick to business. Others feel hemmed in by a sticking-to-business approach. They have what seems to them an important or exciting comment, and they want to say it even if it does not relate directly to the topic under discussion.

How does a person organize a discussion in a realistic and yet productive way? At times, participants want and need the freedom to suggest ideas and mull them over without worrying too much about how they hang together or how they fit into the agenda. At other times, a group needs and wants to get on with the job and to get things organized. At this point, group members seem to feel they know what they want to do and are tired of rehashing things that are clear or decided. A leader should be alert to the alternate needs for freewheeling and for structure. Most groups develop a rhythm in regard to when they want to be loose and easy and when they want to get things organized. Careful attention to verbal and nonverbal cues can help the leader decide about any given group. For example, members of a group may display frustration when the chair reminds them that their discussion is off the topic. A person may accept the suggestion that the comment is out of order in a grumpy fashion, sitting back in his chair and frowning. Another person may say, "I don't want to make a motion or ask for a decision, but I would like to throw out a few ideas and see what you think of them before we get down to business." When, as a leader, you see gestures or hear comments expressing the desire for less concern with the agenda or with structure, you should go along with the group members and give them a chance to kick ideas around.

Other verbal and nonverbal cues indicate that the group wants more structure. A member may look at her watch, shift in her seat, and let her attention wander. When several people seem to be saying, "Let's cut out the talk and get down to business" or "What should we do to get rolling?" the chair, or someone else in the meeting may suggest that they follow an outline, and the group will accept the suggestion and stay with an outline. When they wish to have a more tightly organized meeting, their attention span will continue to be short, but they will welcome attempts to get them back to the business at hand and willingly follow such suggestions.

A realistic picture of how groups work includes the notion that groups do not systematically pick the best solution from a carefully drawn list of possible solutions; rather, they tend to throw out the worst, the not so good, and the fair, until they are left with several good answers, which they mull over until the final decision emerges. The group circles problems, rather than dealing with them in a straight line. Thus, a sensible agenda might well suggest running over topics A, B, and C in about 30 minutes and then returning to the total agenda for a more penetrating discussion. The group needs to find the areas of quick agreement and the points of minor or serious conflict.

Groups tend to approach the real problem, grabbing hold of it almost anywhere in order to get started. Their first pass at the topic results in a rather simple approach. They return again, dig more deeply, and begin to cut closer to the important difficulties. When people start to argue and disagree, they feel social tension and become uncomfortable, so they pull back and turn to less painful matters. After a time they return to the central issue and drive still closer to the solution. The approach-withdrawal action is typical of groups making tough decisions.

A group often appreciates a relatively free and unstructured period early in the meeting to allow a quick survey of all the business and to get some idea of how people feel about things. Some members will need to prod the others to get down to the important arguments, because groups do not like to discuss touchy subjects. If you watch for the tendency to take flight, you as leader can often help the group by pushing for a discussion of the tough issues.

Once a decision has emerged, the group ought to state formally, confirm, and plan details to implement the decision. At the point of getting things in order to carry out a decision, the members are usually pleased to have an outline or an agenda, and they work through these items with fewer digressions during the last stages of the problem-solving process.

KEY IDEAS

- Every organized attempt to get things done in our society requires working with discussion groups.
- The small group is an identifiable social entity with its own patterns of interaction.
- The best size for a group discussion is probably five members.
- Groups composed of even numbers of people tend to be less stable and rewarding than groups of odd numbers.
- Every organization has some meetings that are rituals.
- Discussions may be used to brief or instruct the participants.
- Some group meetings advise the person or persons with the authority to make decisions.

- An extremely important kind of meeting is one called actually to make a decision.
- People in a group that has no history but is expected to meet again size each other up very carefully.
- The participants in a one-time meeting, with no history and no future, are generally willing to accept assigned leadership.
- The people in a one-time meeting take shortcuts to structure their group so they can get on with business.
- The moderator of a one-time meeting is expected to attend to the administrative details of setting up the discussion.
- During the course of a one-time discussion, the moderator is expected to start the meeting, make transitions, summarize, take votes, and generally guide the group.
- The participant in a one-time discussion is expected to follow the moderator's lead, enter into the discussion with enthusiasm, and stick to the point.
- The main reason many people get upset with meetings is that they have a clear, simple, and impossible ideal for a good discussion.
- The ideal discussion is seldom encountered in real life.
- Groups, like individuals, have short attention spans.
- When several people are fighting for control of the channels of communication, they often do not listen to one another.
- Members in discussions have trouble chaining ideas together and getting an overall picture of the topic they are discussing.
- People vary as to how much fooling around they can tolerate in a meeting.
- At times, particularly early in a discussion, participants want and need the freedom to introduce ideas and mull them over without worrying too much about sticking to an agenda.
- Later in a discussion, participants want some structure to organize their work.
- Decisions tend to emerge from group discussions rather than be carefully discussed and voted upon.

SUGGESTED PROJECTS

1. The class is divided into one-time-meeting discussion groups of five or six, and the instructor provides each group with a timely community or campus topic to discuss. A moderator is appointed, and the group plans a brief agenda. The group tries to have a good discussion and, at the same time, to let everybody participate equally. To aid in this equal participation, each group member is given the same number of poker chips or tokens of some sort. Each time a member speaks, he has to "spend" a token. When all his tokens are spent, he can no longer participate. Each group should devote 10 minutes after the discussion to evaluating the effect of striving for absolutely equal participation during the meetings.

2. Attend a one-time meeting of a real-life campus group. Write a short paper describing and evaluating the leadership of the meeting. List the specific techniques used by the leader to keep the discussion moving, on the track, with maximum involvement of the group members.

3. Find three real examples that have occurred in the last month in your community of each of the following kinds of group discussion meetings: (1) ritualistic, (2) briefing session, (3) instructional meeting, (4) consultative meeting, (5) decision-making meeting.

SUGGESTED READINGS

Bormann, Ernest G., and Nancy C. Bormann. *Effective Small Group Communication.* 3d ed. Minneapolis, Minn.: Burgess, 1980.

Brilhart, John K. *Effective Group Discussion.* 4th ed. Dubuque, Iowa: Brown, 1982.

Cathcart, Robert S., and Larry A. Samovar. *Small Group Communication: A Reader.* 4th ed. Dubuque, Iowa: Brown, 1984.

Part Three

PUBLIC SPEAKING

chapter 9

Audience Analysis

A substantial portion of your planning time for any public speech should be given to an analysis of the audience and the situation. A good public speaker is not self-centered or message-centered, but *audience-centered.*

Audience-centered speakers make all their final planning decisions in terms of their analysis of the listeners. Indeed, the art of interpersonal communication as well as the art of public speaking is the adaptation of ideas, world view, information, and arguments to a listener, to several listeners (a small group), or to many listeners (an audience). Let us say that three speakers have essentially the same information to present to an audience. Consider the three ways they might go about preparing the speech.

One might be mostly speaker-centered and give a lecture in which his nonverbal cues indicate that he is worried about how he looks, how his voice sounds, and how his gestures are affecting the audience, and seems concerned that his fingernails are clean. His verbal expressions might indicate he is sure of his own intelligence and superiority and feels he has worked up the material of the speech brilliantly, has accomplished many things, knows many great people personally, and is very important indeed. (Doesn't he sound charming?)

A second speaker might be mostly message-centered and give an obviously laboriously prepared lecture filled with difficult-to-follow statistical information and references to events and people unknown to the audience, all put together in language more suitable for a scholarly journal than a busy college audience.

A third speaker might be audience-centered; she delivers essentially the same information as the other two but uses language that is clear to the audience, supports her ideas with examples that tie into the audience's experience, and holds her hearers' attention by showing how what she is saying relates to their wants, hopes, dreams, heroes, and villains. The essential difference between the first two and the last of our hypothetical lecturers is that the last is skillful in the art of communication.

Audience-centered speakers understand that information has to be adapted to the listener and that the techniques discussed throughout this book are tools to use in adapting ideas to people. They know about hypothetical examples and how they can use these examples to arouse the listeners' interests. They know what the selection of names for people and things means in terms of suggestion, and they choose their words carefully with the audience in mind. They understand the importance of public dramas in which the members of the audience are most likely to participate; they think about their probable heroes and villains and adapt their remarks to all these things. They consider every element of their speech in terms of the people who will be hearing it and the occasion when they will be hearing it. In the parlance of advertising, audience-centered speakers think always in terms of what it (the audience) will or will not *buy*.

GENERAL FEATURES OF AN AUDIENCE FOR A PUBLIC SPEECH

People gathered in a large group to hear a public speech respond differently than they would in two-person conversations or even small discussion groups. Because one person is the center of attention and because a large group of people is listening, the dynamics of the situation are changed in several important ways.

The social pressure of 4 or 5 people is strong, but the power of 50 or 100 is much greater, and when thousands of assembled people stand up or shout, the influence of the crowd upon any individual is immense. Have you ever been part of a large audience at a football game, a student demonstration, or a religious revival, when the crowd began to groan or shout or chant, and felt the emotional impact of thousands of voices moved by a common feeling or emotion?

The audience responds to various details of communication in a fashion that differs in some regards from the more casual and informal interpersonal speech-communication situations. The larger the audience, the more likely it is to expect an elevated style of language from the speaker. The keynote speaker at a political convention generally uses a more careful and formal speech style (and is expected to do so by the audience) than the same politician uses when talking over a strategy move with five staff members in his or her hotel room.

The larger the audience, the more it expects and demands that the speaker appeal to the so-called "higher" motives of human beings. The new president of the United States giving an inaugural address is expected to appeal to the better nature and the more unselfish motives of the American people. President John F. Kennedy said in his inaugural address, "Ask not what your country can do for you—ask what you can do for your country." His statement was in line with the expectations for the occasion as well as for the vast size of the television audience. If the president were to express similar sentiments in the same lofty style in a meeting with an assistant and three leaders of an antipoverty group lobbying for legislation to guarantee an annual income for everybody, he might well get, and deserve, a scornful laugh. On the other hand, the speaker at a high school commencement would receive an outraged reaction from much of his audience if he said he knew the seniors were not interested in a lot of pious baloney from him, that all they wanted was to get out of the auditorium, out of their robes, and into their cars to head for the nearest pot party or beer bust to get stoned out of their heads in celebration of the end of their four miserable years in high school, and that he, for one, thought they had the right idea.

The larger audience enjoys a rosy picture of the world and humanity, whereas the same message in a group of one or two people in a casual setting causes embarrassment or laughter. By the same token, the tough-headed recognition of basic desires that is appropriate to small groups of people sounds crude and disgusting in large assemblies.

One of the reasons we predict the continued importance of public speeches to large groups is that such speeches provide one of the few experiences in our culture in which people expect and get messages about heroes with high motives and where they are appealed to on the basis of their better nature. No matter how shoddy the community or how crude the general mode of conduct, people require some sense of worth and significance. The appeal to the better nature of the audience is a high form of flattery and is a source of pride and significance. Aside from the speech to a large audience, the only other major source of mass communication is television, and it does not provide many rosy depictions of life and of

The influence of a crowd on any of its audience members is immense. (Bermack, Jeroboam)

the community. The predominant style of the newscast and the television documentary, with few exceptions, is the style of the inside dopester (a person who has all the inside information). Television journalists tend to cut all public figures down to size and point out that important people are not larger than life, but ordinary people just like the rest of us, maybe even a little worse in some regards. The general tone of the story presented on television is factual, and what the tone presents as fact is tinged with skepticism about high motivations; the reporters appear to be continually searching for shoddy or unethical behavior. Saints are not dramatic; sinners, on the other hand, make good news copy.

ANALYZING A SPECIFIC AUDIENCE

While the audiences of public speeches share many similarities, each audience is also unique. The first question a skilled public speaker asks about a given audience is how much alike are the audience members in terms of background, experience, interests, and attitudes? If all the audience members at least resemble the typical member on important features related to the speaker, the topic of the speech, and the occasion, the problem for the speaker is clear and can be handled directly. If the audience members are greatly diverse, the problem becomes much more difficult, and the speaker may have to seek some broad and abstract common ground or some overriding goal that can in some way unite such a varied group.

A speaker may start by finding out the composition of the audience in terms of such obvious, but often important, qualities as age, sex, socio-economic class, race, ethnic background, religion, and occupation. Not all factors are always important. For many speeches, the audience's age may be irrelevant, but for other situations, it may be crucial. A speaker planning to adapt language and grammar to his or her audience would need to know if the members were primarily from the working class in an inner city or from an upper-middle-class suburb, if they were predominantly Mexican-American, black, Native American, or white.

A speaker often adapts to an audience by selecting an appropriate example or analogy to clarify a point, and if the audience is composed of farmers and their families, he selects different examples than he would if the listeners are members of the American Medical Association.

Often more important than the general information about age, sex, and social economic background are the audience's attitudes and interests. A person planning a persuasive speech in behalf of more funds for state-supported community colleges would like to know if the audience is generally in agreement that community colleges ought to be supported, hostile to paying more taxes for colleges, interested but undecided, or apathetic to the whole question. Likewise, the speaker would benefit from knowing how many of the audience members hold attitudes toward his or her position that are friendly, hostile, undecided, or apathetic.

A speaker making a thorough analysis of his or her audience finds that specific details are vital; the general features of the audience provide only hints that help when making a more complete study. The speaker with the time and opportunity to study the audience and the occasion would do well to explore their rhetorical visions of the issue.

A *rhetorical vision* is an angle on events that makes sense out of them. It consists of a cluster of interpretative scripts in which human beings, fictitious characters, and supernatural or other forces are personified and proceed to enact a series of actions that explain why things happened as they did. Events are often complicated and chaotic. People dislike a senseless world, so they try to find an explanatory pattern within the chaos. One way to provide an explanation is to portray the events in terms of human dramatic action; you look for the "good guys" and the "bad guys."

It is truly amazing how imaginative we can be when we write our interpretative scripts. It is equally unfortunate how quickly we assume that *our* rhetorical visions are the right, true, only valid ones. An interesting feature of our interpretative scripts is that different people can provide equally plausible stories that make sense out of the very same events but put a different slant on them. You can usually find others who share your perceptions to some degree, however, and when several or many share an interpretative script about events, we say they are sharing a rhetorical vision; they agree about who the heroes are and who the villains are. Until you understand the individual nature of one's rhetorical visions, however, you will have difficulty trying to analyze your audience.

Assume that two students, one male, one female, meet in college and decide to begin living together. Some months later, they are involved in an automobile accident, and the man is tagged for drunken driving. Only in the course of the investigation of the accident do the parents of both students learn they have been living together. The parents of the male develop an interpretative script in which he is the innocent victim and the woman is the corrupting influence. She has seduced their son, who left home for college as an upstanding, decent, admittedly somewhat gullible boy. The parents of the female student have an interpretative script that reverses the roles. As they see it, their daughter fell in with bad company, as personified by the no-good delinquent who moved in with her and introduced her to alcohol, dope, and who-knows-what-all. Undoubtedly the students involved, if asked, would come up with scripts differing from both their parents' and, in some ways, from each other's as well.

Suppose that the Russians invade a neighboring country such as Afghanistan or Poland. The mass-media stories suddenly focus the attention of the American people on these events. Why did the Russians do it? What does it mean for the United States? What does it mean for me? Will I have to register for a draft? go to war? be killed? We want to make sense out of events, and we listen to the various interpretative scripts provided by the president, by newscasters, by our family, and by our friends. There are some old familiar stories still around, which have been used by Americans to explain similar events; we recall these; they form a rhetorical vision that can be thought of as a cold war view of the events. In line with the cold war stories we could explain the invasion in terms of Russian communism out to foment international communism and conquer the world. The only way to stop such aggression is to be militarily strong and mentally tough. The invasion means that somebody must have failed either in strength or toughness. We could further explain the invasion in terms of a failure of nerve on the part of our president. Another way we could explain things would be in terms of a drama in which the leaders of the Russian government had fallen to fighting among themselves for power, and a group of fanatical zealots, paranoid about bordering countries' allegiance, had gained control. Despite the best efforts of our wise and resolute president, these fanatical Russian leaders were causing the international difficulty. Which script would be that of the members of your class? Does some other script fit the audience better?

In addition to the rhetorical visions we form about events, we also have interpretative scripts to explain our own hopes and dreams and many times the hopes and dreams of groups, whole communities of people. Much has been made of the "American dream." The American dream is the drama in which a poor but talented, deserving, hard-working person can climb to success, no matter how humble his or her beginnings. People who believed in the American dream often came from foreign countries to the United States at great sacrifice and hardship and when they arrived in the new country worked hard, often under miserable conditions, to achieve success. Individuals may have personal scripts today much like the widely held American dream of the nineteenth century. You may daydream that you are playing a hero's part and doing interesting and exciting things. All of us want our lives to matter. We want to be appreciated for what we are, for what we can do. The boy who dreams of being a big-league pitcher and sees himself striking out the opponents in an all-star game may practice long hours and live only to achieve his dream. The girl who wants to be a professional basketball player may spend hours shooting baskets in her driveway.

How can you make an audience analysis of the members' rhetorical vision as it relates to a topic for a speech? To illustrate, we will take the most difficult audience situation—one in which most members are hostile to your point of view. How would you go about making a script analysis in preparation for a persuasive speech to a hostile audience?

Suppose a classmate has made a speech against registering women for the military draft. The response of the class has been strongly supportive. You decide that although you may be the only person in the class who feels that way, your next speech will try to persuade the class members to sign a petition in favor of universal registration for women as well as men.

Start by asking, What is their level of understanding of the whole situation? Do they know the current status? Do they know what has already happened? Do they know what is being planned? Do they understand the machinery of registration? Do they know how other countries handle problems of defense and security? Do they understand how various governmental groups must approve a program before it can go into effect?

The preliminaries out of the way, you can raise the most important query regarding the nature of their vision, What is the source of their hostility? Generally, hostility is associated with change. As time goes by, circumstances alter, accidents happen, power shifts, crops fail, people fall ill, things go badly for individuals and groups. They experience a time of troubles. When people have troubles they grow upset, and if their problems continue, they may become frustrated. One response to the troubles and frustrations is to seek change.

We all have scripts on matters that are important to us, and you have your own rhetorical vision to account for the troubles that brought up the issue of registration for women. As part of your preparation for such a speech, you should examine your own script and ask the same questions about it that you ask about the audience's vision.

Where do you find information that relates to the way individuals and groups in the audience interpret events? You can often find out a good deal about them by reading speeches, pamphlets, newspaper accounts, letters to the editor, and editorials, or by actual interviews with potential audience members. In the case of registering for the draft, those who are hostile to it usually use their interpretative scripts in expressing their hostility. If after the first speech a class member said, "I'd like to see us draft some middle-aged senators," you can begin to figure out the interpretative script of that individual. A person who says, "I will not register until the Equal Rights Amendment is passed" also reveals a lot about her rhetorical vision. On the other hand, if a member of the class said, "Phyllis Schlafly was right. I wonder what Gloria Steinem will say now," you would be alert to several conflicting scripts in your audience. Even though both groups might be against registering women, their rhetorical visions are opposites. Schlafly is a personality who symbolizes the women who fought the adoption of the Equal Rights Amendment, whereas Steinem is a symbol of those who fought for it. If you praise Steinem, you please one faction but irritate another.

If you take some time to talk to your classmates, if you learn to listen to them carefully, if you ask a few leading questions, you will often bring out their interpretative scripts. We have an emotional attachment to our favorite scripts. Because human beings are in conflict, we can empathize and identify with them, love and hate them, and watch the outcome of their confrontations with suspenseful, involved interest.

Once you have made some estimate of where your audience members are likely to fall on the continuum, from those who want change immediately to those who are resisting it at all costs, you can make a specific estimate of how best to approach them.

What sort of person will these people be more likely to trust and believe? What can I say to get their confidence? What are the public dramas that excite and move these people? Who are the heroes of their public dreams? Who are their villains? What dramatic actions do they use to build a sense of community and purpose? What attitude do they take toward these lines of action? For example, if all the audience members participate in a public drama that casts the president of the United States into a heroic role, then the speaker who says that the president, whoever he is at the time, is a man of low morals, insincerity, and bad motives will find himself in trouble with that audience. On the other hand, if all the audience members participate in a common drama in which the president is cast as villain, a negative statement about him may draw a strong, positive response from the listeners. If the audience members are strongly divided in their political opinions so that some see the president as a sympathetic figure fighting villainous forces and others see him as a dark and evil personality, the speaker may well decide not to mention the president at all!

GATHERING INFORMATION ABOUT THE AUDIENCE

Often experienced speakers know what sort of information about their audiences would be useful to them but do not have the resources to collect it. In those long-range and important campaigns of persuasion where the success or failure of a new product, the election of a candidate to major office, or the organization, recruitment, and administration of a social or political movement is at stake, the campaign planners generally have sufficient resources for elaborate formal surveys of their potential audiences.

Experts in persuasion have brought scientific marketing and polling techniques to a high state of perfection and proved usefulness. Most public-relations firms, advertising agencies, professional fund-raising companies, and experts in political campaigning and revolutionary organization know how to sample the audience, administer attitude tests or questionnaires relating to opinion, and discover what a target audience thinks about a product or an issue or a particular personality. Some of the public-opinion polls publish their results in newspapers, and even speakers with little time or money can find out how various age groups with various educational backgrounds are currently responding to such general questions as "How well do you think the president has been doing?" When money is available, pressure groups often take their own polls to discover audience attitudes.

Sometimes the main themes of a persuasion campaign are pretested by showing samples of the persuasive material to people, who indicate their reactions by pressing buttons on special monitoring machines or answering questionnaires.

We mention these elaborate and expensive techniques of audience analysis mostly to show how far the art has been developed beyond the mere collection of information about age, sex, and geographic origin. Most of us do not have the resources needed to use these sophisticated audience-survey techniques; yet we can often acquire useful information quickly and cheaply. While the following example is hypothetical and exaggerated, it contains elements that resemble the speech situations in which you might find yourself. In this instance we are dealing with a speaker analyzing an audience that is more likely to be bored than hostile.

Professor Gilbert Johnson, our example, teaches at State University. He has been a lifelong student of the process of eutrophication (too much plant food in a lake causing a lush growth of water plants which, in turn, decay in the late summer sucking the oxygen out of the water). When ecology became an important issue, Johnson suddenly found his specialty popular with the general public. He won several awards and then attracted national notice on a television program. Soon he found himself in great demand as a speaker around the country.

Unfortunately, Professor Johnson's previous speaking experience had been in lecturing to classes of students who were already, at least to some degree, interested in the subject and willing to listen to a detailed, solid presentation. He found his public audiences growing restless, coughing, even dozing off. Gradually, over a period of months, and with the help of a fellow faculty member knowledgeable in speech communication, Johnson discovered that his problem was one of audience adaptation. He began to change his approach and in a while was getting standing ovations and receiving more invitations to speak than he could comfortably accept. (And here the authors indulge in some fantasizing about the value of their field, their careers, and this book!)

Back to Professor Johnson. He has just accepted an invitation to give a speech entitled "Eutrophication and What We Can Do About It" for the Sandy Hill City Commercial Club's bimonthly luncheon. He immediately sends his research assistant to the campus library. He brings back a pad of notes about Sandy Hill City and its surrounding county, Goodwin. The assistant found that the main industry includes the gravel pits and stone quarries south of town; a cement factory has the second most important town payroll. Sandy Hill City is one of the oldest settlements in the state and is the site of the Goodwin County Historical Society Museum, which contains, among other things, the personal effects of the town's most famous son, Brigadier General Allan Snyder, World War I ace of aces and leading proponent of the development of air power prior to World War II. Armed with this information and various devices he has learned about audience adaptation, Johnson begins his speech to the Commercial Club as follows:

> "Eutrophication and What We Can Do About It." [He smiles.] I guess the first thing we can do about it is define it. [Audience chuckles.] I will define it in a minute, but first I'd like to share some of my thoughts with you as I was flying here over the lush farmlands of the central part of the state. I think far too often those of us living in cities forget the contribution the farmers of counties like Goodwin and the thriving towns like Sandy Hill City make to our economy and our quality of life. The countryside was beautiful, fertile, tilled—productive. I could see this as we landed. And as we taxied up to the Goodwin County airport terminal (which is, I was surprised to discover, a remarkably handsome facility, the newest in the five-county area, I'm told), I was impressed by the thriving bustle at the airport. The growth and power of this nation is made up of the dozens of cities such as Sandy Hill City.
>   When my taxi drove north toward the downtown area from the airport, I was struck by the immense size of the Terrara gravel pits. I asked the driver to pull in so I could get out and look at them. Producing, as they do, 35 percent of the gravel and crushed rock used in this state, the Terrara gravel pits make a real contribution to the entire state's economy and progress and really put Sandy Hill City on the map.
>   When we started driving toward town again, we had no sooner gotten under way than we came upon the imposing buildings of the Snyder Cement Works, and I suddenly recalled the name of Allan Snyder, World War I flying ace and far-seeing statesman in the air force—a native son. I had a little time left before I was due at the hotel, so I asked the driver to take me by the Goodwin County Museum. . . .

In the real world, most audiences would consider this much over-done; still, it demonstrates that our professor could find out a great deal about his Commercial Club audience in a short period of time; he combed the public sources of information (libraries, newspapers, and the like) and he allowed some time in the area to talk to the natives themselves before he was to speak.

Often when we are asked to give a speech, we can learn about the audience we will address simply by interviewing the person who contacts us to make the talk. This person will probably be able to tell us about the room or auditorium where we will speak, about who will attend, and what they will expect. As we gain experience speaking to various sorts of audiences, we develop an awareness of what is expected from us in various speaking situations. A PTA meeting in a large urban school presents one kind of audience; a PTA meeting in a suburb presents another kind of audience—similar in many ways, different in some others. The luncheon meeting of a businesspeople's service club is a different audience than a social-business dinner of the same group.

Our best advice, therefore, is to remember that there are many sources of information about audiences and you should collect as much information as you can. Further, you should give public speeches whenever and wherever you can if you want to develop skill in audience analysis and adaptation; by so doing you will gain a personal knowledge about varied audiences, how they respond to you, and how you adjust to control their response. If you have the chance to give a speech to your class, set aside enough time to study your classmates as members of an audience. If you focus on them as potential members of an audience, you will find that you know a lot about them simply from interaction with them as you go to and from the classroom, from class participation, and from discussions. Think of them as individuals in a real audience rather than as "Just our speech-communication class." Try to think through their response to you, quite objectively, and plan and rehearse your speech keeping your specific audience in mind. Adapt your examples, analogies, evidence, and positive and negative suggestions to these people—these individuals collected at a particular time to hear you. Pay particular attention to the analysis of their rhetorical visions.

When giving a public speech, you will often have to work with less complete and precise information about the listeners than you can have when you are speaking in an interview or small-group situation. As a public speaker, you seldom get as much feedback from the audience about how well your messages are comprehended and how they are evaluated as you can get in less formal communication situations. At the same time, however, you do not need as much specific feedback from larger audiences, because the public speaker can use broader strokes and get the desired response with less carefully adjusted messages. Individual members of a large audience adjust their listening to react to someone talking to "us" rather than just to "me." They thus do not expect the same person-to-person adjustment they would demand if you were engaged in a conversation.

While we live in an age of electronic communication, a time in which intimate and informal conversation is prized and common, we also live in a culture that uses the formal public speech for many important occasions and purposes. The complete communicator, in the present age of increased need for quality interpersonal communication, also needs to know about audiences for public speeches and about how to adapt his or her ideas to them.

KEY IDEAS

- A good public speaker is audience-centered.
- Excitement and emotional responses are contagious in a large crowd; the audience response affects the individual listener.
- The larger the audience, the more it appreciates an elevated style of speaking and appeals to higher motives.
- Public speeches fill one's need to celebrate the better side of one's nature and community.
- Television, with its emphasis on shoddy and unethical behavior, is a poor medium for building community-sustaining myths.
- An important question for a speaker is "How diverse is the audience in its attitudes toward my position?"
- More important, often, than the general information about age, sex, and socioeconomic background are the audience members' rhetorical visions.
- If you want to adapt your ideas to your audience, it is a great help if you can analyze their rhetorical vision.
- We can most easily understand events if we see them acted out by people who symbolize complex institutions, organizations, and movements.
- An interesting feature of our interpretative scripts is that a number of plausible stories can account for the same events while putting a very different slant on them.
- Script analysis provides an excellent guide to audience adaptation.
- Begin a script analysis by asking about the audience members, "What is their level of understanding? How interested, supportive, or hostile are they to my topic?"
- The script analysis can reveal the heroes and villains of the audience's rhetorical vision as well as their interpretation of who or what is causing things to happen.
- Remember, there are many sources of information about audiences, and you should collect as much as you can.

SUGGESTED PROJECTS

1. Assume that a visiting speaker asks you to brief him about his or her probable audience. Analyze students at your school. Identify their heroes, villains, and dreams, as well as their general interests and attitudes.

2. Pick some city or town within 100 miles of your school and analyze its chamber of commerce as an audience for a speech, to be made by a student, concerning student attitudes today toward business as a career. What sources would you use in informing yourself about this audience?

3. Select a topic for a persuasive speech suitable for a class assignment. Make a script analysis of the various rhetorical visions that your classmates have in regard to the topic.

SUGGESTED READINGS

Clevenger, Theodore, Jr. *Audience Analysis.* Indianapolis, Ind.: Bobbs-Merrill, 1966.

Eisenson, Jon, J. Jeffery Auer, and John V. Irwin. *The Psychology of Communication.* New York: Prentice-Hall, 1963.

Jeffrey, Robert C., and Owen Peterson. *Speech: A Text with Adapted Readings.* 3d ed. New York: Harper & Row, 1983.

chapter *10*

Speech Preparation

THE NATURE OF PUBLIC SPEAKING

Our speech preparation is aided by the fact that in our culture the public speech is an established communication occasion with well-understood patterns of how we ought to behave and communicate. Once we know what kind of speech occasion it is, we also know a good deal about what is expected of us as a speaker or as an audience member.

For many public speeches the participants anticipate that one individual will deliver an extended message. The audience comes to hear a certain person speak on an advertised subject or title. The public-speaking transaction has a definite format that usually includes a time at which the audience is to gather and the speech is supposed to begin, and quite often a time when the speech is to close. Americans are time-conscious and pay a great deal of attention to the length of a speech. If the speech draws out longer than they have anticipated, audience members often grow restless.

For many public speeches the audience expects and appreciates activities that set the stage for the speaker. A simple format for a speech is to have a local dignitary call the meeting to order and introduce the speaker by identifying his background and experience. The speaker then delivers his message, and the person who introduced him thanks the speaker and closes the meeting. The basic format is often elaborated so that the speaker is preceded by music, group singing, or performances, by lesser personalities, to increase the audience's susceptibility to the main speaker. Big revival meetings, for instance, often have prayers, announcements, songs, and introductions before the evangelist delivers the main message of the evening. Political rallies generally have music, introductions, and some enthusiastic partisan comments before the main speaker comes to the podium.

After the speech, the audience may participate in questioning the speaker or in making comments. The occasion may call for more music or some additional comments by other people.

Generally, the people planning the public speech arrange things so the audience has some place to sit or stand, so distractions are minimized, and so the speaker is provided with a public-address system in good working order that allows everyone present to hear him.

The variety of specific expectations aroused by such situations as the after-dinner speech, the revival speech, the agitator's speech at a political demonstration, and the funeral eulogy praising someone who has died can be identified by such questions as: Does the audience expect and enjoy humor? Does the audience listen quietly to the speaker? Does the audience interrupt and heckle? Does the audience interrupt to reinforce the speaker with shouts such as "Hallelujah! Praise the Lord!" or "Right on!" or "You tell 'em, George!" Does the audience expect the speaker to read a carefully prepared message? Does the audience expect the speaker to deliver an extemporaneous speech with high feeling and vigorous nonverbal communication? To some extent, of course, expectations of audiences are culturebound; more than likely a black rural southern congregation will expect a different funeral eulogy than will a small-town Scandinavian Lutheran congregation in Minnesota.

An adept speaker may sometimes break one or two of the expected conventions that relate to a certain speech occasion and even benefit from the novelty of the violation—people usually enjoy a mild surprise—but if he violates a number of the conventions surrounding a public speech, the audience will often be confused, indignant, bored, or even angry. If a minister, for example, introduces some humor into an ordinarily serious religious meeting, most of the audience will respond as the speaker hopes. If the minister violates other expectations in addition—for example, in way of dress, style of language, dialect, use of profanity or of bald humor, or appearance of drunkenness while delivering the sermon—the audience's responsiveness will be seriously disturbed.

If the audience comes to a public-speaking situation expecting to hear a fire-breathing politician, a hellfire-and-damnation revival preacher, or a violent revolutionary, the members are often predisposed to respond

If a speaker violates the conventions surrounding a public speech, the audience will often be confused, bored, or even sullen. (Reno, Jeroboam)

with high feeling. The planners of the meeting, trying to fulfill these expectations, may precede the main speaker with music and warmup speeches, as we mentioned earlier. By the time the speaker begins, the audience may be quite excited, and if he is skillful, the orator will soon have focused the attention of the listeners upon his speech.

We have, admittedly, taken the above examples from that group of public-speaking situations that conventionally arouse expectations of emotional excitement. The same principles of audience behavior, however, apply to other situations. The audience attending a lecture by a Nobel prize winner, for instance, places equally strong pressures to conform on individual members of the audience. If the speaker is wearing evening dress, if the ushers whisper as though loud and boisterous talk were out of order, if the audience sits upright and with great dignity, the pressure is strong on all audience members to do likewise. If members of the audience begin to cough, grow restless, and look at their watches, all these behaviors put pressure on the speaker and other audience members alike.

The audience is also an important consideration in planning. The audience is not passive. Even listener apathy or disinterest is an important response to a speech. Often the audience members will be interested and respond either positively or negatively to what they hear. Audience responses may cause the speaker problems. If the audience is uninterested, the speaker is expected to use examples, strong delivery, compelling language, and other communication skills to arouse and maintain its interest.

SELECTING A TOPIC

Your planning begins with the selection of a topic for the speech. Someone may assign you a topic area or even provide a specific title for your speech, but often you can pick your own topic. A student speaker often finds picking a topic a major problem, second only to managing communication tension. The two problems are interrelated. Our recommended treatment for developing a positive attitude toward communication tension is to pick the right topic for you and for the audience and to prepare thoroughly before you speak.

We will not provide you with a long list of suggested topics for class speeches. Any list we might prepare now from headlines indicating the current hot news topics would be out of date by the time you read this chapter. You will find a better guide to topics about business, politics, entertainment, government, religion, and military affairs by skimming the headlines in the most recent edition of your local newspaper or the most recent issue of a national news magazine. More important, lists are no substitute for the ability to meet each new speaking occasion with a creative solution to the problem of finding the right topic *for you.*

In our discussion of speech preparation which follows, we will discuss the creative process and how you can learn to use it in planning your speeches. Thinking up topics for a speech that you could give to your classmates is an excellent drill to improve your creativity. We recommend that you take out a few minutes each day for the next few days and write down ten possible speech topics each day. Try to come up with ten topics in the shortest amount of time you can. Write down anything that comes into your head no matter how silly it may seem. Strive for speed; do not worry about quality. The matter of quality can come up later when you have to pick a topic for a specific assignment.

Our best advice is to pick a speech topic that is of interest to you. If you are already well informed on the subject, fine. Even if you are not well informed, if you are curious and excited about learning more about some subject, it can serve as a good topic for a speech. Once you have an established career, people will usually ask you to give a speech because you have specialized knowledge, training, or experience that makes you a person they want to hear.

Even now you probably know more about some topics than most of your classmates. You may know more than they do about hang gliding, making men's ties, or the workings of an automobile engine. Your special knowledge equips you to make a speech whenever you are talking to people who know less about a particular subject than you do. If you are a trained or hobby automotive mechanic, you could make a speech about whether or not efforts to conserve energy by increasing the mileage of American automobiles are likely to succeed.

Even if we have not yet had much special training or study in a technical topic area, we are all experts in some fields because of our personal experiences. We are particular experts in the areas of how we *feel* about a topic, what our responses are, and why, on some issue. Did you attend a high school where belonging to, or not being a member of, certain cliques or groups or gangs was an important factor in your enjoyment of school? You can speak about how such groups function to illustrate the principles of small-group communication, as explained in Chapter 7. Did you attend a high school at which busing for integration and racial balance resulted in an improvement or a decline in the quality of your education? You could speak from personal experience on the effects of busing on the quality of education. Do you know from firsthand experience or from observing friends and acquaintances about drug dependency, teenage sex, or the group pressures that encourage or discourage academic excellence? Perhaps you have a hobby or some consuming interest in a sport. Do you collect coins? records? Do you like some particular kind of music? Are you a movie buff? Are you fascinated with computers? Do you find machines "friends" or "foes" as you look ahead in your lifetime? What do you want from life? How do your goals differ from those of your parents, and what are your personal hopes and dreams? What is your response to the media? Do you feel television has enriched or stifled your growth intellectually? Everyone agrees that reading skills are a basic necessity in today's world; tons of material have been written about "why Johnny can't read." Think back over your years in school; you know who had trouble with basic reading skills. Read some of the research; search your own memory of the process of teaching reading in your own school experience. Your speech topic could then be "I Think I Know Why Johnny Can't Read."

Put your mind to it. Use the tips on creativity that follow. Look on topic selection as a challenge rather than a chore. Skills in creative thinking are elements of your education that you will be able to use for the rest of your life.

MAKING A CREATIVE ANALYSIS OF A TOPIC

A creative analysis is important to understanding a topic. Once a speaker has decided on a general topic for a speech, the next step is to assemble all the information possible within the time available. At this point your ability to use the library, to interview for information, to assemble and remember all the information that you know from personal experience becomes important. Excellent books devoted to library use and research are readily available in your own library. If you want to learn to use your library more effectively, see if a reference librarian will give you a short tour and explain the main reference tools available to you. You will find the skill of using a library effectively important not only for your career as a student but for the rest of your life. A course in speech communication, particularly one that includes the study of public speaking, provides a good stimulus and context for you to learn the very important skills of collecting and recording information for further use in writing and speaking. One expert in the use of the library boasted that given a first-class library and two weeks' time, he could become the second-best authority on any topic in the world. Such claims are probably, like the expert, legendary, but there is a good point to the story. An important part of anyone's education involves learning how to gather information quickly and efficiently.

Once you have an assignment to deliver a speech and have selected (or have been given) a general topic, you should assemble all the information you can and begin to analyze it. *Analysis* is the process of dividing the information into parts, examining the parts, and discovering the important questions that relate to understanding the subject. Some of your thinking ought to be systematic and disciplined, and some ought to be freewheeling and creative. You start by being systematic. Collecting and reading the basic information sets the stage for the more creative analysis later.

Preparation

As you begin the creative "mulling over" of the information you will undoubtedly make false starts and run into dead ends. You may find the topic confusing and be unable to see a pattern in all the information you have collected. You are in the first stage of the creative process, the *preparation phase,* which is a warmup period in which you systematically try to make sense out of the material you have available for the speech. Often you seem to be wasting time, getting nowhere. Do not be discouraged by your seeming lack of progress. You must immerse yourself in the material before you can make a sound analysis of it. Often a person becomes frustrated in the preparation stage and stops working on the analysis. If one has really worked for a sufficient period of time, however, putting the topic aside may be exactly what he or she should do for a while. The key to the successful ongoing creative process is doing each step sufficiently so that the next step can take place. You must prepare thoroughly, gather everything you can find; try to organize it systematically in as many ways as you can. Then, if you have really filled your mind with the material, you are ready for the second stage to happen.

Incubation

As you consciously put the topic of the speech out of your mind for a while and work at other tasks (preferably manual work), the second phase of the creative process, the *incubation period,* should begin. In the incubation period, although you are not apparently working on your speech, your subconscious is mulling it over. Many people are aware of this process when they suddenly see the solution to a personal problem, such as a difficult decision, right in the middle of doing something completely unrelated to the problem itself. But not everyone is aware that this is a natural, creative sequence and that *we can make it happen;* and that the more often we work at it, the more easily it becomes a source of problem solving. In terms of organizing a speech, while you are doing some routine job such as washing dishes, mowing the lawn, or driving the car, you may suddenly find yourself thinking about the speech in a stream-of-consciousness way. Maybe you hear yourself giving parts of the speech. The words sound "right" in your mind. You are not purposely trying to work on the speech, but it just seems to happen as your ideas associate freely, and you combine ideas, seeing yourself give the speech maybe, image following image. At first these ideas and images bubble up to your consciousness in bits and pieces.

Illumination

The bubbling up of ideas signals the beginning of the third part of the creative process, which usually comes after a period of incubation and is a very exciting part of any creative job. When you are thinking of something else, suddenly and unexpectedly you may clearly see the important ideas relating to the topic of your speech and how they fit together. Inspiration seems to strike: you suddenly know what your central theme for the speech will be, and you see how you can best approach it. The answers seem so right and good that you become excited and enthusiastic about the project. The third part of the creative process is this moment of *illumination*.

Verification

The final part of the creative analysis comes after the illumination phase and consists of the careful and conscious checking out of the details of the solution. Sometimes, upon reflection, the moment of illumination will turn out to have been a "flash in the pan"—when you check out the answer for consistency and plausibility, you discover it is not such a good idea after all. Often, however, the moment of illumination turns out to present a good solution to the problem, and your final task then is to verify, check, shape, and fill in minor details. The final part of the creative process of analysis is called the *verification phase*.

Disciplining Creativity

The creative process often seems groping and unstructured. Yet there is a method to the creative madness; it is not completely random, nor is it the same as striving for an answer by trial and error. Creativity requires disciplined work habits. The person who waits for inspiration to strike before beginning to prepare a speech is seldom lucky enough to be struck by the divine lightning. Professional writers who must continually stimulate their creativity to meet deadlines often suggest that the best way to learn to write is *to write*. Successful creative people repeat the slogan endlessly that creativity is 10 percent inspiration and 90 percent perspiration. This advice and the slogan about creativity may seem to be simpleminded, if not question-begging, but they contain the important idea that disciplined work habits are essential to the use of creative talent. Good public speakers also advise that the best way to learn the art is by disciplined practice. One popular slogan that catches the spirit is "If anybody is foolish enough to ask you to give a public speech, be foolish enough to accept."

The more creative you are, of course, the more difficulty you will have getting started on a creative task. Talent acts as though it were lazy, and your creativity will think up all sorts of good excuses for not getting to work. You sit down with a blank piece of paper to begin organizing a speech, and suddenly you remember that you need a glass of water. Having gotten the water, you sit down once more and realize that your typewriter needs a new ribbon. Once the new ribbon is in, you realize it is twelve o'clock and time for lunch. Finally you do get down to work, but as you strike the first key and start the first sentence, you remember that you really ought to go the library and look up some more information before you proceed. All too often, the beginning public speaker puts off the analysis of the topic until the very last minute, and in the rush to meet the deadline the creative process never really has time to get under way. Undoubtedly most of you found some of the above "creative" excuses very familiar. On the other hand, if someone asks you how creative you are, you may not rate yourself too highly. Most people are more creative than they realize; they have simply never learned to use their creative energy in any controlled and accountable way.

You can discipline your creativity by developing systematic work habits. Set aside certain times during the week to do creative work such as writing papers and preparing speeches. Make it an iron rule to spend that time doing your projects. If possible, pick the same desk, worktable, or corner of the library for your preparation and writing. Gradually you will discover that the familiar surroundings and the habit of regular work sessions will make the warmup period less painful, often shorter. You must be faithful to your schedule, however; you must push ahead even when you feel little inspiration and the work is not going well.

Often, with a little planning, you can allow enough time for your analysis to go through all four stages of the creative process. You cannot make a creative analysis all at once in a period of several hours or by cramming it into an all-night session as you might prepare for a final examination. Begin your preparation early and allow time for the incubation period. Set aside some time each day for contemplation. If you can do some routine activity such as walking, running, jogging, sweeping the floor, mowing a lawn, or gardening, the incubation process will be encouraged. Be careful about reading, though; reading occupies your mind too much and keeps it from moving into the free association of ideas and images that is useful for incubation.

When you are in the creative phase of analysis you need the proper mental set. Welcome farfetched ideas and elaborate on them. Imagine as many solutions as you can for a given problem. Modify, change, combine the ones you read about. Play with the ideas and do not worry too much about how stupid or crazy they may seem at first glance.

Once the creative process discovers the basic issues in a body of discourse, you can find a suitable central idea for your speech by answering one or more of the basic questions to your satisfaction. Next, you need to find the most important subpoints that fit under your central theme and the logical relationships that hold among them. When the process of analysis reaches its conclusions, you should have a logical arrangement of reasons in support of your idea, something like a lawyer's brief, which lays out the basic points in a case in a tightly ordered and reasoned fashion.

SPEECH PREPARATION AND USING COMMUNICATION TENSION PRODUCTIVELY

The first rule is to pick topics that excite you. If you talk on subjects you feel strongly about, you will soon discover that your interest in what you are saying is genuine and taking your mind off yourself.

The second rule is to prepare thoroughly. A good way to get the tension under control is to feel satisfied and confident that you are well prepared. A thorough preparation serves to put your mind at ease about that common bugaboo of speakers—forgetting what you want to say.

Some people try to assure that they will not forget by writing out the speech and reading it. Speakers sometimes need a written manuscript for other reasons in addition to making sure they do not forget what they want to say. If you are speaking on radio or television or making an important announcement where you are likely to be quoted in news media, you may need to write all your comments carefully and be sure to read the exact language you have worked out.

The speech manuscript does put your words right in front of you so you need not worry about what you will say, but it also causes some problems. Reading a speech tends to put a barrier between the speaker and the audience. You must be a skillful reader to overcome that barrier and communicate with the audience when you are tied to your manuscript. Few speakers manage to deliver a speech effectively under such conditions. American presidents since the advent of radio have tended to read their broadcast speeches to the nation. Aside from Franklin Roosevelt in the 1930s and Ronald Reagan in the 1980s, almost all the rest have been poor oral readers, and their speeches have often been dull and ineffective as a result. The manuscript itself often becomes a distraction for the audience. Of course, you can use note cards, but a speech of any length written out on cards will grow to quite a deck, too large to handle easily. The way you shuffle this deck and the possibility of getting the cards out of order all contribute to possible difficulties, all easy distractions for an audience.

If you write the speech and memorize it, you can sometimes overcome the barrier put up by the manuscript. If you have the speech memorized, you can practice its delivery and polish up your use of voice, your timing, and your gestures. Memorizing a speech takes a good deal of additional time, however, and you always run the danger of forgetting. When you forget a memorized speech, you often have to be prompted to get back on the right track. For the beginner who tries to memorize a speech, the result may be a patterned use of voice and gesture that seems unnatural to the audience.

The extemporaneous speech is one in which you prepare a careful outline and the supporting ideas you plan to use, but you do not write it out and memorize it word for word. You may rehearse the speech aloud by talking from the outline until you have it well in mind. You might commit the main points of the outline to memory or write them on note cards or a sheet of paper and use these main points to jog your memory while you talk with the audience. If you prepare an extemporaneous speech carefully, you still have the freedom to change your comments as you watch the audience response. Should you forget a point or a story or an example, you can continue on with the next section of your speech without prompting. A well-prepared extemporaneous speech is one of the best ways to deal productively with speech tension.

THE AUDIENCE-ADAPTATION STEP

After you have made a creative analysis of your topic, you should have a thorough understanding of the material. You will have done your "homework" and will have a firm grasp of the ins and outs of the question. You will not yet be ready to speak to a specific audience, however.

Too often, people untrained in public speaking but very knowledgeable and authoritative in a given profession or field will be called on to give lectures; they do a poor job, because they present their logical analysis of the topic, period—no matter what the audience and the occasion. They act as though there is an ideal lecture on their topic, which has universal appeal to all audiences, and they need only find that lecture.

Another problem is that untrained public speakers often want to present everything that led to their own understanding of the question, and since they do not know where to begin cutting down the information, they find time limits frustrating. "You just can't do justice to this topic in one hour," they may say.

A good public speech requires that the speaker take the results of an analysis of a topic and skillfully adapt it to a specific audience and occasion. For the study of public speaking, therefore, the second phase of analysis is of utmost importance. In the second stage, you can turn your attention to analysis of the audience according to the recommendations in the last chapter, and you can then plan how to adapt and arrange the material for the needs of your particular audience.

KEY IDEAS

- In our culture the public speech is an established communication transaction with well-understood patterns of general usage.
- The first step to success as a speaker is careful speech preparation.
- Your planning begins with the selection of a general topic.
- After you have a topic you should gather information relating to it.
- Once you have sufficient information, you should make an analysis of the topic.
- A creative analysis is important to understanding a topic and is the result of the four-phase creative process of *preparation, incubation, illumination,* and *verification.*
- You can discipline your creativity by developing systematic work habits, such as working on a regular schedule at a specific time and place.
- A good speech requires that the speaker take the results of a careful analysis of a topic and skillfully adapt it to a specific audience and occasion.

SUGGESTED PROJECTS

1. For a five-day period take out a few minutes each day and, aiming only for speed, write down 10 topics that could be used for speeches in your class. When you have a list of 50, go through it critically and check off those that you might be able to use.
2. Select the best topic from your list for a five- to eight-minute persuasive speech. Gather information relating to the topic and make an analysis of the material in which you discover a central thesis, main subpoints, and how the subpoints relate to one another and to the central idea.

SUGGESTED READINGS

Bettinghaus, Erwin P. *Message Preparation: The Nature of Proof.* Indianapolis, Ind.: Bobbs-Merrill, 1966.

Mills, Glen E. *Message Preparation.* Indianapolis, Ind.: Bobbs-Merrill, 1966.

Rodman, George. *Public Speaking: An Introduction to Message Preparation.* 2d ed. New York: Holt, Rinehart and Winston, 1981.

Schiff, Roselyn L. et al. *Communication Strategy: A Guide to Message Preparation.* Glenview, Ill.: Scott, Foresman, 1981.

chapter *11*

Organization

QUALITIES OF A WELL-ORGANIZED SPEECH

People who have not studied public speaking are likely to have only a vague notion of what constitutes "organized material" according to the ideal model of that communication perspective. If they can outline a message when they listen to it, or if a speaker presents a message in the form of an outline, they often assume that it is organized. Indeed, many students keep their notebooks in outline format, and many business and professional people present their material in outline form; it *looks* organized. Unless a speaker is trained, however, his material usually is actually disorganized. All you have to do to outline is to list and number some points. You can list points with numbers and letters even though the ideas do not fit logically together. Sound organization, on the other hand, requires more than just listing and using numbers and letters to label items on the list. A well-organized spoken message must have the qualities of unity, coherence, relevance, conciseness, and comprehensiveness.

A good public speech has *unity*. A critic can tell if the speech is unified by looking for a central idea to which each part of the speech relates. Often a speaker helps unify the speech by stating and highlighting the central theme in a way that makes it stand out clearly for the listener. When this is done well, almost all the listeners can later recall the speaker's main point. If the speaker does not state the central theme in so many words, the speech may still be unified if the subpoints are arranged and presented in such a way that the listener is led to figure out the main conclusion by inference.

A well-organized public speech is *coherent*. Coherence refers to the way the parts of the speech cluster or hang together. Each part of a good speech relates to every other part in a way that reveals some clear design. A coherent speech is like a jigsaw puzzle of a picture of, say, a horse; when it is properly put together, the resulting picture is unmistakably a horse. A speech that lacks coherence is like the puzzle when it is only partially put together, with a portion of the head completed but much still missing, and with other parts spread over the table in jumbled fashion.

A well-organized public speech contains main points with supporting information and evidence that clearly and directly *relate to the central theme*. The speaker who feels that something not obviously related to the central idea is nonetheless important and relevant should explain this reasoning to the audience. Speakers who organize a public speech poorly often include much material that is not related to the topic under discussion. When you are first preparing a message, you may "free-associate" ideas and list them just as they come to mind. You may daydream along so that one idea follows another, one image triggers another, one story causes you to think of another, one experience reminds you of another. You may be tempted to include these materials in your speech plan because they interest you at the moment. Rambling and disjointed speeches, however, are undesirable. Everything you say should have clearly understood relevance to your central theme.

A well-organized speech is *concise* in the sense that it does not contain a high proportion of repetitiveness. In a good speech the speaker deals with each point in enough detail for the purposes of the situation and occasion and then does not deal with it again except for emphasis in summaries, transitions, introductions, and conclusions. A common fault in the organization of a public speech is for a speaker to deal with a topic, drop it, take up another topic, perhaps a third, and then return to the first point again. The beginner is learning good technique when he or she can cut a poorly organized message into parts and paste it together again so that all statements about a point are put together and unnecessary repetitions are eliminated. Keeping your speech concise for the listener helps the listener come away with your ideas intact, as you hoped to present them.

A well-organized public speech is *comprehensive* in the sense that it deals with the leading topics relating to its central theme. Of course the speech's comprehensiveness must be evaluated in relation to the audience, the occasion, and the amount of time that the speaker has to discuss the central idea. A skillful speaker will restrict the scope of the speech so that the topic can be dealt with in sufficient detail in the time available. A less skilled person often works out a central theme that is vague or too broad and must then deal with the topics in abstract fashion or leave out so many important ideas that the speech, as heard, is sketchy and lacking in completeness. The public speaker who covers the stated topic as thoroughly as the context warrants has produced a speech with sufficient comprehensiveness.

CONSTRUCTING AN ORGANIZED SPEECH

The speaker constructing a message for an audience has to do three main things in order to organize the speech for maximum effect: *select* the material to include, *arrange* the items in some order, and *proportion* the items by deciding how much time to give to each point.

Although the speech-construction step involves many concrete problems relating to the details of the nuts-and-bolts aspects of fitting a speech together, a speaker still profits from applying our advice about creativity to these matters. Even though you have a general theme for a speech and have analyzed it, you will need to develop a clearly worded central idea for each specific occasion. The central idea for a persuasive speech should be worded as a positive suggestion: "Buy this Bearcat now!" "Picket City Hall tomorrow!" The central idea for a lecture or an informational presentation should be a simple declarative sentence. A central idea for a lecture might be "I will explain the basic model of the message communication perspective."

Vaguely worded central ideas, such as "I will tell you something about communication," are poor guides to use in organizing a speech. Complex sentences that contain several ideas, such as "I will explain a basic model of communication and discuss the nature of communication theory," are likewise troublesome, because they require a speaker to keep *two* main ideas before the audience.

Once the speaker has picked a specific and clear central idea for the speech, he or she can select material that is appropriate for the audience and fits logically under his or her central idea.

The next task in organizing a speech is to arrange the material in some order. As a rule, the speaker should stick to one kind of arrangement only. Later in the chapter we will discuss three important patterns of arrangement in greater detail, and in later chapters, on informative and

Unity, coherence, a central theme, relevance, conciseness, and comprehensiveness are marks of a good organization, even in an impromptu comment. (Franken, Stock, Boston)

persuasive speaking, we will provide additional ways to order the points in a speech.

Deciding how much time to give to each point is a matter of judgment, depending on the total amount of time allotted to the speech and on the audience's attitude and knowledge. The speaker has to think carefully about the arguments to be presented, deciding which is the most important, what material is familiar to the audience, and what is unfamiliar and must be more fully developed.

A good speech has a beginning, a middle, and an end. The beginning is called an *introduction,* the middle is called the *body* of the speech, and the end is called the *conclusion.*

A good introduction catches the audience's attention, arouses and holds its interest, and lets it know what the speech is to be about. Because a speech is different from a theme or essay in that the speaker is talking directly to people sitting in front of him, he must spend some time at the beginning of his remarks just getting everybody's attention. The listeners need a chance to size up the speaker as a person, to get acquainted with him.

The body of the speech contains the main points that make up the message proper. If, instead of speaking, you were writing an article about the same material, the bulk of the article would be similar to the information contained in the body of a speech.

The conclusion of a speech is a brief comment that rounds off the message and gives the audience a feeling that you have finished. A conclusion tends to be a summary of the main ideas in a speech, an appeal for action or reaction, or a summary plus an appeal.

A speaker further achieves unity by clearly and logically relating all major subpoints to the central theme and to one another. You can explain the relationship among ideas to your audience by telling them how you will arrange the main subpoints. "I will begin by . . . Next, I will . . . And, finally, I will . . ." "First I will discuss . . . Second, I will deal with . . . Third, I will . . ." "I want to examine two main questions with you this evening. The first question is . . . The second question is . . ." You can also indicate when you have completed your comments on one point and are moving on to a new part of your speech. "So in summary, my answer to the first question is . . ., but remember that I said the answer to the first question is not enough. We must also answer the question . . ." Finally, you can indicate relationships among points by summarizing what you have said and pointing out to your listeners what you have so far accomplished in terms of your overall plan. "We have now seen that, first, . . . and second, . . . With this evidence I have proved what the lawyers call a prima facie case—that is, a case that, unless answered, gives you enough evidence to render a verdict of 'yes.' But I promised you more than a prima facie case. Let's look now at the most important evidence. . . ."

Transitions are brief comments composed of statements or questions or both that lead the hearer from the point just finished to the next point in the speech. Transitions tie the various points of a speech together.

Inexperienced speakers feel the need for transitions but have a tendency to use one or two words over and over again. Novice speakers say "and another thing" and "another point," or overuse the word "next" or "also." The good speaker has to learn to use varied transitions that summarize the points just made, forecast the point coming next, or better yet, both summarize and forecast.

The speaker who makes comments such as the above helps the listeners see the overall structure of the speech and understand how the details fit together into a meaningful "big picture." The next time you watch a television drama, notice how the director arranges the shots. The drama will often begin with an establishing shot—that is, a picture of the larger scene—so you can understand how the actors are arranged and how they fit into the larger context. Then it may cut to a closer shot of several actors and cut again to a closeup picture of one actor's face as the scene builds to a dramatic climax. At a transition point, another longer shot will often be used to once again establish context before moving the camera to more detailed closeups. Such "big picture" establishing shots are useful for the speaker as well as the television director. You must verbally and nonverbally unify your speech for your listeners throughout.

DEVELOPING BASIC MESSAGE UNITS

The basic building block for messages consists of two parts: the point to be made and the material to support it. The ability to construct basic message units with good supporting material that relates clearly to a well-expressed basic idea is a communication skill that you can use in all your communication, but it is essential in giving a public speech.

When a communicator presents only the main points, without supporting or amplifying them, the speech sounds and reads like a telegram or an outline of the major headings for a theme in an English class. Brief comments on points to be made are hard to understand. Telegraphic talking has the advantage of brevity but usually produces confusion.

Stating a Point

A point to be made clear should be expressed in a complete, simple, declarative sentence. We use the terms *complete, simple,* and *declarative* in their technical meanings for English grammar. Complete sentences include both subject and predicate as in the following: "The operators of the numbers games pick the winning numbers from common experiences." "The moon's gravity affects the way a person can walk on the moon's surface."

Remember that a simple sentence has but one subject and one predicate. Put another way, the point to be made in a message unit ought to contain only one idea. The following sentence would make a poor point for a message unit: "The operators of the numbers games pick the winning numbers from common experiences and generally pay off the police to keep in business."

A declarative sentence states something in contrast to a question, which asks for information, or a command, which tells somebody to do something. "How do they pick the winning numbers for the numbers game?" is not a good point for a basic message unit. Neither is the command "Stop playing the numbers."

Never underestimate the importance of finding a good, clear way to make the point you want to make. If you can express what you want to say in a good, clear, simple sentence, you have gone a long way toward getting your point across.

Supporting a Point

After you have found a good statement of the point to clarify, provide supporting material to make the idea clear. Give an example (real or hypothetical), an analogy (literal or figurative), or a narrative that applies directly to the point. (Of course, if the idea is difficult for the receiver to understand, you may give several examples or analogies or stories to clarify one point.) An important mistake of beginning speakers is to use an example that does not have much to do with the point they are trying to make. Here is a hypothetical example of the does-not-apply mistake:

> The operators of the numbers game in my neighborhood pick the winning numbers from almost anything. For example, I know one bookie who pays protection money all the time, and he's been working one place for a long time and nobody has bothered him or given him any trouble.

In the above instance, the so-called "example" has nothing to do with the point made before it.

Patterns of Forming Message Units

Basic message units can be formed in several ways. The following four patterns are often used:

Type 1

Point to be made clear
Supporting material (examples, analogies, stories)

Type 2

Supporting material (examples, analogies, stories)
Point to be made clear

Type 3

Supporting material (examples, analogies, stories)
Point to be made clear
Further supporting material

Type 4

Supporting material (several examples, analogies, stories)
Point never stated in so many words, but audience supposed to
   be able to figure it out from the mass of supporting material;
   point made between the lines

As a general rule, the patterns that state the point to be made clear
first or last are the best; certainly you seldom will be wrong using message-
building blocks of these first two types. Burying the point in the middle
of a message block often hinders the listener's efforts to dig it out and
follow your comment. Leaving out the point entirely is quite risky. However, if you are reasonably sure of your listener's ability to identify the
point on the basis of your clear examples and analogies, the fourth pattern
can be effective, partly because it provides variety and partly because it
creates the illusion that the point is the listener's own notion and facilitates
his or her willingness to accept it. We recommend, therefore, that you use
the basic message unit without a clear statement of the point primarily for
persuasive situations but that you stick to types 1 and 2 for most messages.

PATTERNS FOR ORGANIZING PUBLIC SPEECHES

The three-part division of a speech into an introduction, body, and conclusion is a good standard way to frame your remarks, but it does not help
you much in selecting and arranging the main points, supporting ideas,
and transitions in the body of the speech. Over the years public speakers
have discovered a number of recurring patterns that have proved useful
in organizing speeches.

If you learn some of the "tried and true" ways of arranging the points
in a speech, you may be able to use them in planning a speech of your own.
At least you will have a place to start. You might buy a coat from the rack

in a clothing store and wear it immediately. The coat is cut to a standard pattern, and it will fit you more or less well. You might buy a coat cut to a standard pattern but have a tailor alter it, modifying it to fit you better. And, finally, you might have a tailor measure you and design a one-of-a-kind coat to your taste, made out of your chosen material. As a speaker, you are in somewhat the same situation as when you buy a coat from the rack in that you can use a good standard outline and often end up with a well-organized speech that fits the audience and occasion more or less well; or you can alter a standard outline and make it fit better; or you can design a unique organizational pattern tailored especially for your specific audience and occasion.

We recommend that for important speeches you try to alter one of the three very basic patterns that follow or that you design a unique outline tailored for your audience alone. An understanding of these three most important and widespread patterns will certainly help you get started in the practice of organizing public speeches.

State Your Case and Prove It

The state-your-case-and-prove-it pattern of organization is the basic, straightforward development where you "tell them what you are going to tell them, tell them, and then tell them what you told them." You begin with an introduction, state your central thesis and the points that you will develop in support of it, take up each point in turn, and end with a summary.

State-Your-Case-and-Prove-It Pattern

   I. Introduction.
  II. Overview, consisting of central idea and listing of points.
 III. Development of each point.
 IV. Conclusion, consisting of a summary.

The pattern of stating a case and proving it is a good one for a speaker dealing with a familiar and much-discussed controversial topic. When a person talks on a well-worn issue, the audience members probably know a good deal about the pros and cons of the subject. The speaker dealing with a much-discussed issue does not need to explore the topic comprehensively and go over as much background information as is often necessary with a fresh topic. If you are dealing with such a topic, you might well just state your position and support it in line with the basic pattern.

Because of the elementary nature of the pattern, you can use it in situations where you have little or no time to prepare your remarks. Have you ever received an honor and been in a situation where, to celebrate the occasion, people began to yell at you to give a speech? "Speech, speech" is a familiar call. Often you can shrug off such a request, and people are good-natured about it and let you off the hook, but sometimes you really must respond. Sometime you may be told before you sit down at a banquet, for instance, that after the meal the sponsors of the banquet would like to have you "say a few words." The technical name for the speech you give when you are asked to say a few words on very short notice is an *impromptu speech.* You can remember a variation of the basic pattern, which is ideal for impromptu situations, and by carefully following the directions for each step of the speech, you can end up with a well-organized speech on the spur of the moment.

The impromptu speaking pattern we recommend consists of the following four steps; you will notice they are essentially a version of the basic state-your-case-and-prove-it pattern.

Impromptu Pattern

    I. Begin with an illustration.
  II. Give an overview consisting of the central idea and listing of points.
 III. Follow through (cover each point in turn).
 IV. Recap, with a twist (conclusion consisting of summary).

By memorizing the key words *illustrate, overview, follow through,* and *recap,* you can recall the directions for quickly organizing your remarks.

You begin the impromptu pattern with an example, preferably a narrative with human interest that illustrates the central idea you want to make. You do not set the stage for the story or example in any way; you simply begin to tell it.

"In the Old West, when they got civilized and stopped hanging the socially undesirable citizens from the nearest tree, they turned to finding a long, thin fence rail, and they'd tie them to it, and then they'd form a long procession and run 'em out of town on a rail. One such individual gained notoriety by asserting, 'If it wasn't for the honor of the occasion, I'd just as soon walk.' "

If you have some ability to dramatize the story, audience members will become interested. Furthermore, they will become curious as to why you are telling the story and what you are driving at. You catch their attention, arouse their interest, and make them want to continue listening.

The second step of the impromptu pattern consists of a statement that leads easily to the central idea of your speech. You then give an overview (state what you will talk about) by listing the two or three points that you will talk about:

> "You really surprised me just now by making me team captain. But I know what it takes to be captain of this team, and I feel a little like the old westerner. Let me tell you why. We can win the title this year, but to do so, we must do two things; first, it's our tradition that the team captain is the leader of the team, not a figurehead, *the leader;* and second, all of us will have to level with one another about any problems we have as a team."

In the third step of the impromptu pattern you take up each point in turn and comment on it, supplying the examples and evidence that come readily to mind.

The fourth step is to conclude the speech with a recap and a twist. The recap is a short reminder of each of the points, phrased in different words than you used when you first made them, and the twist is a surprise ending that makes the speech sound unified and rounded off. A good twist is to refer back to the opening example or story with a tie-in that again shows the relevance of the introduction, thus unifying the speech:

> "If we do those two things, we can win the championship this year. If you are willing to do these two things, I will be willing to ride the narrowest, sharpest rail you can find. If you aren't willing to do these things, despite the honor, I would just as soon get off now."

The state-your-case-and-prove-it basic pattern of organizing a speech is simple but effective. It is an adaptable form, including the impromptu speech outline we used, and it is a straightforward, useful pattern for you to consider.

The Problem-Solving Pattern

The problem-solving pattern is one in which the speaker describes a problem, discusses its causes, suggests possible solutions, and recommends a course of action most likely to solve the problem. In its simplest form the pattern consists of (1) a description of the problem, (2) an analysis of its causes, and (3) an explanation of the best solution. A useful variation is a pattern similar to the one that the philosopher-educator John Dewey introduced at the beginning of the twentieth century. Dewey presented an analysis of what he called *reflective thinking* and discussed the way the trained mind studies problems in the scientific laboratory. According to Dewey, reflective thinking is not random stream-of-consciousness thought, nor is it trial-and-error problem solving. When you daydream, your mind moves from image to image and does not focus on any specific problem. When you solve a problem through trial and error, you simply try everything that pops into your head until finally you reach a solution. Reflective thinking, on the other hand, begins when someone has what Dewey called a *felt difficulty*—a disturbance of the environment or pattern of life that becomes so strong that the individual begins to work to try to do something about it. The person begins to search out the problem and find out what is causing the difficulty. As the individual's vague feeling of puzzlement and difficulty comes under rational analysis, the problem comes into focus and the pattern of reflective thinking begins. As the person gets a clearer picture of the problem, possible solutions come to mind. The individual postpones trying out the solutions, as would be the case in trial and error, and instead *reflects* upon each, weighing the solutions against one another in terms of the causes of the problem. After methodical and reasonable analysis, the individual tries what seems like the best solution, in an effort to relieve the felt difficulty.

Dewey's analysis provides a step-by-step, logical progression that a speaker can use in organizing the materials for a speech. The pattern is as follows:

Problem-Solving Pattern

    I. Introduction.
   II. The nature of the problem.
      A. Definition of problem.
      B. Exploration of causes.
 III. Listing of representative solutions.
 IV. Examination of representative solutions.
   V. Selection of the best solution.

The problem-solving pattern is a particularly good one when the problem is complicated and the audience is hostile to the speaker's proposed solution, or when the problem is complicated and the audience is relatively unfamiliar with the facts of the situation. The pattern gives the listener an easy-to-follow and logical path through what might otherwise be a baffling and chaotic topic.

The problem-solving pattern encourages the listeners to adopt an objective, thoughtful attitude toward the speech, and this can help to disarm them of some of their emotionalism and prejudices. The speaker should adopt an appropriate tone in giving a speech in the problem-solving pattern. When the speaker says, "Let us explore the problem and see if we can decide what is causing it, and let us list all of the good solutions we can think of and compare them to see which is best," the openness of the speaker's approach should lead the audience members to follow along thoughtfully. One must be careful, however, when using the pattern, to adopt a scientific, objective manner and not use emotional or "loaded" language or any of the typical persuasive devices. Use matter-of-fact, direct language that conveys objectivity to the listener.

If you make a speech examining a number of possible solutions to a problem, and then eliminate all but the one you recommend, you will be following the natural tendency of much human decision making and problem solving. Research into the problem-solving dynamics of small task-oriented groups indicates that groups use this method in making decisions and solving problems. People tend to eliminate undesirable solutions first and let the decision emerge as the only remaining option. Often they find it easier to decide which solutions they do *not* want to follow than to decide what they would prefer to do. The pattern of organization that eliminates the undesirable answers until the one best solution is left, is the *method of residues.*

The Envisioning Pattern

The third and final pattern that we will consider in detail is another useful way to organize public speeches. When you organize a speech in this pattern you catch up the audience members in your vision of the problem by artistically arousing their interest, creating understanding, sharing in an interpretative script, and acting in line with your recommendations. We call the pattern the envisioning sequence. The envisioning pattern consists of the following steps: (1) you begin with material that arouses the audience's interest, (2) you next demonstrate that they should be dissatisfied with the way things are going, (3) you move to an explanation of how best to gratify the need you have created in the second step, (4) you dramatize an interpretative script that envisions the way things will be if the audience follows your recommendation, and (5) you move them to action.

The fact that you cannot reverse the parts of a speech that is organized into the steps of the envisioning sequence indicates its organic unity.
The pattern is based on the psychology of consciousness raising or conver-
sion. When people shift from one rhetorical vision to another, they begin
with a feeling that something is not right with their world. They are
restless and dissatisfied. At the point of dissatisfaction, communication
that breaks up the old vision serves to set the stage for a new and more
gratifying consciousness. Persuasive messages that dramatize a new rhetorical vision can provide a new pattern of self-actualization.

An attractive feature of the envisioning sequence is that you can
remember it easily by committing the five key words *(arouse, dissatisfy,
gratify, dramatize, move)* to memory. When you need to develop a persuasive speech, you can think of each key word in turn and begin to draft a
section of a speech aimed at that response. The end effect is a speech
arranged in a proven effective psychological progression.

You might well want to draft your outline by asking the following
questions about your audience: How can I arouse their interest? How can
I make them dissatisfied by showing them the things that are wrong with
their present situation? How can I show them that my solution will meet
the problems and be gratifying to them? How can I dramatize an attractive
future for them once they accept my solution? How can I move them to
implement the plan?

Another good thing about the envisioning pattern is that you can
often eliminate some of the early steps if the audience is already highly
interested in the topic and very dissatisfied. You can then simply remind
them of your common problem and concern and move quickly to the
gratification step. Sometimes, of course, one speech is part of a whole
campaign of persuasion. Much contemporary advertising is planned as a
campaign. Revivalists often talk of a crusade, a campaign that is designed
to create a total persuasive climate through the use of a large number of
integrated messages, prayer meetings, public speeches, revival meetings,
and sermons. If a speech is part of such an ongoing and elaborate campaign, a given speech might concentrate on arousing interest, and subse-
quent messages and speeches could take up the other steps in the envisioning sequence.

HOW TO OUTLINE A SPEECH

We are going to conclude this chapter with a general sample speech
outline that indicates one good way to plan a speech or presentation.

Any speech you give is bound to have individual requirements that you will have to work out for yourself. This outline includes a column (to the left) in which you can comment about the communication techniques you plan to use to achieve your purposes. This method has proved useful to our public-speaking students over the years. It helps develop some objectivity about why you put a speech together in a particular way, and it helps develop a sense of control over material. Many beginning public speakers can dig out much material on a subject for a speech and can make a fair prediction about the probable response of their audience (the other members of the class), but when it comes to deciding what material to use, what to leave out, and how to order the material once they have decided to include it, they are lost without a model outline to follow.

The outline on the following pages is for a persuasive speech, but the same sort of outline can be used for all other forms of public speaking if you modify the content according to the kind of speech.

No one way to organize a speech guarantees its effectiveness. Everything that you learn in this course—about language usage and structure, audience-centered messages, and the many factors involved in persuasion —are vital factors in public speaking. Outlines can aid structure, but the individual art, the creativity, the fun of speechmaking comes when you make the *choices* of what will go into the outline.

To use the outline, start with the left-hand column. Write out what you plan to do. Put in some detail. Then in the right-hand column write a comprehensive outline of the content of your speech.

Introduction

I am starting with a dramatization to catch the audience's attention and bring the problem home to them.

I will begin by asking the audience members to imagine they are canoeing on a deserted lake in the boundary waters of Minnesota. The year is 2000. The wilderness *looks* as it must have looked to the old voyagers who first saw it. They are canoeing through a gentle rain. The lovely wilderness lake is dead. The killer is the gentle rain falling on their ponchos.

This is my central idea.

Urge your representative and senator to support legislation enabling U.S. and Canadian cooperation for stronger regulation of the causes of acid rain.

Body

Point I

I. Our current efforts to deal with acid rain pose a major problem for us, for

    A. Our current laws allow short-sighted pollution of the atmosphere.

    B. At the present rate of destroying lakes we will have few left in the near future.

This is my transition from point I to point II.

Clearly our present laws and practices relating to the control of acid rain are intolerable. What is the answer? The best solution is new legislation with teeth in it.

Point II

II. Strong legislation enabling U.S. and Canadian cooperation in the control of acid rain is a good solution.

    A. Such cooperation can work, for

        1. Canada is willing to cooperate.

        2. (Hypothetical example of how such legislation would work.)

    B. Such cooperation is desirable, for

        1. The long-term economic benefits outweigh the costs

        2. Saving our lakes is important to our environmental system.

This is my transition from point II to point III.

Legislative support for U.S. and Canadian cooperation is a workable solution to our present crisis relating to acid rain. What difference would these changes in the laws make to you? How do you stand to gain from the change?

Point III

III. The new legislation will be beneficial to you, for

    A. It will assure you and coming generations that our fresh water lakes and waterways will be alive and available for recreation and renewal.

B. It will assure you a continued viable environment for your general health and well-being.

Conclusion

I will summarize the main points of my speech and make an appeal referring back to my introduction and I will dramatize a future where if they accept my plan, people can canoe in the boundary waters on lakes that are alive with fish and wildlife.

KEY IDEAS

- It takes some study of public speaking to learn how to organize material for a speech.
- If a public speech is unified, the listeners can usually recall the central idea and the main subpoints.
- In addition to being unified, a good public speech contains only relevant materials, concisely presented in a coherent and comprehensive pattern.
- The basic building blocks for messages consist of a point to be proved and the material that supports, explains, or illustrates it.
- A good speech has a beginning, a middle, and an end, usually called an *introduction, body* and *conclusion.*
- The body of a speech consists of points supporting a clear central idea, all tied together by good transitions.
- The state-your-case-and-prove-it pattern is the one in which you "Tell them what you are going to tell them, tell them, and then tell them what you told them."
- The problem-solving pattern is the one in which the speaker describes a problem, discusses its causes, examines possible solutions, and suggests a course of action.
- The method of residues is the pattern of organization in which the

speaker lists a number of solutions and eliminates the undesirable ones, thus leaving the recommended one as the only remaining alternative.
- The envisioning sequence evolved from revival preaching and is well adapted to persuasive speeches.
- The envisioning sequence consists of the steps of arousing, dissatisfying, gratifying, dramatizing, and moving to action.

SUGGESTED PROJECTS

1. Select a topic of some complexity that will require clear explanations in order for your audience to understand it. Develop a carefully planned speech outline for a five-minute informative speech on the topic. Use the model outline in the chapter as a guide.
2. Select a topic of concern to you and, taking a controversial stand on the matter, develop a five- to eight-minute persuasive speech on the topic. Prepare a carefully planned speech outline to turn in to the instructor prior to giving your speech, as directed in this chapter or as modified by your instructor.
3. Your instructor will have prepared a number of topics suitable for impromptu speeches. Draw three of the topics, pick any one, and return the other two. You will be allowed to step out of the classroom for five minutes to prepare your speech. Follow the directions for an impromptu speech outline in this chapter in preparing your talk.

SUGGESTED READINGS

Howell, William S., and Ernest G. Bormann. *Presentational Speaking for Business and the Professions.* New York: Harper & Row, 1971.
Jeffrey, Robert C., and Owen Peterson. *Speech: A Text with Adapted Readings.* 3d ed. New York: Harper & Row, 1983.

chapter *12*

Language and Meaning

In this chapter we examine the effective use of American English in oral communication. We begin the chapter with a discussion of the denotative and connotative use of language in general and then deal with specific cultural differences in language usage.

DENOTATIVE AND CONNOTATIVE MEANING

When we say a word *denotes* something we mean that the word points to, notes, stands for, or indicates the thing. Thus we can say that the word *chicken* denotes a certain kind of fowl that is a certain general size, is feathered, cackles, and lays our breakfast eggs.

The denotative meanings of a language are the ways the words are plugged into the perceptions of the participants in a communication event. Our decision to use a given word to stand for some object, person, or event is up to us. If the language is to work as a code for communication, however, we must decide which words stand for which objects, and we must agree about it and come to share the *common* code or understanding.

We cannot change the denotative meaning of words willy-nilly, because if we did, we would confuse people. Naturally language is continually changing, and we do change the denotative meanings of some words over time. We have inherited a tradition of using certain words for certain objects, however, and we learn the rules when we learn the vocabulary of our language. We all come to have a number of common denotative meanings for words in a language we use to talk with one another. If a waiter gives us fried dog when we order fried chicken, he has violated our rules for the denotative meaning of *chicken,* to say nothing of our sensibilities.

A common dictionary is a list of rules connecting words with denotative meanings, and we can read, write, and understand dictionaries because we share the same understanding of how words relate to things. We must point out the difference between the denotative meanings that are common to a number of people and the individual responses we all have to words. Although we may all know what animal is meant by the term *dog,* we may respond to that word in different ways because of our past experience. One of you reading about the notion of *fried dog* may respond differently from another one of you, but both of you will have a clear idea of what the words stand for or denote.

Response to language is both individual and cultural. When we say a word *connotes* something, we mean it has additional meanings for a person or a group of persons that go beyond the denotative meaning. Often these additional meanings arouse emotional interpretations. Sometimes we respond to a word or an expression because of our personal experience. The word *chicken* refers to a certain kind of fowl. Both speaker and listener usually understand the denotative meaning for the word to be the same kind of fowl. If the receiver has a violent dislike of fried chicken because of past experience, however, the response to the word will be emotional as well as reasonable. He may not only picture a chicken in his mind but he may feel a shudder of revulsion go through his entire body when he hears the word. Another person using the same dialect and in the same situation might feel a warm, pleasant glow when he pictures the same fowl, because of the favorite pet chicken he had when he was a little boy.

Sometimes a number of people share a common response to language because they share a common situation. Consider the example of two grade school boys arguing during recess. A circle of other children is soon ringed around them. The two boys become angry and one yells at the other, "You're chicken!" Probably none of the children watching the argument, however, think that the first boy is saying to the second that he is really a fowl capable of laying eggs and cackling. Denotative meaning is pushed into the background by the situation. The sentence expresses the source's emotional feeling and attitude, he breaks out with a cry of anger

A common situation, such as a classroom, can help the audience to share a common response to language usage. (Gerba, Jeroboam)

and frustration, and he might have expressed his feelings almost as well with a grunt or a shout as with the sentence. The other boy interprets the sentence in a similarly emotional fashion. The context and the culture which suggests that in a conflict the word *chicken* is a taunt and an insult come into play to form the response to the word. Every student of public speaking learns the importance of analyzing the effect of the situation and the occasion on the response of the audience. The speaker finds that an expression that is appropriate and gains him the desired response on one occasion may well be all wrong on another. Often when we are a message source, we have as our basic purpose telling the receiver something about the world. We are emphasizing the denotative aspect of language. For example, when we tell someone how to get from one place to another, we are informing her about the geographic location of various places. The basic content of a message discussing facts is *information*. A common dictionary definition of *information* is "a message about facts."

What are facts? *Facts* are those things which two or more people can see and agree on. We encode factual messages about such things as chairs, tables, cars, people, buildings, and their relationships to one another.

Someone may come to a meeting, look about the room, and ask, "Where is John?" If you have the information, you may encode a message in reply as follows: "John just called. His car is stuck in the snow in his driveway and he will be late." The information in the message relates to things such as the human being called John, his automobile, his driveway, and the relationships among these things, for example, the relationship contained in the words "he is stuck in his driveway." Further, the message provides information about John's relationship to the building in which the meeting is being held: that he is in his driveway, that the driveway is some distance from the place of the meeting, and that he is there now and will be here somewhat later than expected.

We need to understand and have skills in the denotative use of language in order to make ideas about facts clear. Definition is the basic process we use to create denotative meanings as we communicate.

DEFINITIONS

Among the most important tools a speaker has to help make ideas clear is the ability to define a word. Before a person can tell someone about facts, she must decide whether her listener understands the word she hopes to use. If the listener does not know what is named by a word in the speaker's message, he is likely to misunderstand or be confused by the message.

When a speaker defines a word she tries to make clear to her listener the thing, property, or relationship she means to indicate when she uses the word in their conversation. If the source and receiver have the same meaning for the content words in messages—that is, they both use the same words for naming things and the same words to stand for properties and relationships—they can talk about the facts of their common experience. They can then talk about the things in a room. For example, one person might say, "Please sit in that red chair," or "Be careful of sitting on that red chair, because it is weak and may break." People can also speak about chairs that are not present at the time of their conversation. For instance, a person may describe the color, size, and shape of a chair which he is selling. Should the listener decide to buy the chair, she will expect it to have certain properties because of the information she decoded from the message. If the chair is not what she expected, either the speaker misled her by claiming that the chair had certain properties it did not possess (her information was false) or she did not have the same definition for the words in the message as the speaker did (she misunderstood).

When you are trying to make an idea clear, you must look carefully at the words you use in your messages. You must ask yourself, "Will all the people taking part in the communication decode a name as standing for the same thing?" If not, can you use another word that everybody will understand? If not, you must select the best word, in your opinion, for the thing to be discussed and carefully define it for your listeners.

One way to define a term is to find other words that say the same or nearly the same thing, and by using those other words, clarify how you plan to use the term in the communications to follow. Many of the terms that we have used earlier in the book have been defined in other words. The dictionary definition of a term usually supplies other words that mean the same thing. For example, one meaning of *communicate* in a good dictionary is "to give thoughts, feelings, or information by writing, speaking, and so forth."

If one can describe the thing or events named by a term clearly in other words, the result is a definition. An interesting by-product of the process of definition is that we can describe an imaginary thing, person, or event, and give it a name. For example, we can describe a person who is "the present queen of the United States" and refer to such a person in our messages. Of course, the United States has no queen, so no real person is named by the definition. Yet we can go on talking about "Samantha Regina, the present queen of the United States," as though such a person existed. We can also pick a name such as *unicorn* and supply such a precise description of the beast that an artist can draw a picture of one, even though the animal does not exist.

Take the case of the *rockslide cornberet,* a strange gray bird the size of a crow with a crown of feathers resembling a beret. The rockslide cornberet gets its name from its love of corn, its beretlike headdress, and the female's peculiar practice of laying a single egg in some stones at the top of a mountain and then kicking egg and stones over the edge, thus starting a rockslide. When the rockslide comes to rest in the valley, the pile of stones serves to protect and incubate the egg so the female does not have to sit on it. Since neither speaker nor listener can observe the nonexistent rockslide cornberet, if they argue about it they are talking about individual impressions and not about anything in the world that they can observe to correct their impressions.

We do not get into serious trouble talking about mythical animals or the present queen of the United States, but we do get into difficulties when we talk about *a conspiracy, a racist society, duty,* or *sexism* and cannot find any observations to correct our impressions. Much misunderstanding and many arguments come from discussions of terms that, like the rockslide cornberet, stand for nothing but the meanings we put into them. Equally important is the problem posed by defining terms such as *democracy, capitalism,* or *communism* without reference to actual events.

The process of definition allows us to name a nonexistent economic system called *pure capitalism* or a governmental arrangement called *pure communism.* Having named these fictitious things, we can go on to discuss them as though they were real events with real implications. If we define something called *world communism* in terms of a powerful force of millions of people dedicated to the violent overthrow of capitalism and the destruction of the United States, we may act as though the thing we have defined actually exists in the world. If the thing defined is as unreal as the rockslide cornberet, we might act foolishly because we are responding to definitions and not to things. What of the man who spends years in the Rockies with his camera, trying to get a photograph of the rockslide cornberet? The same thing can happen with definitions such as the *conspiracy* to raise gasoline prices or the *conspiracy* to overthrow the government by violent means.

If you wish to inform people, therefore, you should be sure that both you and your listeners understand whether the terms defined refer to the things of the world that can be observed and whose definitions can be checked or are names for mythical people or events or for abstract concepts.

In our efforts to transmit information we can strive to emphasize denotation and limit the secondary meanings, the connotative aspects of our words, as much as possible. Reporters for newspapers, for example, often try to write their stories in "objective" and evenhanded report language. However, people find connotative meanings even in such straightforward writing as the directions on how to use a product that you find on the label. Speakers may also load up their words with many secondary meanings either on purpose or without being aware they are doing so. Writers of television commercials and poets, for example, often try to pack as much emotion into their words as they can.

We can think of the range of denotation and connotation in messages as varying from report language with a heavy emphasis on denotation (take part A and fasten to part B with bolt of type Y) to the highly connotative words of a television commercial (my man wears Macho cologne or he wears nothing at all). We often refer to the highly connotative message as being *slanted* or containing *loaded* language. In order to sift out the information (denotative meanings), we need to get rid of as much of the slant, or load (connotative meanings), as we can.

Because emotional responses are so important in persuasion, we need to understand how connotative language works its word magic. Such understanding is useful in terms of our playing the role of source according to the message perspective. Often sources fail in their attempts to communicate because they are unaware of the connotative aspects of the words they use. Understanding connotative usage can also help in a positive way in that message sources can use the secondary meanings in a productive fashion.

Even more important, we need, as message receivers, an understanding of connotative language. Once you know how magicians do their tricks, you are no longer fooled by them. If you learn how it works, word magic will no longer arouse the automatic and unthinking response the "snake oil" salespeople hope that it will.

The connotative aspects of language are equally important in public speaking and relationship communication.

THE PERSUASIVE USE OF WORDS

Naming

One important persuasive skill is the ability to select exactly the right suggestive word to name a thing or event. Mark Twain is supposed to have said that the difference between the right word and the almost-right word is the difference between lightning and a lightning bug.

Suppose people are talking about the same thing but are using different names for it. Even with these different names, they may all understand what is being discussed. Say that several people are talking about a college. They might name it *the college, the old alma mater, the institution, the nut house, the playpen with ashtrays, the ivory tower,* or any one of the other names by which this college is known to its many students and alumni. No matter which name the person in the group chooses for labeling the college, all the others present know it is *the college* he is talking about. What, then, do we learn from the different labels? By the selection of a particular label for a thing, the source of a message indicates a lot about how he or she feels about the thing or event in question.

If several men are discussing female acquaintances, a given woman might be referred to as *darling, honey, my old lady, the little woman, that broad, that bitch,* or whatever happens to be the current slang for attractive and unattractive females. And of course, women have a comparable vocabulary to describe the males they know. The name selected for a woman or man is a powerful indirect suggestion to all others present. The words we use are important parts of our persuasive messages.

Propagandists often use names that reflect attitudes. Two hostile bordering countries report an armed clash of their troops. Country number one calls the event "shameless naked aggression," while country number two calls the same event "a defensive retaliation." One country names the government of another "a totalitarian regime," while the latter government refers to itself as "a democratic peoples' republic." Some revolutionaries set off a bomb in a public building. Sympathizers with the revolution call the bombing "a courageous act by heroic freedom fighters." Those who oppose the revolutionaries and dislike the destruction of public buildings call the same bombing "a cowardly, criminal act by mindless terrorists."

Describing

Selecting names heavily loaded with suggestion is but one way in which choice of words is important. The words a speaker uses to describe the properties or qualities of the things, events, or people designated by the names are equally important. One person says, "This cheese has a rich bouquet." Another remarks, "This cheese stinks to high heaven."

Compare the following ways of describing the qualities of a given individual, and see how words work to carry suggestion to the listener:

John is prudent.
versus
John is a tightwad.

Mary is courageous.
versus
Mary is reckless.

John is sensitive.
versus
John is emotionally unstable.

We can also suggest attitudes by the words and phrases we use to describe relationships among things, people, and events. Consider these examples:

John was a love child.
versus
John is a bastard.

John and Mary have a deep and satisfying personal relationship.
versus
John and Mary are living together like a couple of alley cats.

185

In the last example we used a figure of speech to describe the relationship. Figures of speech are important techniques to suggest or state a comparison between two things. By associating a thing, person, or event with something pleasant, admirable, or good, we suggest that the thing itself is also desirable. By associating the thing with something unpleasant, or bad, we make the opposite impression. Compare "This cigarette has a springlike freshness" with "This cigarette reeks like a dumpyard incinerator."

One important persuasive technique is to describe a person in terms of an adjective or noun that connotes a positive or negative attitude toward that individual. Much of what people do when they persuade is to attack or defend other people and their actions. We often say that a friend has good qualities and an enemy has bad character traits. When a propagandist uses words with negative connotations to describe an enemy, we call the technique *name calling.* A politician using the name-calling technique might refer to an opponent as a *political hack,* a *crook,* a *left-winger,* or an *arch conservative.*

CONNOTATIVE MEANINGS LINKED TO CULTURAL DIFFERENCES

Some words and statements are closely tied to the structure of society and tend to arouse a common reaction from entire groups of people. Look at the following examples:

> Drive slow.
> She played it as she should.
> Whom did you wish to see?
> It is I.
> It don't neither.
> Dese cigarettes are better'n dose.
> Andy, he be with us.
> Y'all come back soon, heah?
> I hain't seen 'im.

You probably found some of the examples odd and somehow not right, while others seemed quite right and comfortable. You might decide that some of the expressions were incorrect or bad grammar or showoff ways of talking that only affected people would use, or people speaking with a southern dialect or an urban-ghetto dialect. Your response to the expression reflects your response to the culture, the way of life, of those who speak the various dialects. Do you like the southern geographic region? Do you feel it is an area of pleasant, cultured, and gracious life?

Do you feel the South is a closed society, racist and bigoted? All these feelings come into play when you hear a person speak in a southern dialect. Some critics of political speaking argued that former President Lyndon Johnson's Texas drawl damaged the effect of his television talks to the nation. Jimmy Carter's Georgia dialect and the Kennedy family's Boston speech also influenced the response of various segments of the American public to their speeches. Your response to an expression in black English likewise reflects your attitude toward race relations and your feelings about black culture. Whoever you are, wherever you live, you have to accept the fact that you speak a dialect. To someone from a different heritage and environment, the way you speak is strange.

Speech often reflects geographic regions, social classes, and economic, ethnic, religious, and racial differences. People in different geographic regions have developed different styles of speaking; working-class people use different forms of expression, different vocal inflections, and different rules to form sentences than do upper-middle-class people. People who live in the black urban ghettos of the North develop some unique patterns of speech, as do bilingual members, such as our Mexican-American and Puerto Rican populations.

All the different ways of talking within the United States make up a single complicated system in which people move around from place to place, from one social and economic class to another. We must add to the system the effect of the mass media—film, television, and radio—which transmit a steady flow of messages in a standard dialect. Even within the same geographic regions, such as the southeastern United States, the lower class speaks differently from the upper middle class; the black worker speaks differently from the white worker. In practice, however, since all classes within a region talk with one another and all are exposed to radio, television, and film, the various expressions and ways of speaking rub off on one another. Thus you probably shift back and forth in your style of speaking, depending on how formal the situation is and on the people with whom you happen to be speaking at the time.

KEY IDEAS

- When a word denotes something, it points to, notes, stands for, or indicates the thing.
- The denotative meanings of language relate to the descriptions of the world.
- We make a decision to use a word to stand for some object, person, or event.

- A dictionary is a list of rules connecting words with their denotative meanings.
- When a word connotes something, it has additional meanings for a person or a group that go beyond its denotative meaning.
- The basic content of a message discussing facts is information.
- Definition is an important process we can use to create denotative meanings as we communicate with one another.
- A description of a thing or event named by a term results in a definition of the term.
- Definition can also be the process that creates imaginary things or abstract concepts and assigns names to them.
- Abstract names such as *democracy, capitalism, communism, youth,* and *nationalism* can cause communication problems when used without reference to actual events and things.
- The highly connotative message is slanted, or loaded, to suggest a positive or negative interpretation of the information.
- An important persuasive skill is the ability to pick the right word to suggest the connotative meaning the speaker has in mind.
- Speakers can arouse connotative meanings by skillful use of descriptive words to characterize people, things, or events.

SUGGESTED PROJECTS

1. Select a newspaper article that reports some dramatic news event involving interesting people. Rewrite the news story in two ways. First, emphasize the denotative factual reporting of the event. Try to keep the names, the relational terms, and the descriptions as neutral as possible. Second, slant the message to create an emotional response to the event. If time permits, tape record the two versions for playback to the class.
2. Select a highly persuasive television commercial, printed advertisement, or political speech and analyze the word choice and descriptive language to discover how the copywriter or speechwriter manipulated connotative meanings to suggest that the message receiver do or think or believe something.

SUGGESTED READINGS

Farb, Peter. *Word Play: What Happens When People Talk.* New York: Knopf, 1974.
Flesch, Rudolf. *Say What You Mean.* New York: Harper & Row, 1973.

chapter *13*

Delivery

We have now gone through the process of finding a suitable topic, analyzing the topic and the audience, adapting the topic to the audience, constructing a suitable organization, and using suitable language. The final step comes when you face the audience and, using suitable verbal and nonverbal communication, present the speech. We discussed the basic principles of language usage in Chapter 12, and here we will only note some of the ways in which the delivery of the speech translates words into an oral message composed of both verbal and nonverbal elements.

Delivery is the presentation of the speech and consists of the paralinguistic, kinesic, and proxemic factors that the speaker employs to communicate with the audience. It includes the way the speaker uses voice elements such as pitch, rate, loudness, articulation, and pronunciation; delivery also includes body movement such as posture, gesture, eye contact, and facial expression.

APPROACHES TO DELIVERY

Over the years scholars who study public speaking have argued about which of two general approaches to delivery is better. One approach stresses thinking the thought as you speak it and feeling the emotion as you express it. The idea is that you should work from the inside out, because the best way to decide how to express disgust, for instance, is to feel disgusted, and then you will naturally find the vocal intonations and gestures to communicate that emotion. You may have heard of "method" acting; this is much the same approach. The second approach is one where you study, plan, and rehearse the nonverbal communication carefully. In this approach, you work more from the outside in, on the assumption that most speakers are somewhat clumsy and inept and that for them to trust to feeling alone will only result in mumbling monotony and awkward gestures. In the second approach it is often helpful to have the advice of someone trained to tell you how effectively you are speaking.

Much of the controversy comes down to the question of how much and in what manner you should rehearse your speech. The advantage of concentrating on your meaning, as in the first approach, is that when you do it well, you appear natural and direct, unstudied; you project a lively sense of here-and-now communicativeness. The disadvantage is that if you have not worked on the basic skills of voice, articulation, and gesture, you may not have the techniques to enjoy the advantages of the approach. Few of us are natural actors or speakers. You do not want to appear inarticulate, inept, and unprepared.

The advantages of rehearsing key lines and gestures carefully are that when you do it well, you *appear* spontaneous, expressive, and confident. You project grace and an attractive vocal presence. The disadvantages are that, poorly done, you may come across as a kind of wooden-gestured, singsong-voiced, mechanical person, almost devoid of personality and vitality.

Both approaches can work if done well; both have problems to keep in mind as you experiment to see which appears to work better for you. Obviously, we feel that someone trained to help people become effective speakers can help you get better faster as you experiment. Many really effective speakers we know use elements of both approaches. Either approach should include practice in basic skills in delivery and careful rehearsal before you deliver your speech.

In Chapter 10 we described a speaker's main rehearsal options. Speakers may write out their manuscripts and read them, they may prepare the speech and memorize it word for word, or they may prepare an outline and speak extemporaneously. If you read from manuscript or deliver the speech from memory, it is essential that you rehearse the speech a number of times. As you rehearse, watch your language for difficult phrases. You should practice different ways of saying the lines in

Careful rehearsal can pay off if the advantages and disadvantages of rehearsing are considered. (Southwick, Stock, Boston)

order to make the key ideas stand out. Make sure your posture, gestures, and facial expressions support your meaning. Strive for naturalness. The best art conceals itself. If the audience gets nonverbal clues that you have labored long and hard over your delivery, you will have failed to some extent. Try to convey the illusion that the lines and gestures that you have rehearsed a dozen times are spontaneous, spur-of-the-moment reactions to the situation.

Rehearsal is also important in extemporaneous speaking. Here you do not have to overcome the barrier of the written manuscript or the memorized speech, but your delivery may be rough as you fumble for a word, repeat yourself, look away awkwardly, or start a gesture and stop it in a jerky way. Rehearsal can make the words flow more easily, even though you have not memorized them and can smooth out and polish your delivery.

When you write or memorize a speech, you can go over the language very carefully to make sure that you are taking the connotative and denotative aspects into account and to define, name, and describe things in a way designed to achieve your objectives. You must be careful, however, not to produce a written essay rather than a speech. A paragraph that reads well may not sound good when spoken to an audience. Sometimes a speech that works for an audience seems unduly redundant when read silently. Written and oral language usage differ; your ear cannot reread a confusing sentence.

We strongly urge that you get into the practice of recording speeches and listening to them to see for yourself how well your ideas come through. Better yet, ask someone who has not seen your manuscript to listen to the tape and then tell you what he or she got out of it. Even when you expect to speak extemporaneously, you will have some time for rehearsal; give some thought to specific word choice and sentence structure as well as the nonverbal elements of your speech. If a particularly effective phrase occurs to you, add it to your outline in the margin; you may want to use it when the time comes.

PRINCIPLES OF EFFECTIVE DELIVERY

One important goal in delivering your speech should be to communicate as effectively as possible with the audience. A basic principle of delivery is that any feature of your nonverbal communication that serves to distract the audience from the message is undesirable. You should work to rid yourself of all such distractions. Those of us who lecture to college classes have learned again and again how tempting it is for audience members to be distracted by nonverbal tics and random movements. We have run across the student who carefully notes down every "uh" and "err" and reports to his friends after class that the "speech" instructor used 52 "uhs" during the course of the hour. We know of students who discuss the speaker's tendency to pace back and forth in random fashion, to lean on the podium, to look at the floor or out the window, to purse her lips or look at her notes, or fool with her pencil.

Among the more distracting features of a speaker's delivery are regular vocal tricks, facial tics, or physical movements, such as swaying from foot to foot, which have no relation to what the speaker is saying. The technical term for "uhs" and "errs" is *vocalized pauses.* Vocalized pauses are among the most disturbing features of delivery and can be remedied with some attention and practice. Many times speakers use words much as they might use vocalized pauses. Some years ago students experienced a "you know" epidemic of large proportions. We heard some speeches in which every idea was cluttered with "you knows." Other terms go in and out of style. "Man" is another term that often serves only as a distraction when used as a verbal crutch. Overused, *any* word or phrase can become a distraction.

Many times we are unaware of the aimless patterns of voice and gesture that distract our audience. If you have an opportunity to see yourself giving a speech on videotape, it is often a revelation.

The second principle of effective delivery is to speak in a manner that is appropriate to the topic, the audience, and the occasion. If you are speaking to a small audience of 25 in a classroom, your manner should be different from what it would be if you were speaking to 2500 people in an auditorium or to 25,000 people at an open-air rally. Public-address systems enable us to speak in more conversational tones to the largest of audiences, but the larger audience requires a broader and more impressive manner. The broad gesture, which seems appropriate before the large rally audience, would seem overwhelming in the small classroom. Likewise, the manner of delivery appropriate to a highly emotional occasion would be inappropriate to a calm or solemn occasion. There are cultural expectations for every speech occasion, and the rule is to use an appropriate manner of delivery, one that fits the audience and the occasion.

The third principle of effective delivery is to use nonverbal elements to reinforce the meanings in your message. The way you orchestrate the vocal melody and the accompanying body movements in relation to your words can strengthen or weaken your communicativeness. A good delivery will make it easier for the audience members to listen to and decode your message.

The fourth principle is that your manner should increase your credibility as a person. Much of your credibility, or believability, as a source of ideas and advice depends upon the kind of person you seem to be. Members of your audience who are unacquainted with you or only know you by reputation will often decide whether you are likable, trustworthy, active, and knowledgeable on the basis of your nonverbal communication.

Speakers can use nonverbal suggestion to make themselves more influential, more persuasive with their listeners. You should work hard to appear to be in charge of the situation and your material, though in a relaxed and friendly way, not in a dictatorial or wise-guy manner. Remember that we are more likely to be persuaded by someone we accept as a person—a person we feel we could like. If the speaker's manner conveys the impression that he is calm, confident, sincere, and honest, we are more likely to trust and believe him. In a question-and-answer period after a formal speech, or in any face-to-face communication event, if the speaker's manner of fielding questions, dealing with disagreements, and handling challenges is confident, her credibility with the listeners is increased. If, under such stress, she loses her temper, her credibility often correspondingly plunges. If, further, the speaker can communicate to the listener that she genuinely appreciates questions and respects the questioner, and if she responds fairly and candidly to the best of her ability, admitting honestly when she is stumped, she tends to build good will. If the speaker's manner suggests that she has something to hide, or if she hedges in such a way that she appears insecure and afraid of making a mistake, then her ethos is damaged. All these instances refer mostly to the manner in which the speaker conducts herself, to her nonverbal signals.

If a person communicates verbally and nonverbally that he is trying to control us, that he is trying to outwit us and make us do something *he* wants but that we do not know about, that he is not really interested in us but in what he can get out of us, that he thinks he is a lot better and smarter than we are, or that he is so set in his ways he will not be changed, no matter how wrong others may feel him to be, then we are likely to reject him as a person and to reject his message as well. He will not persuade us, because we do not think much of him or his ideas.

On the other hand, if the speaker communicates verbally and nonverbally that he is absolutely fair, candid, and honest; that he is not defensive about his status or his expertness; that he is deeply involved with and dedicated to our common objectives; that he is willing to make personal sacrifices for our common good; that he is competent; that his advice is good and is given in our best interest—then his ethos is likely to be persuasive for us. He just may persuade us as he speaks, because he inspires confidence that he knows what he is talking about and wants to share his knowhow with us for our own good.

IMPROVING GESTURES AND MOVEMENT

Posture

The way a speaker stands and holds his shoulders and his head as he speaks communicates a good deal nonverbally to the audience. If the speaker is delivering a speech in a relatively formal setting, the audience expects him to stand erect, with his weight evenly balanced on both feet. The feet should be relatively close together, with one foot slightly in front of the other.

The speaker should not lean on the speaker's stand, slouch first on one foot and then the other, rock back and forth or from side to side, or stand with feet widespread.

If the speaker is in a relatively informal setting, and if he wishes to communicate nonverbally that he does not want to give a carefully prepared speech, but plans to ramble on a bit and throw out a few ideas and then ask for questions and comments, he may sit on the edge of a table, sit in a chair, lean on the speaker's stand, take off his coat, and so on.

Facial Expression

One of the most important tools any speaker has for nonverbal communication with an audience is his range of facial expressions. Smiles, grins, smirks, frowns, grimaces, and raised eyebrows can all add emphasis or, conversely, suggest that the descriptive words in the message are to be discounted. Unfortunately, one of the beginner's most common reactions to nervousness is failure to use facial expressions. As a result, the anxious speaker often talks in a monotone, sighs a great deal, and has a blank expression on his face.

The person who is vivacious in conversation, whose face is alive every second in animated talk with one or two others, often tones down his facial expressions when giving a public speech. He should do just the opposite. A slight smile or grin is often lost on an audience 12 feet or more away. Thus, you ought to overdo the smile, the grin, the frown when you are giving a public speech in a good-sized room or auditorium. You have to overdo your platform personality to achieve the effect you ordinarily produce in the more informal and intimate situations.

Eye Contact

One of the most expressive regions of the face is the area around the eyes. Again and again the eyewitnesses who reported their impressions of such great American speakers as Daniel Webster, Henry Clay, Stephen Douglas, and William Jennings Bryan noted the arresting and powerful effect of the speakers' eyes.

Generally the speaker ought to give the illusion that he is looking directly at the members of the audience. To be sure, direct eye contact may be a culturebound nonverbal convention, and you may wish to modify the advice for special situations; however, you are well advised to look a middle-class North American audience in the eye.

In almost all situations, random eye movements are distracting. Looking over the listeners' heads for no clear purpose, looking out the window, looking at the corner of the room, looking at the floor, or looking always at your speech notes can prove distracting. When the speaker looks away from the audience for the greater part of his speech, he has no way of judging its response, of utilizing the feedback from nonverbal cues.

Gesture

The beginning speaker often makes an unsettling discovery when he gets in front of an audience. He finds that attached to his shoulders are two arms to which he normally pays little attention, but which now suddenly cannot be ignored. At the ends of his arms are two conspicuous hands. His first thought is to hide his hands, so he puts them both behind his back. When he does this, he feels tied up, and every move he makes with his shoulders seems awkward. He then tries to hide his hands in his pockets, but he still feels restricted, and his hands seem as obvious and as useless as ever. He may fold his arms over his chest or try to hold them rigidly by his sides, in the hope that nobody will notice them, but there is no hiding either the arms or the hands. The only solution is for the speaker to learn to use his arms and hands to make gestures in support of the material in his speech.

Once the beginner realizes he must move his hands and arms, he may make a second mistake by keeping his elbows close to his sides, using the forearms for short, jerky gestures. His nonverbal communication at this point is that he wants to use some gestures but feels inhibited in front of his listeners.

You can get the feel of good ways to gesture by practicing at home in front of a mirror. When you practice gestures suitable for a speech, you should make them broader than you first feel necessary. Experiment with gesturing with both arms. Remember to use the space above your shoulders, particularly if you are speaking from a stage and are some distance from your audience. Move your hands to express ideas. Make sure the movement flows through the entire arm to the tips of your fingers. Do not let your hands and fingers flop about loosely; do not use gestures that distract from, rather than add to, the meaning of what you are saying.

The entire body can gesture to suggest nonverbal meanings. The speaker may hunch his shoulders and crouch to suggest a certain mood or feeling. He may step toward the audience, pull back, turn to one side or another, or stand on tiptoe. A good speaker may use the techniques of pantomime, the art of getting across emotions, actions, and feelings by mute gestures. He may turn slightly, crouch, and make an imaginary pistol out of his extended index finger to suggest to the audience the character of a holdup man in a story. He might next turn, stand rigidly erect, and hold both hands high, this time suggesting his own response to the feeling of having the gun in his back.

THE USE OF NOTES

The question of whether to have notes for a public speech may seem a minor matter. Yet in the hands of a speaker who does not know how best to use them, notes can inhibit eye contact, facial expression, posture, and gesturing, and thereby affect the speaker's total skill at nonverbal communication. Many speech instructors prefer that students not use notes in class, simply because notes hinder development of good habits of nonverbal communication through body language. Some instructors also feel that beginning speakers should learn to keep the outline of their ideas in mind, without notes, as they speak. We do not use notes in most informal communication situations. We may use notes for formal speaking situations, however, and the Teleprompter and other devices provide ready notes, even whole speeches, for television performers. It seems to us that the situations calling for speeches without any notes are rare. However, listeners are impressed when a speaker uses no notes, and you should keep this in mind for your most polished and important speeches. If you can develop a way to prepare speeches that allows you to keep the main points of your outline in mind, you can usually easily remember the examples and other supporting material that fit under the main point. If you can speak extemporaneously without notes, you can keep your eyes on the audience and gesture more freely.

Many students find it difficult to speak without notes, and plan to use notes in the speaking they will do after they finish the class, so they prefer learning to speak well using them. The most important point about using notes in a speech is not to pretend that you have no notes. Few things a speaker can do distract an audience as much as the pretense that she has no notes. Sometimes a speaker writes her notes on small cards and stacks them on the speaker's stand or holds them hidden in the palm of her hand. She cannot fool anyone. The first time she sneaks a look at her notes the audience picks up the cue and watches for her to steal another look; she may create more suspense with this nonverbal behavior than with what she is trying to say! So if you need notes, bring them out into the open, then use them naturally, trying not to cut down on eye contact and facial expressiveness any more than necessary. Perhaps in the instance of quoting a statistic or a special sentence from some authority, the speaker can even hold up the notes and point to the place where she has her information; this communicates nonverbally that what she is saying is absolutely correct and she has it written down to make sure she says it correctly.

Avoid the common pitfalls of using notes. Do not look at them whenever you feel embarrassed; look at the audience, keep your poise, and pause to collect yourself. To the audience, your poised look at them as you pause communicates that you are about to say something important and are thinking about exactly the right way to say it best. Do not play with your notes; a nervous speaker with something in his hand is often tempted to fold it, roll it, tap it, or bend it. The audience may, again, become more interested in what you may do next with your note cards than in what you are saying.

Do not clutch your notes tightly in front of you with both hands; you cannot gesture with your hands if they are in this rigid position. Hold the notes in one hand and use the other arm and hand for gesturing, although you may certainly gesture with both arms if it seems appropriate—the notes, held up in one hand, will not distract from the gesture; if anything, a vigorous arm gesture that includes the display of notes may communicate that you are prepared, you have in your hand what you are going to say, and you are very much in charge of the situation.

The more imagination you can develop to enable you to see yourself as the audience does, the better your nonverbal communication will become.

CONTROLLING SPEECH TENSION

If the beginning speaker is anxious and the audience finds out about it, it is largely through nonverbal cues. The speaker's hands may shake, his voice may quiver, he may have difficulty looking at the audience, and he may remain poker-faced, wooden-looking. An audience is quick to pick up cues about the way a speaker feels about himself. If the speaker regards his own nonverbal cues as showing that he is worried about his performance, the audience will get the correct impression that the speaker has stage fright. They will begin to worry about him and his feelings and be distracted from the ideas in his speech. Then the speaker not only has trouble getting his ideas across to the audience but also must combat their view of him as someone with not much to offer them, someone they need to help through the difficult task of giving a speech. Interestingly enough, the same body motions, if perceived by the speaker as symptoms of his intense involvement with, and high regard for, his subject and the occasion, can make a strong positive impression on an audience. We cannot stress too much the importance of how the speaker perceives himself. This perception of yourself is the first thing you communicate to any audience.

If the speaker can control her tension so that her gestures, posture, and facial expression are appropriate to what she is saying, the audience will seldom know she is anxious. Every good speaker gets keyed up before she goes on. But like the athlete who is nervous and keyed up in the dressing room but feels fine two minutes after the game starts, the good speaker uses these feelings of nervousness and tension to key her up to do a better job.

The point is that you do not want to stop feeling excited and keyed up about giving a speech or standing before a crowd. You want to learn to use this tension to make your mind sharper and less likely to forget, and to give your whole body more focus and concentration on communicating with your audience.

While waiting for your turn to speak, force yourself to sit erect and gaze about with confidence. Pick a spot in the front of the audience and when you are introduced, get up from your chair, pause, pull yourself erect, and firmly and calmly force yourself to walk to the spot. When you reach the spot you picked, pause again, stand erect, and with the weight balanced comfortably on both feet, look out at the audience and, for just a moment, let your eyes run over the listeners. Be sure and look at the people in the audience *until you can see them.* Some beginners, when they feel particularly nervous at the start of the speech, are unwilling actually to look at the audience. Since they do not know what the people look like or what they are doing, they find themselves growing more and more nervous as they proceed. We are all afraid of the unknown, and if the speaker is not watching the audience, he has no way of knowing what it is doing. In all speaking situations, it is far better for you, the speaker, to look at your audience, to see the friendly faces, the smiles, the frowns, the questioning looks—to realize that an audience is made up of human beings much like yourself, that they usually wish you well (particularly in a speech-communication class), and that they want you to be a good speaker.

And so, having looked directly during this pause at the people to whom you will be talking, take a good deep breath as quietly as you can and begin your speech in a strong voice. By standing erect, by acting confident, by pausing, and by beginning in a good strong voice, you complete the illusion of confidence for your audience.

Furthermore, you will discover that if you can give the audience the impression that you are a poised and confident speaker, their impression will affect you, and you may soon feel more confidence and find that you can keep your tension under control.

Nonverbal communication is sometimes called the silent language. We are all vaguely aware of the implications of gesture, facial expression, and body attitudes when we talk with people from day to day. When we are involved in public communication events, we need to become more sophisticated about the implications of nonverbal body-motion codes, so that if we are speaking, we know what to do to make our nonverbal communication support our intention. If we are viewing and hearing someone else speak, we need to be aware of the many signals given by the speaker's body, eyes, and vocal intonations. All these are elements of nonverbal communication, and they are important components of messages; there is much truth in the saying, "What you *do* speaks so loud, I can't hear what you say."

KEY IDEAS

- Delivery includes the way the speaker uses voice elements (such as pitch, rate, loudness, articulation, and pronunciation) and body movements (such as posture, gesture, eye contact, and facial expression).
- One approach to delivering a speech is to think the thought and feel the emotion at the time of presentation.
- Another approach is to study, plan, and rehearse the delivery carefully.

- Either basic approach or some combination of the two can work for a speaker if he or she learns to use it well.
- No matter what form of preparation a speaker uses—manuscript, memorization, or outline—rehearsal is essential.
- The goal of rehearsal of the speech should be a delivery that appears to be natural and spontaneous.
- Any feature of your nonverbal communication that distracts your audience from the message is undesirable.
- Your delivery should be adjusted so it is appropriate to the topic, audience, and occasion.
- Your delivery should reinforce the meanings in your message.
- Your delivery should increase your credibility as a message source.
- One of the most important tools any speaker has for communicating with the audience is the skillful use of facial expressions.
- Generally the speaker ought to give the illusion that he or she is looking directly at the members of the audience.
- You can get the feel of good ways to gesture by practicing at home in front of a mirror.
- The most important point about using notes in a speech is not to pretend that you have no notes.
- The more imagination you can develop to enable you to see yourself as the audience does, the better your delivery will become.

SUGGESTED PROJECTS

1. Select an emotional passage from a human interest story, novel, or short story and prepare a three-minute (450 or so words) oral reading. Rehearse carefully and experiment with various approaches to communicating ideas and feelings. Read your selection to the class, striving for an illusion of naturalness and spontaneity.
2. Select some person that you admire very much and write a three-minute speech about him or her. Commit your speech to memory and polish the delivery in rehearsal. Deliver your speech to the class, striving to communicate directly with your audience.
3. Pick a dramatic personal experience that touched you emotionally. With or without notes prepare to tell the class about your experience in extemporaneous fashion. The experience can be as violent as an automobile accident or as tranquil as the sunset on a wilderness area lake. Try to make the audience experience your feelings at the time.

SUGGESTED READINGS

Boebe, Steven A. "Eye Contact: A Nonverbal Determinant of Speaker Credibility." *Speech Teacher* 23 (1974): 21–25.

Eisonson, Jon. *Voice and Diction: A Program for Improvement.* 4th ed. New York:
Macmillan, 1979.

Jeffrey, Robert C., and Owen Peterson. *Speech: A Text with Adapted Readings.* 2d ed. New York: Harper & Row, 1983.

chapter *14*

The Informative Speech

Throughout this book we have stressed that in our culture the public speech is an established communicative occasion with a long tradition going back to our earliest history. Indeed, if we could take a time machine back to a meetinghouse in New England in the seventeenth century and listen to what was going on, we would soon be able to tell that a Protestant minister was delivering a sermon. There is much similarity in the main features of public-speaking occasions and in the nature of the speaking itself down through the years. The similarities carry over into different geographical regions as well. You could attend a college lecture in California, in Florida, in New Mexico, or in New York and soon be able to tell that they were all of a type and that they were all given for a similar occasion.

Just as we learn the general grammatical usage and dialect features of how to use a language, so we learn the general usages of people in public-speaking occasions and can communicate more easily because we do know what to expect.

Although there are some common general features to all public-speaking occasions, there are more specific requirements for special types and occasions. If we learn the details that have to do with the persuasive speech, the informative speech, the organizational presentation, and the more specialized types of speaking, we can do an even better job of listening to and giving such speeches. In this chapter we describe the essential features of the informative speech.

THE NATURE OF THE INFORMATIVE SPEECH

A common public-speaking situation is one in which a speaker has important information or knowhow to give to an audience. The audience comes to learn from the expert. The speech form expected under the above circumstances is the *speech to inform.*

In our culture, we expect a lecture to be an objective and many-sided view of the material. The lecturer does not intend to narrow the choices of the listener but rather aims to open up new horizons and give the listeners new perspectives for viewing the topic. Of course, few of the real-life speeches we attend are just what we expect them to be. Every speaker has some biases, and often is not as objective as the model suggests. Still, though we tolerate some departure from the ideal cultural norm, if a speaker advertised as a lecturer gives, instead, a powerful persuasive pitch for a pet project, we are disturbed by this violation of a cultural norm.

The informative speaker is supposed to encourage feedback and strive to achieve understanding by answering questions in a complete and open way. We expect the speaker's language to be a clear and careful reporting of denotative meanings and descriptions of factual information. While we anticipate that the persuasive speaker will select language to slant the speech in favor of his bias, we expect the informative speaker to use language in a way that represents various positions and arguments fairly; his tone is "These are the facts, and these are the various ways people look at the subject, and you can draw your own conclusions after I have given you all the information."

PURPOSES OF INFORMATIVE SPEAKING

Explaining What Is the Case

Speakers who give informative speeches may have one of several more specific purposes in mind. They may have the purpose of explaining what is the case. That is, they have information because of special personal knowledge that the audience members do not have. They may have been eyewitnesses because of an unusual personal opportunity or they may have been sent on a fact-finding mission. They might report on such matters as what it was like to walk on the surface of the moon, the conditions in Antarctica in regard to fresh water, the conditions in the Australian outback in terms of agriculture, or the learning opportunities for American students in Spanish Universities. Such informative speeches are often organized around spatial topics such as the different regions of Australia; in time sequences such as what I first learned, my next impressions, and my final conclusions; or around related topics such as learning the Spanish language, learning about Spanish culture today, or learning about Spanish history.

Explaining How to Do It

People may give informative speeches because they have special abilities and talents that they can hand on to their listeners by giving how-to-do-it speeches. The speakers may explain how to prepare gourmet foods, run a microcomputer, explore a wilderness trail, or perform a laboratory experiment. These speeches are often speeches of application and are frequently organized around step-by-step directions or recipes.

Sharing Knowledge

People may give informative speeches because they have knowledge gained from study and research, and they can give their listeners an understanding of the topic that serves to satisfy curiosity about basic processes, lawful relations, and historical forces. The speakers may explain the structure of the atom, the Big Bang theory of the creation of the universe, the way federal deficits relate to interest rates, or the way the cohesiveness of a small group interacts with communication processes. Informative speeches aimed at creating understanding are often the most difficult and interesting for the speakers, but in the best of such speeches the organizational structure tends to grow out of the material. It is difficult for us to give you a how-to-do-it recipe, to take some typical order of materials, and apply it to such informative speeches.

GENERAL APPROACHES AND PROCEDURES IN GIVING INFORMATION

We can provide some general directions about approaches to informative speeches that should help you at least get started on developing your

A speaker with special information can tell an audience how to do a specific task. (© Buck, 1980, The Picture Cube)

message units and integrating them into a good speech outline adapted to your specific audience.

One way for the speaker seeking understanding to proceed is to go from the simple to the complex. The speaker might begin with the freezing of fresh water in a local pond, move to the freezing of salt water, and then go on to the freezing patterns of the Antarctica.

The speaker might also move from the known to the unknown. If the audience knows nothing about algebra, but does understand arithmetic, the speaker might start with some basic axioms of arithmetic before going on to algebra, building on the similarities to arithmetic. Or if the audience knows something about personal banking, the speaker might start with banking and then move to the federal government's budgeting and borrowing as related to interest rates and deficits.

A speaker might begin with big-picture overviews of the topic, then move to subpoints that deal with specifics, and conclude with a review of the big picture. The speaker could begin with an overview of the structure of the atom, move to explanations of subatomic particles, and conclude with the way the system functions.

Expository procedures include definitions, descriptions, and explanations. In Chapter 12 we discussed the process of definition of terms in some detail. The speaker who defines words and concepts provides the audience with the language and ideas needed to understand further analysis. Descriptions are word pictures of what the speaker has seen or accounts that make clear other sense experiences related to the phenomenon such as smell, hearing, touch, and taste. Explanations often give an account of how something works, the laws that govern a process, the purposes or motives behind human action, or the forces that resulted in an effect.

To become a good informative speaker you must work on skills in inventing and applying supporting material to implement the general approaches and procedures. The remainder of this chapter explains the specifics of expository supporting material.

EXPOSITORY SUPPORTING MATERIAL

Specialists in communication have long debated the question of whether or not information is different from persuasion. Probably there is no such thing as neutral objective information. Still there are some important differences between understanding an explanation and accepting it. We might understand that someone is explaining an automobile accident as resulting from an evil eye, but we may not be persuaded that the explanation is a good one. At any rate whether you're primarily interested in transmitting information or in getting someone to follow your advice, you often need to get some points across so they are clearly understood.

We define *exposition* as the process of setting forth, spelling out, clearing up, making plain, and shedding light on. The speaker's basic expository tools are examples, analogies, and narratives.

Examples

One of the most important skills you should develop to improve your communication is the ability to recognize and use examples. What we call *examples* are sometimes also called *illustrations*.

An example is one (of a number of things) taken to show (the nature or character of) all. The example illustrates some important points about all the things like it. An example may also be an instance that illustrates the operation of a law or a general principle.

Real and Hypothetical Examples   When speakers use examples to make points clear, they may select an instance that actually happened, or may invent an example, much as an author makes up a story. When speakers use nonfictional accounts of actual events or people, they are using *real* examples. When they dream up a fictitious incident that might have happened, but in fact did not, they are using a hypothetical example.

Real examples are useful in making a point clear, but they may also be evidence to prove a point in an argument. If a person wants to prove that the smoking of marijuana does not necessarily lead to the use of heroin, he may submit as proof the real examples of a number of people who have smoked marijuana but have not used heroin. *Hypothetical* examples, on the other hand, are not proof, because if you were in an argument and made up a number of examples to support your side, another person could make up an equal number of examples to support the other side. Suppose one person argues that juvenile delinquency is caused by poverty and miserable living conditions in the inner city. "Take the case of Johnnie," he says, "growing up in the ghetto. Johnnie is much more likely to become delinquent than a child in the suburbs." "Not at all," answers the other person. "Take the case of rich Billy, whose parents have no time for him and who give him every material thing he wants instead of giving him enough love, time, guidance, and discipline." Both parties in such an argument can dream up make-believe characters such as Johnnie and Billy as long as they like and match hypothetical example with hypothetical example. When using real examples, however, the debaters can submit only actual happenings as evidence.

Real examples carry more weight, because they are factual and because the person in a conference, interview, group discussion, or public speech who explains ideas by using real examples gives her listeners the feeling that she is speaking from a firm basis of facts and that she is an expert.

We may have trouble using real examples, however, when we take part in informal talks and do not have notes with us. If a point comes up in a conversation or an interview and we need an example to make the idea clear, we may not remember the details of a real example and may not have time to look them up. Even when we have time to prepare for a public speech, we may search the library in vain for exactly the right example to make a point. We can tailor the hypothetical example to the needs of the audience, the point to be clarified, and the time available. Thus, although hypothetical examples are not evidence, they are a good way to make a point clear.

The Artful Use of Examples   Why are examples so important to basic communication skills, no matter what the setting or the occasion? Examples are concrete and make broad principles and laws easy to hear, smell, see, taste, and feel; when we stop talking about the law of gravity and start using the example of the falling basketball, the listener can visualize the event and see how the law works in actual practice. Examples add interest to a message. A good example makes a difficult idea easier to understand. We enjoy the understanding that comes from seeing how or why something works. We like to be able to understand things, and so an example that brings understanding also brings interest.

People appreciate the skillful use of example. Most of us enjoy watching an expert perform. Even though we may not be good musicians, we probably enjoy watching and hearing a skillful pianist. Although we may not care much for baseball, we may enjoy watching a talented shortstop field ground balls. When a talented and skillful speaker uses a good example—one well suited to the listener, the occasion, and the point under discussion—we get a similar sense of interest and appreciation.

The use of examples is an art that can be acquired through practice. Any speaker can pick an example to clarify a given idea. Good speakers are able to pick examples that interest the listeners and are within the listeners' experience and level of understanding. By skillful use of examples they can connect even abstract, difficult ideas to the experience of the other person.

When you pick examples to clarify a point, you ought to be listener-oriented. A good speaker has a number of different examples available for illustrating the same point. He invents examples from different situations. The speaker who picks an example that interests the listener helps ensure the success of his attempts to inform. By selecting examples of different lengths, the speaker can make his comments shorter or longer. The speaker who has a good supply of examples can be guided by feedback and supply the listener with additional examples until he is sure he has been understood.

Suppose we wish to clarify the point that each person should carefully decide whether to learn the standard general American dialect if he does not already speak it. Suppose, too, that we know quite a bit about the people who will hear our speech. We know how old they are, whether they are male or female, what jobs they have, their hobbies, their social and economic class, and whether they are from the South or the North, from the city, the suburbs, or a rural area. We have available the following examples to clarify the point about the decision to learn a new dialect:

An actual person who is a network television announcer and grew up in Tidewater, Virginia

A hypothetical person who is an education major from Brooklyn and plans to teach in Brooklyn

An actual person who is a business major at Louisiana State University and speaks with a Cajun accent

An actual person who is a community-college student with no major as yet and who comes from a suburb in Los Angeles

An actual person who is a black star in the National Basketball Association, attended a Big Ten university, and was originally from a ghetto of New York City

A hypothetical person who is a Chicano from New Mexico and attends a community college there

An actual person who is from an aristocratic old family in North Carolina, is proud of her background, and is studying art

An actual person who is a militant black from an inner-city ghetto in Detroit, studying to be a social worker

Each of the above examples contains a great deal of information in addition to what we have described. Some are quite detailed and take longer to explain than others. Some are humorous, some serious, and some full of conflict. When we prepare to talk to a given group of people, we have to pick the example that seems best for this audience in this setting, at this time. Decide which of the above examples would be best for each of the following occasions:

A meeting of the Parent-Teachers Association in a wealthy suburb of Detroit

A meeting of the Parent-Teachers Association in an inner-city school in New York City

A speech-communication class in a Los Angeles College

A group of students at a high school careers-day convocation in Atlanta

A meeting of black students at a Big Ten university

Since examples can add interest and emotional tone to a message, the speaker must consider the occasion as well as the audience when selecting which examples to use. If a person plans to discuss a topic in an informal two-person conversation over coffee in a cafeteria, a light, humorous example might be used. If the person plans to clarify the point in an important presentation before a large group in a formal setting, he or she should pick an example that has a different tone and treatment. One should not use humorous or sexy examples on solemn occasions, nor should one use serious, weighty, or complicated examples in an after-dinner speech.

Analogies

The analogy is another important way to clarify ideas. If you become good at using examples and analogies, you will be able to meet 80 to 90 percent of your needs in making a point clear. An *analogy* is an extended comparison. When a speaker takes two things or two events and points out that they are the same in important respects, he is making a comparison. If he continues to point out several similarities, he makes an analogy. The short comparison is a figure of speech. "She has a neck like a swan's" is a figure of speech, a simile. If we take the figure of speech about the woman's neck and extend the comparison of woman to swan, we may invent an analogy: "She has a neck like a swan's. She swims with the grace of a swan, but when she walks she waddles like a swan. Her voice is a swanlike screech, and her nose looks like a swan's beak."

Analogies are like examples in many respects. Like examples, analogies come in two major types—the literal and the figurative. A *literal* analogy resembles a real example. The literal analogy is a comparison between two things, people, or incidents drawn from the same class or genus. The speaker who compares Metropolitan Community College to North Oaks Community College in regard to size of student body, quality of instruction, courses offered, and extracurricular activities available is using a literal analogy. He can find and verify this information. A *figurative* analogy, on the other hand, resembles a hypothetical example. It is a comparison between two things that, at first glance, do not seem comparable. A woman's neck is not really like a swan's neck. A woman does not have feathers on her neck, nor is a woman's neck as thin and long as a swan's. And yet the listener understands when we say that the woman's neck is like a swan's. Life is not really like a football game, although many a coach has used that figurative analogy in his annual speech for the team.

The literal analogy can build on the past experience of a listener. A good way to make a new idea or a new situation clear to another person is to compare the new idea to the old. Moving the listener from the familiar to the unfamiliar creates interest and understanding. The listener often finds familiar material dull. If the content of a message is unfamiliar, on the other hand, the listener is often so confused that he or she rejects the material and makes no attempt to understand it. In a good message the content is familiar enough so the listener can keep his or her bearings, yet is novel enough to create interest. If a recent graduate returns to her high school after her first semester at college, a young friend still in high school might ask, "What is college like?" The college student might answer with a literal analogy comparing the high school they both know to the college only the speaker knows.

Literal analogies, like real examples, usually depend on factual material for their development. You cannot always find a good literal analogy to use in an informal conversation or discussion. When you do find an apt literal analogy, however, you have a powerful tool for making ideas clear.

Figurative analogies resemble hypothetical examples in that they are largely fictitious. Often the message source can express an emotion or an attitude toward some person or event more by comparing two things that might not, on the surface, seem comparable. For example, the president of a large oil company might argue:

> My company is criticized because we have a large share of the market for gasoline. I can't understand the criticism. The oil industry is like the National Football Conference. If a team wins a large share of its games in the conference, everybody thinks it is a great team, because that is what football is all about—winning games. But when we win a large share of the gasoline market, we are criticized for being a monopoly. Yet that is what the oil industry is all about— winning a share of the market.

The comparison of the oil industry to the football league expresses a strong positive attitude toward the industry on the part of the speaker. Try to invent an analogy that would express a different attitude toward the oil industry on the basis of this following hint: "Big oil companies are like octopuses that have their tentacles into every aspect of our lives, including the government!"

Figurative analogies add interest to a comment designed to clarify an idea. They reveal the speaker's basic communicative skill, and we enjoy the artistry of a good comparison, whether it is a short figure of speech or an extended figurative analogy. Figurative analogies can help make complex notions and principles easier to understand.

Narratives

The final important device for making a point clear is the narrative. *Narratives* are stories, either true or fictitious, long or short, that contain characters, situations, and action. Stories are about one central character who draws the audience's interest. Usually the main character has a clear object in view and attempts to achieve his goal; in the process he runs into trouble, and the story tells about his good and bad times as he works for his objective. The old formula for a love story, for example, is boy meets girl, boy falls in love with girl, boy loses girl, boy gets girl. The fun of the story is in the many different ways in which the boy may lose the girl and the unusual ways in which he may win her back. In a good story, the forces that keep the boy from getting the girl ought to be evenly balanced with the chance the hero will get the girl. Conflict and suspense result from the hurdles the character must overcome to win his objectives and the even odds on his success or failure.

Narratives may be factual; among real-life stories, some of the most effective are the speaker's personal experiences. Perhaps it would be appropriate to tell about the time she was supposed to get to school for a big examination but had stayed up late studying and slept through her alarm. When she did wake up she had only a short time to get to school. Racing to make it in time, she was stopped by a policeman, and so forth. The personal-experience story is one of the most common and effective ways to make a point clear. A well-told personal-experience story can amuse, illustrate, clarify, and present the speaker in an attractive light as a person of insight and humor.

The *anecdote* is a short narrative concerning one particular happening of an interesting or amusing nature. When the anecdote is amusing, it also may be called a *joke*. Both serious anecdotes and jokes tend to have a sudden twist at the end, which is called the *punch line*.

We can explain some things by telling a *plausible story* that includes all the facts to be explained and makes them hang together so they sound plausible. In Chapter 9 we discussed the way groups of people come to share interpretative scripts that account for their experience and provide them with a rhetorical vision of their social reality. Speakers often use interpretative scripts to explain and persuade in the hope that the audience will participate in the story.

As we noted at the beginning of this section, it is often difficult to decide whether a given speech or piece of supporting material is primarily an explanation or an argument. We have pointed out in our description of real examples that they can be used as evidence and that the literal analogy is one way to reason from what we know to what we think might happen.

Interpretative scripts not only throw light upon the subject but always give events a slant. Nonetheless we find it useful to think of the rhetorical devices in terms of their ability to explain and convince in teaching students how to use them. We have now explored the ways in which examples, analogies, and narratives can be used to clarify ideas.

KEY IDEAS

- Although there are some general features common to all public-speaking occasions in our culture, there are more specific requirements for special types and occasions.
- The participants in one common public-speaking situation come with the expectation that the speaker has important information to give to the audience.
- The audience attending the informative speech comes to learn from the expert.
- In our culture, we expect a lecture to be an objective and many-sided view of the material.
- Speakers who give informative speeches may have the purpose of informing about what is the case, about how to do something, or about how to understand something.
- An informative speaker might approach the subject by moving from the simple to the complex, from the known to the unknown, or from the big-picture to the details.
- The most important tools for making ideas clear are the example, the analogy, and the narrative.
- The example illustrates some important points about a group of like things, or provides an instance of the operation of a general law, rule, or principle.
- When people use examples they may select ones that actually happened (real) or ones that are made up (hypothetical).
- We can tailor hypothetical examples to the needs of the listener, the point we are making, and the time available.
- A good example makes a difficult idea easier to understand and arouses the interest of the listener.
- The choice and use of examples is an art that can be learned.
- A short comparison is a figure of speech; an extended comparison is an analogy.

- Literal analogies are comparisons between things from the same class or genus.
- The literal analogy can build on the listener's past experience by comparing the thing to be explained to something the listener already knows.
- Figurative analogies are based on comparisons that are unusual; they add interest to a message because of their novelty.
- In a narrative, conflict and suspense result from the hurdles the main character must overcome to win his or her goal.
- Stories useful in informative speaking may be factual or fictitious.
- Among the most effective factual narratives for a speaker are those dealing with his or her personal experiences.

SUGGESTED PROJECTS

1. This is an oral exercise in making ideas clear. Select a complex concept from one of your other courses, such as the concept of comparative cost advantage in economics, or the concept of valence in chemistry, or the concept of mitosis in biology. State the point to be made clear, and using only one extended real example or one extended hypothetical example, make the point clear to the class. Your example should be two minutes in length. You should announce to the class before you begin the form of example you will use.

2. This is another oral exercise in making ideas clear. Select a concept similar to the one used in project 1 above. State the point to be made clear, and using only one extended figurative analogy or one extended literal analogy, make the point clear to the class. Again your analogy should be two minutes in length, and you should announce which analogy you will use before you begin.

3. Select a topic area in which you have special knowledge which your classmates are unlikely to share. Do not pick something like the proper way to serve in tennis. If you know how computers are used to project voting outcomes during network coverage of elections or how the law of comparative cost advantages is supposed to work in economics, these would be good topics. Prepare a five- to eight-minute speech to inform for delivery to your class.

SUGGESTED READINGS

Olbricht, Thomas. *Informative Speaking.* Glenview, Ill.: Scott, Foresman, 1968.
Walter, Otis M. *Speaking to Inform and Persuade.* 2d ed. New York: Macmillan, 1982.

chapter *15*

The Argumentative Speech

The participants in one common public-speaking situation come with the general expectation that the speaker will make an argument in support of a debatable position. The audience expects the speaker to take a controversial stand and present a well-reasoned analysis of the question in a logically coherent fashion.

THE NATURE OF ARGUMENT

The communication event may be billed as a debate, or the setting may be such that the emphasis is placed on reasoned argument as in the case of a lawyer arguing a brief before a judge. Often the members expect that speeches given to legislative sessions of state governments or the U.S. Congress or to legislative sessions of churches, fraternal organizations, and professional associations will be based on evidence and will downplay emotionalism.

Arguments and Persuasion

Of course, it is probably impossible to draw a clear distinction between emotional and logical proofs. Likewise past efforts to distinguish between

convincing an audience and persuading an audience have failed to with-
stand the test of more careful social scientific study. In an important sense,
a good argument has a strong persuasive appeal for many people. The
point of dealing with argument in a separate chapter is to focus your
attention on that important aspect of public communication for special
drill and study. The ability to present good reasons in cogent fashion in
support of a point to be proved or of a general position is an important
one that you can use in many communication contexts.

Argumentative Issues

People ought not argue about things they agree on, so arguments should
be organized around areas of disagreement. When people disagree, they
should clarify both their agreements and disagreements and then focus
their differences clearly. The focus of a disagreement is an *issue*. In our
political campaigns much is made of candidates debating the issues, but
the term has been used in so many different ways that it has lost much
of its usefulness. For example, it makes little sense in terms of argument
to refer to the "image issue" or the "personality issue" or the "sleaze
issue." Even so the basic idea remains sound, namely, that people who
disagree should clearly phrase their disagreement in the form of a question.

Arguments can relate to issues phrased as questions of fact. Lawyers
may argue, for example, on the question of what happened in the past,
such as whether or not Mr. John Doe did willfully and with malice
aforethought murder his wife? Others might debate whether or not a
single assassin killed President John Kennedy or whether there are still
American servicemen listed as missing in action alive in Vietnam. We
might also argue and predict future facts, such as whether or not an
accidental nuclear war will break out within the next 20 years or whether
or not the federal government will repudiate its debt.

Arguments can relate to questions of value. Thus, we might argue
whether or not the death penalty is justified, whether or not abortion on
demand is immoral, or whether or not society should practice euthanasia
on the hopelessly ill elderly.

Finally, arguments can relate to questions of policy. Thus, we might
argue whether or not to amend the constitution to guarantee women's
rights, to deny abortion on demand, or to require a balanced budget.

Arguments consist of good reasons made up of evidence and logic
integrated into a coherent case that portrays an overall position pro or con
on an issue. We will begin with an analysis of practical reason or logic and

then examine the details of evidence and proof as exemplified in argumentative supporting material.

MAKING A LOGICAL CASE

For our purposes we will define logic as the process of drawing a conclusion from one or more points that serve as the assumptions or premises or that need to be proved with evidence.

Lawyers call the paper they write that contains the logic of an argument a *brief*. Someone working on an important argumentative or persuasive project might well outline the main conclusions and the points that support it, much as a lawyer briefs a case. By following an outline, a person can clearly see the connections from reasons to conclusions and decide whether they fit together logically.

Checking Logic

When people question our logic, they often ask the short but troublesome question "Why?" When we answer a *why* question, we usually provide a *because* response. One good way to check the logic of a conclusion following from reasons is to write the conclusion clearly at the top of a sheet of paper and list the reasons supporting the conclusion under it, beginning each reason with *because*. If—keeping in mind our common-sense meaning of because—the outline makes good sense, the logic is probably all right.

For instance, here is a conclusion with its supporting reasons, using *because* to indicate logical connections:

> A high federal budget deficit will result in high interest rates
> *because* the government will borrow large amounts of money,
> causing demand to exceed supply and driving up interest rates
> *because* a high deficit forces the government to borrow large
> amounts of money to pay its bills.

One can also test the logic of conclusions drawn from a set of reasons by listing first the reasons and then the conclusions introduced by the word *therefore,* as in the following example:

> Many businessmen believe that women are by nature not tough
> enough for top management positions, and many male personnel
> directors assign women to positions that are traditional women's

A well-organized argument allows an audience to see the logic of the speaker's points and conclusions. (Vilms, Jeroboam)

roles in society; therefore, many women are discriminated against in business and industry.

When checking your own logic, keep in mind that the evidence must relate to the point you want to prove and that the reasons you present must support your conclusion. One of the most difficult things to do when trying to think clearly and logically is to make sure that every step of an argument is to the point. Here is an example of an argument that makes a mistake by trying to fit two related reasons together, as reason and conclusion:

> Computer crime is on the rise because many young people use computers for recreational purposes.

Although both ideas are related to the general topic of computers, they do not fit together as main point and supporting reason.

When we prove to someone the wisdom of acting, believing, or thinking in a certain way by means of evidence and logic, we have used one of the most powerful means of persuasion. Often the decision based on facts and careful inferences from evidence is better than the decision made solely on the basis of the advice of a person we like and trust or on the basis of suggestion. Most important, as consumers of persuasion, we need to be skillful in testing messages for their factual content and the soundness of their logic.

Faulty Analysis of Causation

The error of assuming that because one event followed another the first caused the second is a very common one. In general, the entire question of causation is a difficult one for the public speaker. Usually events are interrelated in very complex ways, and when a person assumes that event A caused event B, many factors that contributed to event B are probably ignored. Generally you should be suspicious of any argument that asserts that a single cause brought about a complicated event. Consider the following faulty argument:

> Herbert Hoover was elected as a Republican president before the depression of the 1930s; Dwight Eisenhower was elected as a Republican president before the recession of the 1950s; Richard Nixon was elected as a Republican president before the recession of the 1970s; therefore, Hoover, Eisenhower, and Nixon caused the economic problems.

If we were to indulge in another common fallacy, which is to make a hasty generalization on the basis of too few examples, we could assert that Republicans cause economic depressions and recessions. Both fallacies are present in the next argument:

> Woodrow Wilson was elected as a Democratic president before the United States entered World War I; Franklin Roosevelt was a Democratic president when we entered World War II; Harry Truman was a Democratic president when we entered the Korean War; and John F. Kennedy was a Democratic president when we escalated the Vietnam War; therefore, the Democrats always get us into war.

The error of assuming that because one thing preceded another it caused the event that followed is an easy one to make. You ought to be careful in evaluating the arguments you hear as well as those you use yourself to be sure they do not contain the fallacy.

Circular Reasoning

The fallacy of arguing in a circle is illustrated by the following assertions:

> "Liz is in the movies not because she is a good actress but because she is a personality."
> "Why is she a personality?"
> "Because she is so widely known."
> "Why is she so widely known?"
> "Because she is in the movies."

The above example may seem rather trivial, even though it illustrates the fallacy clearly, but the circular argument can crop up in important political and economic discussions as well:

> "Détente with the Russians will not work."
> "Why?"
> "Because you cannot trust the Communists."
> "Why?"
> "Because the Communists will never keep their treaty obligations."
> "Why?"
> "Because Communists are untrustworthy."

The Contradictory Argument

The inconsistent or contradictory argument is probably the most basic logical fallacy. In the study of formal logic, an argument that contradicts itself is always invalid, and on that basis, public speakers should put a premium on logical consistency. The debater who can convincingly point out that the opponent's argument is contradictory carries the issue. In the debates at the Virginia Convention, called to consider approval of the new Constitution of the United States, Patrick Henry argued against Virginia joining the new government, and James Madison argued for the Constitution. During the course of the long debate, Henry presented a great many different arguments against the proposal, and Madison was able to challenge Henry's reasoning on the grounds that he contradicted himself. For example, Madison first pointed out that Henry had argued that the provision that three-fourths of the states would be sufficient to start the new government was a bad one, because this would allow too few states to form the new government. Next, Madison pointed out that Henry had later argued that the stipulation that two-thirds of the states be required to ratify amendments would make it too difficult to change the government. Madison argued that Henry's argument was inconsistent in that Henry said three-fourths of the states were too few to start the government, but two-thirds were too many to amend it.

EVIDENCE AND PROOF

When we discuss proving a point for an audience, we must remember that we cannot tell whether a given piece of information is proof until we look at it in relation to the point to be proved.

Evidence is material that furnishes grounds for belief or makes evident the truth or falsity, rightness or wrongness, wisdom or folly of a proposition. In law, *evidence* is a technical term that refers to material supplied by lawyers in support of their arguments in court. Legal evidence may include testimony of witnesses, written documents, or actual items, such as pistols, knives, or clothing.

Proof is the process of gathering together, ordering, and presenting enough evidence to convince the judge or jury (or us, the listener-consumers) to accept a given proposition.

Although we evaluate evidence in terms of general rules about good evidence, we must look at proof in terms of a given audience. Proof has to convince somebody. A given message unit, consisting of proposition and supporting evidence, may convince one individual but not another. An old folk saying claims that "the proof of the pudding is in the eating." Even though the cook thinks the ingredients are good and his recipe interesting, if the people eating the pudding do not like it, for them anyway the pudding is no good. No matter how good the speaker thinks his evidence is, no matter how sound his reasoning, if the listener is not convinced, his proof has failed.

In the next section we emphasize ways to make an argument in behalf of a proposition by use of statistics supplemented with real examples and by use of the testimony of eyewitness observers and experts.

ARGUMENTATIVE SUPPORTING MATERIAL

Statistics

Statistics are numerical comments about facts. A person may comment that Bill is tall. A similar statement may say that Bill is 6 feet 6 inches tall. This last statement includes numbers and is thus a statistical comment. When the statistics are accurate, they give us more precise information about facts than can most other forms of description. When a person wants to talk about many things and has only a short interview or conference in which to make his or her statement, the use of statistical description enables the person to pack a lot of information into a few sentences.

Suppose a student asks the dean, "What are my chances of going on to the university if I enroll at Pleasant Hills Community College?" If the dean answers, "Of every 1000 freshmen who start at Pleasant Hills, 300 go on to the university," she covers a large number of facts (implicit in her answer is the information that while 300 go on, 700 do not), and she has given this information in a short sentence.

However, because the answer provides only a little information about a lot of students, we may get an incomplete picture. How many of the 700 who do not go on for further education wanted to or planned to? Many community-college programs are designed as two-year programs and are complete in themselves. How many of the 300 who go on for more education finish with university or four-year college degrees? In other words, many things are left unsaid by the dean's initial statistical statement. Many persuaders and pressure groups use figures to fool the public as well as to inform people. Even when used carefully and honestly, as in the dean's statement, statistics are abstract and present only a part of a larger picture. In our discussion of statistics, we will particularly look at both the sound use of statistics and the dangers of presenting factual information in the form of figures without explaining exactly what these figures mean or, almost more important, without explaining what the figures do *not* mean.

Numbers suggest precision and accuracy. Most of us think of figures as being factual and scientific. We do not know how to answer a statement such as "Twenty percent of inner-city teenagers use heroin" unless we have some statistical information of our own. We may say, "I find that hard to believe," or "That figure seems awfully high," but if the other person repeats the statement, the suggestive power of the number itself, "20 percent," is persuasive, making it difficult for us to answer.

Numbers as Measures   We all use numbers to talk about such things as our age, height, and weight. We count things like apples, pennies, and oranges, and we know how useful counting and measuring can be. One important way to reason is to count things and then—applying addition, subtraction, multiplication, and division to the numbers we have—compute further answers for ourselves. If I make $100 a week, and $22 is deducted in taxes and insurance, I figure that I will have $78 in my weekly pay check. As long as my basic premises are right (I make $100 and $22 is deducted), then when I make my mathematical computations, my experience will agree with my predicted outcome. I calculate that I will have a $78 paycheck, and when payday arrives, I *do* have a check for $78.

All this seems somewhat obvious to us at this stage in our lives. We have no difficulty counting apples or people, because we can tell one apple from another and we can differentiate people. But the use of numbers becomes much more complicated as soon as we leave individual, single items. Counting the length of a table, for example, is more difficult than counting the number of tables in a room. A table is one long uninterrupted length. We have, then, to make arbitrary divisions or units along the length of the table, so that we can count each division just as we counted the apples. In spite of the complications of measuring and counting, however, we can achieve fairly accurate results when we measure a table or count apples. We can compare lengths of various tables, and we can compare the total number of apples in one box with the total number of apples in another.

Numbers As Evaluations   Because numbers are such useful labels, we tend to use numbers for many things that cannot be counted in the simple way apples and inches can. When we do this, the accuracy with which the numbers represent the real world is decreased. You have all taken essay-type tests in which the instructor assigns points for each answer. Question 1, you are told, is worth 25 points. The instructor has the job of deciding whether the answer given by a particular student is worth all 25 points, or only 20 points, or 10, and so on. What can the instructor count to arrive at a conclusion that the answer is worth 20 points? Nothing, really. The number 20 is an evaluation that corresponds to a word evaluation of the answer, such as *good* or *fair,* and the instructor is simply using the convenience of a number to make his general evaluation of the answer.

If you say that Mary is 5 feet tall and weighs 100 pounds, you have made a measurable, accurate statistical statement. Suppose you are told that Mary has an IQ *(intelligence quotient)* of 140. Is this an accurate, dependable statistical statement? Not so much so. We are impressed that Mary's IQ is 140, because we know that this value borders on the genius range of human intelligence, but what have the testers counted to arrive at the number 140? They have certainly not been able to count anything like apples or inches or pounds. Mary has done certain tasks, and the tester has assigned number values to them. He has added up the number values of the tasks Mary completed correctly (her score) and has compared her score with those of others her age who have taken similar tests, in order to determine her mental age. On that basis he has assigned the number 140 as a measure of Mary's intelligence. To say Mary has an IQ of 140 is a less valid statistic than to say Mary is 5 feet tall and weighs 100 pounds.

When we use or listen to statistics, we must make sure we know how the people who observed the facts picked the numbers they assigned to the facts as statistics about them. Did the person gathering the statistics count something that could easily be counted by you or by anyone else, so that several people would come up with the same numbers, or did he use the number as an evaluation or a name? Numbers that come from counting tend to be more useful and accurate than numbers used as names or evaluations.

Many people and organizations are engaged in counting and evaluating things and publishing statistics. Today's student acquires facts and figures from many different sources. In organizing communication messages, we seldom have any trouble finding statistics; the newsstands are full of magazines that are, in turn, full of statistics we can repeat in a communication class. Our trouble comes when we begin to puzzle out what the numbers we find actually mean.

The basic information we need to understand something or to make a wise decision is often a comparison of how two things are similar or how they are different or how they are changing in relation to one another. The things we want to know can often be described by such terms as *enough, too much, on time, gaining, out of reach, leveling off, losing ground, the weakest regions, the strongest area, ahead of schedule, above average,* and *less than we expected.*

Using Figures in Comparison   One of the most important ways people use figures is to make comparisons. Basically, we compare figures to get a clear indication of *more* or *less.* We can use figures to find out about more or less by looking at two things at about the same point in time (we measure Joe's height and Harry's height and say that Joe is at this moment 2 inches taller than Harry) and by looking at the same thing at different times (Metropolitan College had an enrollment of 1500 in 1975, 2200 in 1980, and currently has 2100).

When we compare figures, we must be sure not only that the numbers are a result of counting and not of naming or evaluating, but also that the units counted are comparable in terms of the point we wish to prove. The most common thing people try to count that is not comparable from time to time, is the dollar. Usually the dollar buys less this year than last, although in some periods of American history the reverse was true. Suppose an older person says to a high school student, "When I started my first job I made only $1 an hour and here you are beginning at $4. Are you lucky! You're making four times what I made then." The idea that a student making $4 an hour today is earning four times as much as a man making $1 an hour in 1945 is wrong, because the value of a dollar depends on its buying power—how many hours a person has to work to buy a good dinner in a restaurant, a car, or a bag of groceries. Someone making $4 an hour today can buy little, if anything, more than a person making $1 an hour in 1945.

Even on the same day in different parts of the country, the dollar is not comparable in terms of buying power. If someone says welfare payments are much higher in New York City than in Jackson, Mississippi, what is he saying? Maybe the dollars paid in New York City buy less than the dollars in Jackson. What you buy for a dollar in one part of the country often costs more, or less, in another part of the country. This is even more true when one compares cities around the world.

Even when the things compared are the same size, or are corrected to make them comparable, the people who compare figures for today with statistics from the past often ignore the effect of the increasing or decreasing numbers of people in a given city or region. For example, the latest figures regarding deaths in automobile accidents, arrests for using illegal drugs, or the occurrence of venereal disease are usually larger than the same statistics from 10 to 20 years ago simply because the population of the United States has increased in the last 20 years. Comparisons of absolute numbers are poor evidence to prove a trend toward better or worse. Comparing the total number of deaths on the highways 10 years ago with the total number this year is not as valid a statistic for proving the increased rate of automobile-related deaths as is the number of deaths per 1000 cars in those years or, better yet, the number of deaths per 100,000 automobile-miles driven in those years. Because some cars are driven so much more every year than others, a comparison of car-miles driven is more meaningful than a comparison of deaths per so many automobiles. Airlines usually present safety statistics in terms of passenger-miles rather than in terms of number of flights or length of flights.

The Random Sample To this point we have assumed that the figures under discussion are the result of observing everything we want to know about. That is, if we want to know how many students are enrolled at our college, we find out the number by tabulating every student. Many important statistics are the result of such complete counts. If the counting is complete and no item is overlooked, the numbers that result are the most useful kind of statistics. Much statistical information, however, comes from observing only part of the total and then trying to figure out what the whole picture looks like by making educated guesses about the whole from the part actually counted. The argument is that you do not have to drink the whole glassful to know the milk is sour.

A good way to take a sample is by picking items in such a way that every member of the total population has an equal chance of being selected. The result is a *random sample* that allows statisticians to compute with a specified margin of error the nature of the parent population.

Most polls of public opinion are based on the answers of several hundred or perhaps several thousand people to various questions. Surveys of television viewers also record the responses of a sample of the total viewing audience. Often surveyors report their results in specific figures. One may read that the most recent poll shows that 53 percent of the American people approve the way the president is doing his job. These same polls may not also indicate that, given the number of people polled and the error that creeps into such sampling, the results are accurate only within 2 or 3 percentage points.

Averages In addition to describing numerically the whole of a group, statistics can be used to describe the average of a group. For instance, the average student at a state college is 21 years old. We often want to know what is typical, and averages help us find out. But an average can be misleading as well as useful. For example, if all 20 members of a class have part-time or full-time jobs, we may not discover the typical salary if we add all the salaries and divide by 20 because, for one thing, those with full-time jobs probably earn more than those with part-time work. Even if we limit our group to 10 students with part-time jobs, averaging may be misleading. For example, if one student is a highly successful door-to-door salesman who makes $20,000 per year, including this high salary in the averaging gives us a misleading figure. Say the 9 remaining students have salaries between $4000 and $8000 a year, averaging for the 9 people about $6000 per year. Including the single $20,000 salary produces an average of $7400 per year, which is higher than the earnings of most members of the sample and lower than the earnings of only a few.

All numerical statistical evidence must be carefully examined when you use it or hear it as part of a persuasive campaign to prove a point.

Determining What Is Typical

The notion of typicality ties together the use of statistics and examples. An important part of statistical analysis is the discovery of the fact or facts that are the most usual or that are in the middle of a range. We have mentioned the average—the sum of all the numbers divided by the frequency of their occurrence—which is often an appropriate device for indicating what is typical. It is called the *mean.* If we take the weight of each of the 11 players on a football team, add them to find the total weight of all players, and divide by 11, we have the average weight of a player on the team. If the average turns out to be 220 pounds, that statistic gives us a better impression of how heavy the players are than would the extreme example of Harry Potter, a 180-pound quarterback, or William Jones, a 167-pound scatback. As the two lightest-weight players on the team, Harry and William would be poor examples of the weight of the team as a whole. There may not even be a player who weighs the exact average, 220 pounds, but if we use Fred Smith, a 223-pound end, or Elbert Reed, a 217-pound running back, for our example, we have selected an example close to the actual average weight.

Another way statisticians discover the typical is by arranging all of a group of statistics in order from larger to smaller, and then picking the statistic at the middle point and using this to show what is usual. If we made a list of the incomes of all the students in our sample of 10 and arranged the incomes in order from the highest to the lowest, we could count halfway down (or up) and consider the income in the middle of the list to be the typical example of the income. In the case of the 10 students, a midpoint, or *median,* example would give a more accurate indication of what was typical than would a numerical average. The median example is often a good statistic to use when the figures you are discussing range from unusually high to unusually low. These extremes are accounted for when you pick the point in the middle.

Real examples add interest to statistics because they relate the dry figures to the human world. Statistics can express many facts in a short statement, but without examples they often seem dull and boring. Facts presented in terms of people who are heroes or villains, who suffer and have moments of joy and happiness, are more interesting and more understandable.

Examples that are factual can also support a point as evidence of its truth or wisdom. A person trying to find out the truth about a particular problem must weigh the real examples carefully to be sure they are factually accurate and typical of the things they are supposed to illustrate or represent. We can take one or two examples as being representative of a class of people or events. We imply that the examples are able to stand for a great many more just like them that we could use if we had the time to discuss them all. The danger, therefore, is that we may, in the interest of proving a point, use an extreme example. In the early 1970s, two dramatic and compelling events caught the imagination of the American public. The first was a series of bloody murders of Hollywood personalities, for which a long-haired commune leader named Charles Manson and several of the women in his "family" were convicted. The second was a war atrocity in which a number of Vietnamese women and children were killed at a village called My Lai, for which an infantry lieutenant named Calley was convicted. Some people argued that the hippy culture was morally bankrupt and vicious, and they submitted the Manson murders as an example to prove their point. Other people argued that the military-industrial complex was morally bankrupt and vicious, and they submitted the My Lai massacre as an example to prove their point. Both groups were guilty of using extreme, rather than typical, examples.

The use of extreme examples as proof is characteristic of popular-magazine articles. A writer in search of an attention-catching device for his opening paragraph often describes a dramatic but unusual case and implies that it is typical.

Students of straight thinking have found so many instances of the use of a few extreme examples to prove points that they call such errors of thinking the fallacy of *hasty generalization*. If one of your friends did something your parents thought was out of line, they may have made a hasty generalization about your whole group of acquaintances. When someone submits an extreme example to another person in a conversation or discussion and then jumps to the conclusion that the example is typical, both speaker and listener may be misled about the facts of the case. When we make such mistakes, we can usually expect a rude awakening sooner or later.

Testimony

Eyewitness Testimony   "When in doubt, go see for yourself" is generally good advice. In other words, if you don't believe someone, go find out with your own two eyes and ears. We depend on the evidence of our senses in deciding many factual questions. If you want to know if it is raining, you go to the window and look outside. Say that a fight breaks out in the hallway. You run to see what is going on. Someone else runs up after the fight is over and asks, "What happened?" You describe the fight. This other person says, "I don't believe you." You shrug your shoulders and say, "Suit yourself. But that is what happened." We believe the evidence of our own senses.

However, many times in our communications with others we want to prove a point about some facts but have not had the time or the chance to see the particular facts for ourselves. Maybe the facts, such as what happened in the fight in the hallway, occurred at only one place in time, so that unless we happened to be there, we have to depend for information on the story of a person who did see the event. Some facts are complicated and occur over a period of time or at a considerable distance, so that we would need much time to observe them all. During the years the United States did not have diplomatic relations with Communist China, the facts about what was going on in China existed but could not be observed by Americans. If we wanted to know how things were going in China during those years, we had to rely on the testimony of people who were there—foreign correspondents from countries that did have diplomatic exchanges with China; we often read reports about China that were written, for example, by Canadians who went there to observe at first hand.

Thus an important source of evidence is the testimony or word of an eyewitness. In a court of law, the only testimony about facts allowed is that of an eyewitness. Sometimes in everyday living, we are willing to depend upon what the law terms *hearsay* (second-hand information, gossip, or rumor; the word of somebody who got a story from someone else), but when we are trying to prove something, rumor is a shaky substitute for eyewitness accounts. Think of several rumors you have heard recently. How many turned out to be entirely accurate?

Many times we quote testimony from a witness who has written up an account of what he saw in a newspaper or magazine. Sometimes we refer to a statement made on radio or television by an alleged eyewitness. When using the testimony of a witness to prove a point, we ought not to assume that just because the person saw the event he is necessarily telling the truth about it or giving a good picture of what happened.

Suppose we ask a friend of Bill's what happened in the hallway fight between Bill and Harry. Bill's friend may well say that Harry did not knock Bill down, but that Bill slipped. Another eyewitness who has no stake in the matter, such as friendship with one of the participants, may say that Bill provoked Harry, and Harry hit Bill a solid blow to the jaw and knocked him down. Which eyewitness do you believe? How do you decide which reporter is the more reliable witness to what actually happened?

When trying to decide what happened in any given instance, we have to examine the testimony of eyewitnesses carefully. You should ask yourself such questions as:

What exactly did the witness intend to say?

Was the story a put-on? Was it supposed to be funny?

Was the person able to make a good report? Was he in a position to see? Did he have the training that would make him better able to keep track of what was going on? Is he a reliable person?

Was the person willing and able to tell the truth?

Was there any reason for the witness to lie or distort the truth?

Did the witness have a bias? What did the witness expect to see? (We all have a tendency to see what we expect to see. Each of us has a personal bias built in when we view or hear an event.)

Expert Testimony   Speakers frequently use direct quotations from well-known authorities in interpreting facts. Usually we use *expert* witnesses to testify about what the facts mean. If we go to a doctor and he shows us our X rays, we may still ask, "What does it mean?" He could then tell us that the X rays indicate there is a fracture of a small bone in the right foot. Many facts are difficult to interpret, and people who specialize in a given area can often help us decide what the facts mean. An expert in foods may testify that the diet of the poor people in an area is not good enough to keep them healthy; he may testify, further, that studies have shown a direct relationship between diet and intelligence in young children. Another expert on drug usage may testify that the facts indicate that the use of marijuana does not affect a person's physical ability to drive a car as much as does the use of alcohol in comparable amounts. Speakers often quote the interpretation of facts by widely known experts to support their case.

Another way in which we may use testimony is to decide what we ought to do in a given case. We might ask the doctor who told us we have a fractured bone in the foot, "What shall I do?" He might advise us to have the foot put into a cast to keep it immobilized for six weeks while it heals. We often depend upon an expert's advice; in the case of the doctor, his advice is testimony you should consider as you decide what to do about the facts. Obviously, when you want advice, you must ask the right expert. Suppose an unmarried pregnant teenager asks her mother, "What should I do?" Suppose she asks her boyfriend, a girlfriend, or her doctor the same question. Her mother might say, "Get married." The boyfriend might say, "Have an abortion." The girlfriend might say, "Keep the baby." The doctor might say, "Take these pills, they're vitamins; don't gain too much weight, and come back to see me in a month." The teenager has received testimony from four sources. Whose testimony is more persuasive? Whose testimony ought to be more persuasive? Has she perhaps not asked the right expert or the right questions yet? Consider the involved interests of her sources. A speaker may quote or allude to advice from leading authorities who recommend the same proposals as does the speaker.

One widely used propaganda technique features the testimony of glamorous and famous people telling us we ought to buy or do something. The form of the argument is similar to the legitimate use of the testimony of experts to support a case. However, the persuasive power of the testimony comes from the old propaganda device of nonrational transfer of glamor and prestige of a popular or famous name to a product or proposal. We often see baseball or basketball or football players advising us to buy a certain kind of shaving cream, cologne, or breakfast food. Movie stars advise us what political candidates to vote for. Supposedly, if we admire and value the opinions of a sports or television star, we will transfer our liking to the product he tells us to use and will buy it.

When an expert tells us what to do about a health problem, getting an education, or voting for or against a tax increase or school bond, or to support an antinuclear position or candidate, or to support a disarmament conference or an antipollution effort, we should be sure that the person is an expert *in the field* he is talking about. We should not follow a person's advice just because he is likable or glamorous. If the person talking about facts has a vested interest in how he interprets the facts to us, we must keep that in mind when we consider his testimony. Remember most personalities are paid handsomely when they make commercials advising you to buy a service or a product.

KEY IDEAS

- The participants in one form of public-speaking come with the general expectation that the speaker will give an argumentative speech by taking a controversial stand and presenting a well-reasoned analysis of his position.
- It is difficult to draw a clear distinction between logical and emotional proofs, between argument and persuasion.
- The focus of a disagreement is an *issue.*
- Arguments can relate to questions of fact, of value, or of policy.
- Logic is the process of drawing conclusions from one or more points.
- Decisions based on careful inferences from evidence are often better than those made on the basis of the persuasive power of personality and suggestion.
- One common logical fallacy is to assume that because one event followed another the first caused the second.
- Other common logical fallacies include arguing in a circle and being inconsistent or contradictory.
- Evidence is material that furnishes grounds for belief or makes evident the truth or falsity, rightness or wrongness, wisdom or folly of a proposition.
- Proof is the process of gathering together, ordering, and presenting enough evidence to convince the listener to accept a given proposition.
- Statistical descriptions of factual material often contain much information in a few words.
- Even when carefully and honestly presented, statistics often give the listener an incomplete picture.
- Numbers that come from counting tend to be more useful in informing about the world than figures used as names or as evaluations.
- Some units, such as the American dollar, are not comparable from time to time.
- The latest figures regarding any vital statistic are usually larger than the same figures for several years ago simply because the population has increased.
- Much statistical information comes from observing a sample of the total population and making an educated guess about the whole on that basis.
- A random sample allows a more precise guess about the total population than most other kinds of samples.

- Extreme examples are poor evidence.
- The fallacy of hasty generalization results from jumping to a conclusion on the basis of a few extreme examples.
- An important part of statistical analysis is the discovery of facts that are usual or typical of a wide range of things.
- Real examples are a good way to add interest to statistics, and statistics provide a good guide to typical examples.
- We depend on the evidence of our senses in deciding many factual questions.
- The testimony of reliable eyewitnesses is an important source of evidence about factual matters.
- In an age of specialization, expert testimony interpreting complicated factual matters is often an important part of persuasion.
- A widely used propaganda technique is to cite the testimonial of a famous and glamorous person in behalf of a product or service.
- If someone testifies that we ought to do or believe something, we should examine that person's authority carefully.

SUGGESTED PROJECTS

1. This is a project in proving a point. Select a controversial point, phrase it in suitable form, and then, using only statistical information, support the point for two minutes.
2. Select an argument presented in a newspaper, magazine, or on television. Note the point to be proved and then analyze the supporting material critically. How could the argument have been better supported, in your estimation?
3. Select a topic you feel strongly about and prepare a five- to eight-minute argumentative speech for delivery to the class.

SUGGESTED READINGS

Huff, Darrel, *How to Lie with Statistics.* New York: Norton, 1954.

Jensen, J. Vernon. *Argumentation: Reasoning in Communication.* Belmont, Calif.: Wadsworth, 1981.

Newman, Robert P., and Dale R. Newman. *Evidence.* Boston: Houghton Mifflin, 1969.

chapter *16*

The Persuasive Speech

No aspect of communication is more important to our daily lives than persuasion. We are urged to vote for political candidates, to support reforms, to buy products, and to establish relationships with other people. The message with persuasive intent comes at us in two-person conversations and interviews; in face-to-face small-group conferences; in public speeches and business presentations; in newspapers, magazines, letters; and in films, radio shows, and television programs. Billboards proclaim suggestions about how we should act or believe; neon signs entice us to drink, eat, or buy. The lyrics of popular songs sell a point of view or a lifestyle. We go to a job interview and try to persuade the interviewer to hire us. We take a job as a salesman and try to get a customer to make a purchase. We see an attractive person and try to persuade her or him to go to a movie with us.

PERSUASION DEFINED

Persuasion is sometimes called changing behavior. It can also be defined as changing attitudes or beliefs, winning friends, influencing people, gaining cooperation, or selling a product or an idea. When we talk somebody into doing something, we have persuaded him. When we suggest ideas or

237

beliefs or argue for a position with evidence and logic in such a way that the listeners change their behavior, attitudes, or beliefs, we have persuaded them.

We will define *persuasion* as communication to influence choice. When we speak to inform (make a point clear), we often provide the listener with information that opens up new horizons and increases choices, but when we speak to persuade we try to influence the listener's choices and narrow them to the one we prefer.

Notice that persuasion is communication intended to get a response from the receiver, to change the listener's attitude or beliefs. The source of the message, the person giving a persuasive comment or making a persuasive speech, has a specific purpose in mind and drafts the persuasive message to achieve that goal.

Persuasion is not the same as force. We can control human beings to some extent with the use of force or the threat of force. If you are forced to do something, your options are closed. Coercion eliminates choice, while persuasion influences it. Coercion does not require artistry. "Do this or I will bash in your head" may get results but requires little skill—only the brute strength and the desire to deliver the blow. A good salesperson, on the other hand, is skillful and has developed the art of persuasion to a high level. If selling were as easy as bashing in heads, more people would be making $50,000 a year in commissions.

Persuasion is not the same as inducing somebody to do something by offering a powerful reward. A father might get his son to cut his hair by promising him a new car. Offering a large reward is similar to offering a threat of force. Neither offering a large reward (the carrot) nor threatening punishment (the stick) nor using both the carrot and the stick involves much communication skill or selling ability.

In this chapter we begin by dealing specifically with the most challenging of speaking situations—the occasion requiring a persuasive speech. We then discuss some general features of persuasion directly applicable to the public-speaking situation but also important in other contexts and when you are listening to and evaluating persuasion.

THE NATURE OF THE PERSUASIVE SPEECH

The participants in one common public-speaking situation come with the general expectation that the speaker will deliver a persuasive message. The audience expects a persuasive speech when a speaker known to take a definite stand is scheduled to talk on a controversial subject and we expect an all-out effort to convert people to the speaker's position. In many respects the persuasion occasion is similar to that of the argumentative. The main difference is that while we expect the debater to emphasize evidence, logic, and proof, we expect the persuader not only to make a good argument but also to be credible, emotional, and motivating.

Persuasion and Motivation

The concept of motive, properly defined, can help the person preparing a speech. Our concern here is with motive in the sense of what, in fact, drives members of the audience to act the way they do. Many people talk of motivating other people. When a salesperson says he or she must motivate the customer to buy the product and a teacher says he or she must motivate the student to study for a test, they seem to be saying that they can install within the customer or the student a motor that will impel the customer to buy and the student to study. We must realize that whatever basic motives the listeners possess are in them already, and as persuasive speakers, we have to adapt to the motives present in the audience. We cannot install motives in people, because motives develop in a complex way, usually over a period of time. People's motives are influenced by their heredity, their upbringing, and the people after whom they have decided to model themselves. When we manage to persuade a member of an audience, we do so largely by attaching our suggestions to the motives already present. Only by hooking into previously held motives can we make individuals in an audience want to do or believe what we are trying to persuade them to do or believe.

People tend to do what they want, even though, upon careful study of the facts, what they want at the moment may not always be the best thing in the long run. A good automobile salesperson tries to make the customer *want* his car first; then he suggests logical reasons why the person should buy it. The salesperson often suggests, "Why don't you get in and drive it around awhile?" He hopes that when the customer gets behind the wheel and drives the car, he will come to want to have the car for his own. Persuasive speakers should carefully evaluate the wants of their audience and then present their ideas in such a way that they make the audience *want* to do what they suggest.

Dealing with Audience Habits

We all perform much of our daily routine out of habit, those learned behavior patterns that are repeated so often they become almost involuntary. When you first started senior high school, or later, college, your old habits and patterns were torn up, and you had to develop new ones. Usually such periods of our lives are troublesome for us. We do not know where to go next, what to do. We often feel homesick for the good old days, or really for the good old ways. When you analyze the audience for your persuasive speech, remember that if you can show that by following your advice the members of the audience can continue in the same comfortable ways, they will often choose your suggestion. On the other hand, if you want to change things, you will have to shake up your listeners and make them believe that their present habits cause serious trouble and that they must change their ways. If a person is in the habit of smoking cigarettes, then before you can persuade him to change his habit, you have to prove to him that he may be in for serious trouble if he does not stop smoking. You must remember that your persuasive message may "cost" the listener a comfortable habit; you have to be ready to meet the challenge of his resistance to change.

The Two Types of Persuasive Speech

Persuasive speeches arise in two main situations. First, a number of people have grown increasingly restless with the way something is being done. They are unsatisfied with some basic part of their lives. These people begin to think up new and, to them, better ways to do something about it. They are now ready to attempt to persuade other people to support their drive for a change. Once a substantial number of people begin to argue and persuade the community to change things, the second situation arises: Another group becomes disturbed because it feels the present situation is satisfactory, and fears the proponents of change will succeed. This group begins to take steps to persuade the community to reject the proposals for new programs. Persuasive speeches are given either (1) to get the audience to work for, vote for, or in some way help adopt a new law, program, or way of doing things, or (2) to get the audience to work against, vote against, or in some way prevent the adoption of a new law, program, or way of doing things.

The Speech for Change   If you are disturbed or upset by the way things are going and wish to advocate change, you should develop a speech outline that has three main parts. The first point in a persuasive speech

A persuasive speaker may effectively bring about change in a part of the audience.
(Skytta, Jeroboam)

for change is "Things are a mess." Take the topic of the current state of
the educational system. Someone who wishes to change it should begin
with the point, "The present educational system is a mess," and then use
the basic building blocks of communication (a point to be proved and the
evidence, examples, statistics, and testimony of experts that support the
point) to build his case against some aspect of current educational practices. The second point in a persuasive speech for change is "Here is my
program to solve the problem." In developing this point, the speaker for
change explains his recommendations. He describes his recommended
changes and urges the audience to take some positive action to help get
the changes made. The third point in a persuasive speech for change is "If
you do as I say, here is what is in it for you." The speaker then describes
in graphic detail the benefits that will accrue if the listeners follow his
advice and support his proposal.

Persuasive Speech to Change Things

   I. Things are a mess.
      A. Point to be proved (statistics, testimony, examples)
      B. Point to be proved (statistics, testimony, examples)
  II. Here is my program to solve the problem.
      A. Point to be made clear (examples, analogies, narrations)
      B. Point to be made clear (examples, analogies, narrations)
 III. Here is what is in it *for you* if you adopt my program.

Notice that this basic framework can easily be expanded to use the envisioning pattern explained in Chapter 11.

Of course, you will not find many occasions when the exact phrases "Things are a mess" and "Here is my program to solve the problem" can be used in your speech. You will need to phrase the points differently for each specific occasion.

The proof of the case tends to come in the first point, where the speaker describes the present conditions and explains the nature of the problem. The persuasive impact tends to come in the third point, where the speaker describes how the wants of the audience will be satisfied by the new program. Here, in shorthand form, is a quick, persuasive speech:

> Your present car is a mess. The paint is scratched, the tires are shot, the motor needs overhauling. The repairs will soon cost more than new-car payments, and in the meantime you can't count on your transportation. Here's my program for you. Let me put you into this neat little Rattlesnake four-cylinder convertible. You not only get dependable transportation, but you get a whole new outlook on life. The women who won't date you now will begin to flock around you. You'll get a new sense of zest for life as you tool down the freeway in this sweet little sports car.

The Speech Against Change The speaker who wishes to persuade an audience *not* to adopt a new proposal has several different options in planning his or her speech. Essentially, the basic outline consists of three points that take issue with the three main points of the speech advocating the change. Thus the first point is "Things are going along just fine"; the second point is "The proposal would not work"; and the third point is "The proposal would make things a lot rougher on you." The speaker need not use all three points, however. For some arguments, he or she may select only one and argue simply that things are just fine and submit two or three major reasons for believing change is unnecessary. He or she may pick several points and argue, for example, that there is no need for a proposal as drastic as the one under consideration, and even if there were a need, this plan would not help matters any.

Let us see how the entire outline works:

Persuasive Speech Against Changing Things

   I. Things are going along just fine.
      A. Point to be proved (evidence)
      B. Point to be proved (evidence)
  II. The proposal would not work.
      A. Point to be proved (evidence)
      B. Point to be proved (evidence)
 III. The proposal would make things a lot rougher on you.
      A. Point to be proved (evidence)
      B. Point to be proved (evidence)

The persuasive part of the speech against a proposal can come in the first point, if the speaker describes the desirable aspects of the way things are and makes the audience appreciate and want to keep the good things they have. Of course, the speaker can also be persuasive in the third point, by presenting the dangers in vivid and graphic terms, so that the audience is repelled by the results of the new plan as the opponent presents them.

THE PERSUASIVE POWER OF PERSONALITY

Persuasion and Personal Relationships

One of the most important factors for persuasion in a communication situation is the quality of the personal relationships that are established. If the people who are discussing a topic like and trust one another, attempts of either one to influence the other are more likely to succeed.

Persuasion often consists of advice. When we receive advice, we usually face some risky choices. Many of the big decisions in life pose some risks. Should I enlist in the army? Should I take a job with Pulver Motors? Should I get married? Should I go to college? Should I take a shot of heroin? When the choices are risky and I need advice, I turn to someone I trust. Trust assumes that the other person will give me advice that to that person seems best for me. When I trust a person, I can count on that person's strength, integrity, sincerity, expertness, and concern for me.

Persuasion and Likability

Often liking and trusting go together, but they are not necessarily always connected. We might find some people likable but not trustworthy in important matters because we know they are forgetful, unreliable, or easily swayed by emotions. On the other hand, some people whose advice we take and whom we trust are not likable. We might trust a certain medical doctor because we know she is well trained, sober, and a talented physician, even though we do not like her much as a person.

Nonetheless, if we like a person, we are tempted to believe and accept his or her ideas and advice. We often *feel* better about taking the advice of someone we like than about accepting the recommendation of someone we dislike. An important part of the study of persuasion, therefore, concerns how people who talk with one another come to *like* one another.

Physical beauty is a factor in being likable. People's ideas about what is beautiful are as individual as people. Just the same, Americans spend billions of dollars each year in the search for beauty because, for many, physical attractiveness is the key to popularity and friendship. Physical beauty is not enough by itself to assure likability, but other things being equal, the beautiful people have an advantage. Advertisers often use the persuasive power of handsome men and beautiful women shown using the product or simply being present in the same picture with an advertising slogan.

Speaking ability is a factor in being likable. A pleasant, flexible, resonant voice quality communicates a dynamic personality, an alive and vibrant person. The person who can find the right word at the right time and who can express an idea clearly and with interesting examples or analogies draws attention and interest. The person with a lively and vivid imagination, who can make small talk, spin out dreams or fantasies, dramatize characters, tell interesting stories, and ask unusual questions, is interesting and can be likable.

Listening ability is a factor in being likable. Listening is a real talent and is often underestimated. The person who is willing to listen to others and find out who they are, what they are interested in, and what they are worried about is often liked. Genuinely good listeners are always welcome.

The Importance of Our Attitude Toward Others

An attitude of willingness and ability to help creates a feeling of trust and liking in others. A genuine offer of help is a powerful force of persuasion.

Well-managed stores instruct the salespeople to ask, "May I help you?" The may-I-help attitude in reverse works to build trust also. "I *need* your help" is another persuasive message. A person who asks for help, accepts it without bitterness, and then thanks us makes us feel good.

Persuasion and Source Competence

In addition to being likable and working to engender trust, the speaker should suggest competence, expertness, credibility, and conviction if his or her advice is to be persuasive. We expect a competent person's talk to contain a wealth of good and relevant information about the topic under discussion. The speaker who is clear, whose comments are easy to follow because they are well organized, whose language is precise, and who has a fluent and expressive way of speaking further suggests to us that he or she is competent. This is as true of the person talking to us face to face as of the person giving a public speech.

Finally, a powerful force for persuasion is the speaker's deep personal conviction that he or she is right. The first persons good sales representatives persuade are themselves. The father who discusses the dangers of the use of tobacco and advises his son not to start smoking as he himself drags on a cigarette is not persuasive. The persuasive power of dedicated reformers is in large part a result of their willingness to make great personal sacrifices for the cause.

Persuasion and the Speaker's Reputation

When we study the persuasiveness of well-known public figures, therefore, we must examine both the effect of the speaker's reputation and the impact of the message itself. The reputation of a speaker influences our acceptance of his or her ideas, but our final decision usually depends upon what he or she says to us.

Scholars have used a number of different terms for the concept of the source's reputation. A popular term is *image*. Most politicians have professional help in building an image (reputation) that will gain votes. Business firms, motion-picture stars, rock musicians, government agencies, and other institutions often try to create a favorable image of themselves.

Another term for the speaker's reputation often used in communication research is *source credibility*. A large number of studies have examined the influence of a source's reputation on audience attitudes. The researchers first gave the experimental subjects a test to find out their attitude on a topic. Next the investigators told different groups of subjects that different people (sources) had produced the message they were about to hear. (The message was tape-recorded, so it was the same for each group.) They then played the message to the subjects and tested them again to determine whether listening to the recording had changed the listeners' attitudes. Since the content of the message was the same (controlled), the investigators argued that measurable changes in the attitudes from group to group resulted from the fact that each group believed a different person had been speaking.

A listener's prior opinion of a speaker comes from many sources: previous in-person communications between them, what others have said to the listener about the speaker, what the listener has read about the speaker, and biographical information the listener may know about the speaker. Sources of information need not be individuals, of course. We receive communication from organizations, as well, and they too have prior reputations. The CIA has a reputation that affects all messages sent out by that particular unit of government, just as the Civil Liberties Union, the Ku Klux Klan, Exxon, the Communist party, and the Republican party, have images or reputations that affect the persuasive impact of messages they send.

Consider the images of two mythical candidates as they have been created on television and in the national publications. One is a senatorial candidate named Wayland, who is said to be young, slim, attractive, educated at Radcliffe College, dynamic, polished, a woman who inherited wealth but who has been giving her life to public service. Photographs of Wayland and her husband attending cultural and social events often appear in the slick magazines. They have several attractive young children. Wayland has appeared more and more frequently in recent months on television news shows in brief scenes that show her stepping off airplanes, talking informally to reporters at airports, or speaking before audiences. Her voice is pleasant, her manner serious but with some lightness and humor. She has a good smile and looks like someone you would enjoy knowing. Wayland's enemies say she is a lightweight and has gotten as far as she has largely through the power of her inherited wealth and social connections. There are ugly rumors about an impending divorce and about her extramarital sex life. Wayland is a liberal and strongly committed to a nuclear freeze.

Wayland's opponent, also mythical, is the incumbent Senator Homer Beardsley. Beardsley is approaching 60 but is said by his friends to be amazingly vigorous and young at heart. He is frequently shown jogging, playing tennis, and chopping wood for the fireplace of his cabin in the western mountains. Beardsley is a self-made man, the son of a poor tenant farmer; he worked his way through college and law school, won a scholarship, and went abroad to study. Beardsley is said to be a brilliant man, but he has some difficulty expressing himself in speeches. He is a man of few words, and he has something of a poker face. He is by no means a charmer. He has the reputation of being a powerful member of senate committees, although he does not get many headlines. Mrs. Beardsley is a plain but pleasant woman who likes to recall her farm background. They both enjoy country music and camping trips in wilderness areas. Their children are grown; they have grandchildren. Beardsley has been a strong defender of what he calls "preparedness" and is suspicious of all plans to disarm the country.

Some students in a speech class (with our myth in mind) are presenting a debate on the nuclear freeze, and the student speaking *for* the freeze quotes candidate Wayland. The student speaking *against* the freeze quotes Senator Beardsley. The reputation of each authority influences your, the listener's, response to the statements. However, should Wayland appear on campus to give a speech, her reputation would be a factor as you *begin* to listen to her, but her platform personality and her demonstration of the personality traits others have attributed to her would be important factors in your final image of the speaker.

The Building of Images

Building a good image of candidates and institutions is the object of much organized persuasive campaigning. As an individual, you are projecting a public image every day. You can learn much about how your own image appears to others and how you can improve your projection of it by studying the professional imagemakers' techniques. What are they primarily interested in doing? Professional persuaders often go to great lengths to discover attractive images for clients. Obviously, you are also trying to project your own image in the most favorable way.

Interestingly enough, images for persuasive impact vary from audience to audience and from culture to culture. You will certainly try to project your most responsible image to your father when you ask for the family car for the evening, but 10 minutes later, on the telephone, you may try to project your most exciting, devil-may-care image to the date you expect to pick up in an hour. Consider our mythical political candidates once more. Did you find Wayland's image more attractive than Beardsley's? If so, you might well be from the suburbs of a metropolitan area. If you found Beardsley more attractive, you are probably from a small town, rural, or midwestern area. Psychologists tell us that we identify with people with whom we feel we have much in common. In this instance, the word *identification* refers to the feeling that you and another person could walk a while in each other's shoes. Consider a black candidate who was raised in an urban ghetto, went to college on a basketball scholarship, became a star in the National Basketball Association, and subsequently worked with ghetto youths and became a militant advocate of minority rights. Would you find his image attractive? Anyone wise in the arts of persuasion takes a close look at the image he or she wishes to project and then works hard to find out what images will be attractive to the audience he or she hopes to persuade.

From all this, however, you must not conclude that imagemakers are creating false impressions of candidates or institutions. Persuasion must work within the limits of possibility. The basic personality of the candidate, or the nature of the institution being "sold," forms a framework within which the persuaders must operate. The best public-relations firm in the world cannot make Homer Beardsley appear to be a member of the jet set or socialite Wayland appear as a blue-collar worker. If a public realizes it has been fooled, the reaction is always swift and disastrous for the unwise candidate. All the persuaders can do—but this is of considerable value to candidates and to you as an individual—is to learn what is attractive in a personality being "sold" and to help a person stress the attractive portions of his or her image and minimize the less attractive elements.

Our society has been undergoing a refreshing scourging of phonies. If you consider it hypocritical to sell yourself when you wish to persuade, you should remember that there are times when people believe in a cause strongly and find that their personalities are alienating people; they will then work hard to change their images in order to build more favorable response for the cause they are promoting. Accenting the positive is no sin; accenting what does not exist, on the other hand, is unethical. If a potential candidate sells himself to the voters as a churchgoing, sober man, when in fact he never goes to church and drinks heavily in secret, he will be found out and his ethos will be damaged.

What happens when we know little or nothing about the source of the communication? We often decide how much to accept from such a source on the basis of the stereotypes we have all built in our minds since childhood.

We accept or reject messages because they come from people whose roles in society we accept or reject. We know that many professional people have spent years acquiring the knowledge needed to label themselves landscape architects, medical doctors, lawyers, certified public accountants, or college instructors, and when they speak to us as professionals, we tend to accept what they say as being useful (truthful or persuasive) whether or not we find them personally attractive. We are accepting the image of the expert rather than the image as a personality, and we accept messages from such experts more readily when they are speaking about their particular area of competence. When a professor of economics argues that the Federal Reserve Board is following the wrong policy, we listen to her and tend to think she knows what she is talking about. We expect her judgment to be professional and based on careful research. When this same professor argues that the salaries of economics professors ought to be increased, we may not accept her message as being as persuasive, since in this second instance, she is speaking as a person with vested self-interest and not as a scholar making an objective study of a subject. The authors watched with interest one evening as a well-known surgeon nearly tore up his hat in anger and frustration after the elementary school building committee wisely declined his carefully worked out plans for the new school. Used to having his judgments accepted immediately in his day-to-day hospital world, his expertise dropped dramatically when he spoke as another parent in the school meeting. The parents preferred the opinions of the teachers, administrators, architects, and city planners present, and wisely so. Experts, to be persuasive, have to stay within their area of competence.

Direct Knowledge of the Source

In the final analysis, of course, a great deal of any speaker's credibility is generated by how he talks and what he says. Any speaker can do much to make his image more attractive right at the moment he is communicating.

The speaker may well create an advantage by reminding the audience of factors in her background, experience, and training that make her particularly competent to discuss the topic. This should not be done in a boastful way, of course. Often the speaker's expertise is known beforehand, either from advance publicity or from an introduction before she speaks.

The speaker may also imply her status. For example, she can add as she talks about what kind of tires we should use on our cars, "I've been racing stock cars for some years, and I've found that . . ." A speaker can dramatize his or her expertise as in the following example. A woman, a special counselor in the welfare department, was being introduced as a speaker to a group of young mothers, all newly receiving benefits in the form of aid to dependent children. These mothers were more than a little wary of listening to another expert tell them how to manage their lives, particularly their finances, now that they were on welfare. The program chairperson introduced the speaker as a woman who had earned a degree in social work from the university and whose experience in the field was extensive. The listeners were only mildly impressed. The speaker won their attention and hearts at once when she began. "Fifteen years ago I was sitting in your seat. I'll tell you how I got up here, and I'll tell you how you can get yourself back on your own two feet, and I know that's where you want to be. I *know* each of you wants to do the absolute best you can for your children, and for yourself, and that's why you are here." Wiping away the feelings of guilt that had washed over the young mothers as they had filled out the myriad papers necessary to obtain public assistance, the speaker had immediately told them: "You are great women with problems; I had the same problem a while back, and I learned a lot of answers, which I am going to pass on to you."

One final element always useful in constructing the persuasive ethos of a speaker comes from the fact that we all like to laugh. If a speaker can amuse us, if she can share her sense of humor with us, we are going to find her more likable. If she can communicate to us that she takes the subject, but not herself, seriously, we will be drawn toward her. If her humor is gentle rather than cutting or sarcastic, if she turns her humor back on herself rather than using it against others, we will trust her more. A person who can amuse her audience seems secure and in command of the situation. You must be careful not to overdo the use of humor, of course, particularly if you have a serious point to make. People love comics and clowns and try to place in that role any person who has some talent for comedy. The rewards for amusing speakers are great—laughter, congeniality, and the knowledge that they are well liked. But just as experts must stay in their area of expertness, so comics are expected to stay comics. If clowns try to make a serious point, to give advice about important matters, we feel uncomfortable and tend to ignore their advice. Use humor in your persuasive speeches, then, but keep in mind your overall purpose. There is much persuasive power in the personality of the source of the message.

THE PERSUASIVE POWER OF SUGGESTION

Persuasion and Aping Behavior

People often do or believe something because other people around them are doing or believing it. Follow-the-leader behavior is so primitive, we will call it *aping* behavior because the stereotype of an ape is that it will mimic behavior. If a person walking down a street stops and peers up toward the sky, some people may walk on past the sky watcher, but several other people will stop to see what has caught his attention, and soon a knot of people will be standing, peering upward.

How often have you been a part of this next scene? A siren sounds in a quiet neighborhood. People go to their windows or doors or out on their porches to see what is happening. One person runs from a house and dashes up the street. Soon several more follow, and if enough of the watchers are pulled into the parade, the pressure for you to go along with them grows strong. You probably go, too.

Beliefs and ideas can develop in the same fashion. So can norms or ways of behaving. Laboratory studies have shown the extent to which the behavior of others persuades us to do things we otherwise would not do.

A candid film made in the 1960s included a scene in which, when actors planted in a doctor's office waiting room began taking off their clothes in a matter-of-fact way, as though this were the usual procedure in that situation, a number of unsuspecting clients, after initial reactions of surprise and bewilderment, also began to remove their clothes.

You are probably not enjoying this evidence of how often we simply ape others in how we behave, what we do, even what we think. But human beings *do* behave this way. Aping behavior is often harmless and normal. However, you should resist being manipulated by propaganda that is designed to induce you to ape behavior which, if you stopped to consider, you would *not* choose. You should particularly watch for the propagandist's use of the so-called "bandwagon" technique, which asserts that "everybody is doing it, so come on along."

Persuasion and Following Directions

Another common human behavior pattern is to do and believe as we are told. Again, this is an immediate and natural response. If one person gives another directions about what to do or what to believe, the second person tends to do or believe as directed. Directed behavior occurs without thinking. If the sign says STOP, you stop. Often people are hardly aware of what has taken place when they unthinkingly accept directions. As parents, you will tell your children what to do. As children, you were told by your parents what to do. Much of our educational process is a matter of following directions. Carried to extreme lengths, controlling people by telling them what to do and think is like pushing buttons to direct the movements of a mechanical toy. Under deep hypnosis, people blindly follow the directions of the hypnotist, reacting much as a machine would to programmed instructions.

Even so-called "rational" human beings are surrounded by persuasive messages capitalizing upon this tendency to follow directions. Particularly on radio and television we are ordered to:

Buy Buick!
Elect John Doe!
Vote Republicrat!
Shop downtown!
Throw the rascals out!
Save today!

Persuasion and Accepting Suggestions

Directions, as shown above, are clear, blunt, and unequivocal. You are given no option. Directions are phrased and delivered as commands. Suggestions, on the other hand, recommend a belief or an action, but are phrased in such a way that the receiver has an option, some choice about doing or not doing what is suggested. The direction "Quit your job!" becomes the suggestion "May I suggest that you consider resigning?" Suggestion slips the idea into the mind more gently than the jarring direction, and although suggestions encourage the growth of the idea or action, they do so less directly.

Thinking up and developing good suggestion requires considerable artistry. Suggestion skillfully done is efficient. Suggestion puts positions or points into the mind so they are hard to attack logically. We have observed many student discussion groups trying to find a good topic to present as a group for a class discussion. One member suggests a topic, and immediately another makes a face, showing his disgust with the idea, and says, "Let's not do that. Let's do something new and interesting for a change." The first participant then has to present good reasons and make a big effort to overcome the effect of the second member's suggestion that the topic is trite and uninteresting.

The process of suggestion, however, like that of direction, involves getting the listener to accept without thinking an idea, belief, or action. Suggestion is one of the most commonly used persuasive techniques in advertising and propaganda. See if you can think up a strong suggestion in behalf of some service or product in 25 words or less. Can you better these paraphrases of Madison Avenue masterpieces? "Glamour toilet tissue is like facial tissue. It doesn't *feel* like toilet paper." "If she kisses you once, will she kiss you twice?" "Clean odor, the Cologne of Mouthwashes." One we have always liked is the brief persuasive spiel of the hawker selling cheap inflatable pillows to people attending the big show in the state fair ground grandstand. "Four hours on a board," he drones, "Four hours on a board. May we suggest a pillow?"

Many of the people who bought pillows after hearing about the four hours on a board probably never consciously reasoned through their decision. This board-and-pillow example is of further interest because the hawker's spiel contains the two major kinds of suggestion used in persuasion, direct and indirect. The sentence, "May we suggest a pillow?" is *direct suggestion,* telling the potential customers what the seller wants them to do. The phrase "Four hours on a board" is *indirect suggestion* that the potential customers will be uncomfortable shortly if they do not buy the pillow and, moreover, will be quite comfortable throughout the show if they do.

Directions and suggestions may be positive or negative. Positive persuasion results when a belief or a course of action is urged. "Save today at the Anniversary sale!" Negative direction and suggestion urges the listener not to believe, or not to do something, as in the slogan "If you smoke, stop! If you don't smoke, don't start!" Positive suggestion and strong direct urgings have persuasive impact. Negative suggestions or directions are often less effective than positive ones. Negative urgings call attention to the belief or action you do *not* want to encourage and, in so doing, may arouse a curiosity about the subject that had not been in the listener's mind before. There is a line from a Carl Sandburg poem we often quoted to one another when our children were toddlers. The line well describes the unwanted effects of negative suggestion. Paraphrased a little, it reads, "Why does the child put molasses on the cat when the one thing I told the child *not* to do was put molasses on the cat?" The sign "Do Not Open This Door" often prompts more than one person to open the door simply out of curiosity. You would be wise to consider *all* possible results when you use negative suggestions in persuasive communication.

When speakers hint at a point without actually saying it, the suggestion they are using is indirect. The listener is led to discover the point rather than told directly about it. If a propaganda campaign maintains a steady barrage of indirect suggestion over a long time, the listeners may gradually come to believe something or begin to form a new attitude, almost without knowing what has been happening to them. When television was still advertising cigarettes, one brand was sold for some time as the cigarette for sophisticates. Its advertisements showed a woman dressed in the current high fashion, surrounded by luxurious furnishings, holding this particular brand in a long cigarette holder. Then, the company decided to change the cigarette's image, and a whole new advertising campaign was launched. Sophistication was out, and the ads now showed virile he-men working in oil fields, punching cattle, fighting forest fires, logging, or building huge bridges in high mountains. Gradually many viewers came to associate this brand of cigarettes with strong young outdoorsmen. Little was said in either campaign about the cigarette's flavor or its nicotine content. Both advertising pitches were expensive campaigns of indirect suggestion designed to persuade people to smoke the brand if they, too, wanted to be, at first, sophisticated and, later, ruggedly masculine.

Indirect Suggestion and Dramatizing

In Chapter 9 we discussed the importance of discovering the rhetorical visions of the members of your audience as you analyze their values and motives. Here we turn to the ways speakers use narratives and dramatizations to adapt to the rhetorical visions of the audience members and convey a position by indirect suggestion.

One powerful means of persuasion is the dramatization of interpretative scripts that hook into the audience's dreams (rhetorical visions). Often the speaker will portray his or her position in a persuasive speech in terms of real people acting in such a way that their behavior explains what happened. Once you have discovered the interpretative scripts of the listeners, you can search for ways to dramatize your subject that fit into their rhetorical visions.

Successful persuasion not only relies on real-life people but also uses fictitious characters who have admirable or hateful characteristics to serve as hypothetical examples. Superman brings certain qualities to mind; so does Caspar Milquetoast. Finally, a persuasive speaker may use the figure of speech called *personification* to create emotional responses to abstract propositions. When a speaker uses personification, he endows an abstract idea, institution, or government with human characteristics so it begins to act like a person in a drama. Mark Twain once suggested that a lie could travel around the world while the truth was still pulling on its boots. Suggesting that truth can pull on its boots gives truth the attributes of a person. In nineteenth century oratory, the personification of such abstract notions as *truth, virtue, beauty,* and *eloquence* was common.

Persuasive messages may contain personifications of abstractions such as the United States of America in the form of Liberty or Uncle Sam or of Great Britain in the person of John Bull. Political cartoonists, who often work with suggestion to achieve their persuasive impact, frequently personify John Q. Public or give the atomic bomb the characteristics of a human being.

In addition to characters, a propaganda or persuasive campaign must provide a setting for the drama. Watch several television commercials or clip several advertisements from a magazine. Notice the scene or location of the action. Although only a small number of people still work as cowhands in our country, a high percentage of characters in advertising campaigns ride horses, wear large western hats, and herd and brand cattle. Many commercial advertisements are set in "pluperfect" homes—gorgeous and in perfect order. Much political persuasion derives its impact from the particular setting in which the drama takes place. The John F. Kennedy drama of Camelot was played out at Hyannisport, Palm Springs, and the White House. Jesse Jackson's Operation Push was set in the black ghettos of Chicago. Skillful propagandists planning a dramatic action for symbolic effect take pains to select the proper scene for their drama. Do you demonstrate in front of the federal building or at the site of a large nuclear energy plant? Do you go to Washington, D.C., and march on the Pentagon, or do you go to the state capital?

Finally, the characters placed in a scene and situation must participate in a dramatic action that arouses our emotions and causes us to become involved imaginatively in what is happening. Persuaders often can take actual events and with a bit of imagination remake them into dramatic actions to fit their purposes. Persuaders and propagandists are in an important sense dream merchants, and to the extent they can catch their audiences up into a dream, they can often persuade them to act and believe in certain ways. One legend has it that in the early days of the automobile, the tendency was to advertise cars in terms of engineering details and facts about their performance. Then an advertising genius developed an ad consisting of a photograph of a handsome young man in his driving togs and goggles, his scarf flying in the wind, a beautiful girl at his side, driving an open car on a road that led across a green valley to the mountains beyond. When asked what in the world he was trying to sell with such a layout, he is alleged to have replied, "A dream"; and modern advertising was on its way.

The heroes of our public dreams are likable and believable and tend to be credible. The villains of our dramatization of events can seldom persuade us. Thus the dramatic interpretation of events provides the audience with emotional involvement as well as with credible sources. The positive and negative suggestions inherent in an attractive drama presented as part of a persuasive or propaganda campaign are among the most powerful forces for changing attitudes and behavior.

As consumers of persuasion, and as persuaders ourselves, we should be much aware of the importance of public dreams in relation to positive and negative suggestion. We should learn to look for the rhetorical visions that seem to be operating currently in our culture because the interpretative scripts change as events around us reshape our priorities. Much of advertising and of the selling of political candidates is shaped by what the dream merchants think the public is buying this year.

We should be alert consumers of persuasion and constantly evaluate messages. As we develop our own persuasive efforts, we should be aware that even the most skillful dream merchants cannot always predict the public's response to their campaign. Nor is what we see and hear in the mass media necessarily the most persuasive communication we receive.

Much of our motivation to be and to do is contained within the dreams that become real and exciting to us. Our rhetorical vision is often shaped by the positive and negative suggestion inherent in the messages of the mass media; many of our personal fantasies are these messages after they have been discussed, recreated, reshaped in our talk with other people we like and enjoy; some of our dreams are the product of shared group fantasies.

We are not necessarily persuaded by reason. We are often persuaded by suggestion that ties in with or creates our rhetorical visions. To limit communication to factual information is to deny the powerful influence we all feel when those things we hold most dear, our innermost hopes and dreams, are involved.

KEY IDEAS

- Persuasion is communication designed to influence choice. Coercion, like persuasion, restricts choice but, unlike persuasion, requires little artistry.

- Little persuasive skill is involved in offering a reward or threatening punishment.
- The participants in one form of public-speaking come with the expectation that the speaker will deliver a persuasive message.
- The persuasive speech aims to influence the listeners' choices and to narrow audience responses to the one the speaker recommends.
- The speaker should remember that people tend to do what they want at a given moment, even if the evidence indicates it will be bad for them in the long run.
- The speaker who wishes to change an audience's habitual routine has the burden of proving that change is necessary.
- Much persuasion is dependent on the quality of the personal relationships established among the people involved in a communication.
- When the choices are risky and people need advice, they turn to someone they can trust.
- A genuine offer to help is a powerful force for persuasion.
- We tend to believe people we think are competent, expert, and interested in our welfare.
- A powerful force for persuasion is a person's deep personal conviction that he or she is right. Sincerity is persuasive.
- The image of a public figure is closely related to his or her credibility as a source of messages.
- Organizations and business corporations also have images that affect their believability when they issue corporate messages.
- The persuasive impact of a public figure's image varies from audience to audience.
- If a public realizes it has been fooled by misleading image building, the reaction is usually swift and disastrous for those involved.
- We accept persuasive messages from some sources because they have professional credentials that we respect.
- Much of people's credibility is created by how they talk and act in our presence.
- A message source creates a credible image to a large extent by nonverbal communication suggesting that he or she is interested in the listener, expert in the subject, and admirable as a person.
- Funny people are not listened to on serious matters, but a judicious use of humor in a speech increases a speaker's credibility as a human being.
- The principle of aping behavior is simple: what one person starts, others tend to follow.
- People tend to do and believe as they are told.
- Suggestion plants positions or points in the mind so that they are hard to attack logically.

- Whereas direct suggestion tells listeners clearly what they may do or believe, indirect suggestion only hints at it.
- Negative forms of persuasion sometimes backfire, because listeners may be tempted to do what they are told not to do.
- When speakers use the figure of speech called personification, they endow an abstract idea or institution with human characteristics.
- Persuaders are in an important sense dream merchants, in that they can propagate a certain dream and can sell products and ideas that promise to fulfill the dream.

SUGGESTED PROJECTS

1. Select some important personal decision, such as which college to attend, whether to get married, whether to buy a car, or which career to pursue. Think of the one person whose advice you would be most likely to accept in regard to the decision. Make a list of reasons why this person is a credible authority for you in regard to the particular decision.

2. Write a short paper in which you describe and discuss six techniques of indirect suggestion that you have noticed in current television ads or in magazines and newspapers.

3. This is to be your most thoroughly prepared, carefully written, and well-rehearsed speech—the equivalent of an oral term paper. Select a topic that you feel strongly about and prepare a five- to eight-minute persuasive speech for delivery to the class.

SUGGESTED READINGS

Brembeck, Winston, and William S. Howell. *Persuasion: A Means of Social Influence.* 2d ed. Englewood Cliffs, N.J.: Prentice-Hall, 1976.
Clark, Ruth Ann. *Persuasive Messages.* New York: Harper & Row, 1984.
Larson, Charles U. *Persuasion: Reception and Responsibility.* 3d ed. Belmont, Calif.: Wadsworth, 1983.

Appendix

Evaluating Communication

DAY-TO-DAY CRITICISM

We all evaluate communication events. Communication is such a vital activity that we all discuss our successful and unsuccessful communication attempts informally, just as we discuss films, plays, novels, and other artistic works if they are important to us. Our discussion may be of the basic I-like-it or I-don't-like-it variety. "I hate it when he asks me questions in class." "I just can't talk to my mother." "We had a great discussion in the dorm last night." "Can't you get something else on television? Politics is so boring." Or as we become more sophisticated about our communication, we may provide more specific and detailed explanations of our evaluations: "I hate it when he asks me questions in class. Nonverbally he comes across to me as saying he is better than I am, like he is continually evaluating what I say. He also strikes me as manipulating me —trying to use me to make a point with the class. I get very defensive, but I'm in a one-down position, and if I told him what I really think he'd probably cut my grade." Or we may say about the politician on television: "Man, is he boring! His language is so abstract and filled with clichés. He never dramatizes. His organization is clear enough; fact is, it's so simple and he keeps repeating the points so often I begin to get the feeling he thinks I have the mind of a twelve-year-old. For a politician in national

259

office, that man has got to have the most monotonous voice of anyone in Washington in the last twenty years. It's a real chore to keep your attention on what he's saying."

In this chapter we provide you with the basics you need to begin evaluating communication. We provide a step-by-step analysis of the evaluative process you can apply to your communication assignments and to those of your classmates. We also discuss the uses of rhetorical criticism and provide directions on how to evaluate messages that are of special importance.

THE BASIC EVALUATIVE PROCESS

In order to evaluate communication, you must learn the basic principles relating to the processes involved. Once you learn the theory, you can examine a given communication event and apply the appropriate standards to it. The basic evaluative process consists of three steps: (1) selecting criteria for evaluation, (2) describing the communication event, and (3) applying the criteria to the description and making the evaluation.

Selecting Criteria

Once you have picked the communication you wish to study, you can turn to the evaluation proper. The first step is to take from the applicable principles of communication a number of criteria to use in the evaluation. The process applies to casual conversations, interviews, business meetings, television programs, public speeches, and all other forms and contexts of communication. To illustrate our point, we will look at how you might criticize a public speech.

You could pick a number of criteria from the public-speaking perspective to use in evaluating a speech. You could evaluate how the speaker analyzes the audience and adapts the ideas in the speech to the audience. You could select the way the speaker argues the case, the quality of the evidence, the plausibility and consistency of the reasoning. You could pick the skill with which the speaker develops a persuasive platform personality. You could concentrate on the speaker's delivery, including gestures, facial expressions, voice projection, articulation, and so forth. You could focus on how the speaker dramatizes his or her avowed position and evokes emotions, creates positive and negative suggestions, gives directions, and arouses the listeners to action.

Usually we do not raise every possible critical issue that we can about every speech. For example, if your instructor gave you an assignment to give a public speech, he or she might emphasize the delivery or the organization or the persuasive content; when you delivered the speech, then, your classmates and instructor would look for the particular aspect assigned when evaluating the speech.

Describing a Communication Event

The second step in criticizing communication is to use the criteria as guidelines in examining a communication event (as it unfolds or as it is represented in a recording) and describing its features. Let us say that an assignment emphasized making ideas clear. You would then look at the speech and ask such questions as: "Did the speaker use definitions? If so, what kind of definitions were used? Did the speaker use any of the techniques of explanation, such as listing parts and so forth? Did the speaker use any examples? If so, were they real or hypothetical examples? On the basis of the criteria, you would then describe the techniques that the speaker used in the speech in some detail. You might note: "The speaker tried to clarify the point about how high unemployment and economic recession could be accompanied by a high rate of inflation with a hypothetical example about a dairy farm that was losing money, was not milking all of its cows, and was still charging more for its milk."

Evaluating the Event

The last step in the critical process is to make an evaluation of the speech according to the criteria. You might decide that the speaker did a poor job of clarifying the concept of recession and inflation because the example drawn from agriculture was poorly adapted to the audience, which was composed of students who were all from the core-city areas of a large metropolitan center and were unfamiliar with some of the technical details of dairy farming. The same sort of critical judgments could be made about delivery—"poor eye contact, mumbled, lots of fidgeting; I thought she was going to break her pencil in two at least five times during the speech"; about the audience—"The audience really sat there like a bunch of zombies; they did not respond at all"; and so forth.

The same essential critical process is used in all communication contexts. The critic evaluating organizational communication events from the message perspective might select as criterion the fidelity of information transmission and might make her evaluation by conducting a survey of how much information the employees of a company receive from messages that are sent downward through the organization's formal channels of communication. She might conclude, for instance, that employees comprehend or can recall only 25 percent of the information that upper management transmits down through channels to them. Another critic might examine the amount of information that a jury gets from the judge's charge by giving them a test of their comprehension of key ideas. The critic might also study videotapes of conversations or small group meetings for evidence of nonverbal feedback, which she could evaluate as to quantity and effectiveness.

A student might recall a deep discussion with close friends that dealt with important questions of human relationships and examine it from the relationship communication perspective by asking how well the participants expressed authentic feelings, developed trust, self-disclosed, and confronted and worked through their conflicts.

Evaluation is important in your role as a student in a communication class. Without evaluation of our communication so that we can discover what we are doing well and what we still need to work on, we cannot improve. Your evaluations can help your fellow students improve their communication. Learning to evaluate communication gives you an added understanding that you can then apply to your own speaking and listening.

We go beyond the basic principles of classroom criticism in this chapter, because as important as evaluation is to your own improvement as a message source it is even more important to your role as message consumer. You spend much more of your time listening, reading, and watching messages than you spend in writing and speaking. Unfortunately in our modern mass-communication world the slogan "Listener beware" is often the order of the day.

THE CRITIC AS CONSUMER OF COMMUNICATION

One of your purposes in this course should be to become a skillful and perceptive critic of the messages that bombard you so you can be a wise consumer of information, persuasion, and propaganda.

We live in an age in which we get messages from public speakers, but we also get messages while being hammered by disco music as we see images projected on a screen. Perhaps most effective of all modern persuasive messages is the television commercial—using music, slogans, dance, drama, still pictures, moving pictures, animated cartoons, poetry, and argument, all orchestrated into a tight, smooth sales pitch, crammed into 60 seconds or less. How many TV commercial ditties can you sing? Did you try to memorize the words? Or did the catchy tunes insinuate the persuasive message into your mind without your paying much attention?

Communication events are frequently aimed at mass audiences; messages are brief and polished, and they have to compete for our attention with hundreds of other messages. This fight for attention leads communicators to use every avenue of the senses to reach us, hold our attention, and persuade us to buy a particular model car, adopt a new hemline, or wash with a certain brand of soap.

Gullible consumers of film, radio, and television may come to live in a world of images, impressions, and stereotypes without being aware of how they got there. What kinds of people do what sorts of things in the messages we daily consume? Are the old people decrepit and useless, the butt of jokes about shuffling walks and squeaky voices? Are the drug users cool and admirable or sad and bewildered? Are women portrayed as superwomen easily juggling career, home, and family? Do you gradually get the impression that the mayor is a fool as you watch him answer reporters on news shows? Do you begin to wonder if the marines are vicious and the cops corrupt? Much of what we believe and much of how we act derive from the sometimes fringe impressions we get from the messages we see on the mass media—impressions that are reinforced when we talk informally with family and friends.

We pointed out in some detail in Chapter 1 the importance of developing skill at critically evaluating the political messages that we receive in order to function as citizens. We could make the same point in regard to religious messages; the rise of cults, the charges and countercharges of brainwashing and deprogramming indicate the importance of your becoming an aware consumer in that area. Similar concerns apply to our responses to advertisements about products, to messages relating to self-improvement, to leisure-time activities, and to a wide range of other topics.

We are all plugged in to so many message sources through the mass media that we are in danger of suffering from information overload. Most of us protect ourselves against such overload by ignoring the bulk of the messages that surround us. We simply do not have time to listen, let alone evaluate it all carefully. Some of these messages, however, are vital to our interests. We seek out these messages and pay careful attention to them. The vital and interesting messages are the ones we should learn how to examine with care.

USES OF RHETORICAL CRITICISM

The technical term for carefully criticizing important messages is *rhetorical criticism.* Rhetoric is the study of the arts of persuasion. Scholars have developed some techniques to guide the evaluation of important messages and have published studies that can help the general public in their role as consumers of information. Rhetorical criticism has three major uses: (1) you may criticize messages as a way to present and defend your position in a discussion or debate, (2) you may criticize messages to upgrade the general quality of communication in society, and (3) you may criticize messages to discover how communication works to shape our dreams, impel us to act, and provide us with a vision of the world. All these uses of rhetorical criticism help us become wiser consumers of communication. Once we understand how the word magic works, it loses its spell over us. We begin to control our communication rather than to be controlled by it.

One good basic approach to rhetorical criticism is to take the steps of evaluating a communication event, described earlier in this appendix, and apply them to the messages you wish to study. The difference between applying these steps to classroom evaluations and rhetorical criticism is largely one of degree. The rhetorical critic will take more time and be more careful and rigorous in applying the steps. Rhetorical criticism begins with the selection of a set of messages to evaluate. Just as you might turn to information from consumer groups when you are about to make an expensive purchase such as a car or stereo set to see how they evaluate a product, so you might criticize in detail a particularly important article, book, speech, television program, radio message, or other source of information.

If the country is in the midst of a political campaign and you are interested in it, you might select a televised debate among the candidates or a speech or news conference for your rhetorical criticism. Following the steps of selecting criteria, describing the message, and applying the criteria, you might examine such things as the credibility of the message sources, the soundness of the ideas, and the propaganda elements in the communication.

Criticism As Advocacy

In your discussions with others you may use the criticism of messages as a way to debate the pros and cons of a question. One way to make your point is to emphasize the high quality of the communication of those who are leading speakers for your position. Another way is to attack the shoddy communication of a person who symbolizes the opposition. Such criticism helps clarify public debate on important issues. When a number of people examine the communication surrounding a public issue, they often succeed in carefully and systematically evaluating the communication of pressure groups, one-issue movements, and established political and social institutions.

Another technique for taking an "advocate's" position by means of communication criticism is to examine how communication contributes to an undesirable condition in society. Critics might examine how the language of the mass media or the dramatizations of the media gives an undesirable impression of a particular ethnic or minority group. In this regard, a critic might analyze the negative connotations of the terms associated with darkness or blackness (e.g., blackhearted) and argue that black people are victims of the language of a racist society. Or a critic might argue that Polish jokes reflect prejudice against Polish people. Or the critic might argue that the commercials on television present male parents as simpleminded dolts who are continually duped by their spouses and children. Or the critic might argue that girls are dramatized in the mass-media magazines as nurturing, selfless, soft, and defenseless, while boys are portrayed as assertive, tough, and selfish. Or the critic might argue that sexist bias is built into the language in that all terms for positions of power are associated with the male gender—*chairman,* for example. (Under the impact of the latter sort of criticism, at our schools we now have *chairpersons* and *chair-ones.* One of our daughters received a letter from a college she was considering attending addressed to "Dear Freshperson.")

Criticism As Social Corrective

You will find rhetorical criticism useful in still another way. Some critics of communication are not involved as participants in an ongoing debate but are interested in criticizing the general quality of communication in a society. Their aim is to be objective and look at the communication on all sides and criticize it in an evenhanded manner. They strike out at shoddy communication no matter where they find it. They may examine the gobbledygook of bureaucratic communication or the murky, jargon-ridden style of some textbook writers. They may evaluate the decline in the quality of imagination and dramatization resulting from television commercials or the dull English created by ghostwriters for the television broadcasts of the president.

Criticism As an Avenue to Knowledge

The final kind of rhetorical criticism aims at discovering knowledge about human communication. Scholars criticizing public communication in this way are trying to understand human communications in all its varied forms. Rhetorical criticism thus takes its place as a liberal and humanizing art, a scholarly endeavor that aims to illuminate the human condition. It is particularly concerned with human symbolizing, which works to divide and integrate human beings, to interpret human problems, and to enable cooperative efforts to be made to solve them and to provide self and group concepts for human beings searching for meaning in their existence and endeavors.

We do not expect you to become a professional rhetorical critic, but we recommend that if you want to become a knowledgeable consumer of persuasion you might develop a habit of reading criticism and learn to appreciate good criticism. Just as someone who enjoys reading can profit from reading book reviews and literary criticism, so, too, can the individual with an interest in communication profit from reading rhetorical criticism. Continued reading of criticism is a good way for you to keep current in your thinking about persuasion and communication. We seldom learn all we need to know about any subject in one or even several courses, and we need to keep reading and updating our thinking after we finish the courses and continue to do so after we graduate.

Index